D0852820

220,7
Boa   BIBLE COMMENTARY

Boa, Kenneth

Talk thru the Old Testament

220,7
Boa

BIBLE COMMENTARY

Boa, Kenneth

Talk thru the Old Testament

Library of the
CHRISTIAN CHURCH (DISCIPLES OF CHRIST)
KALAMAZOO, MICHIGAN

TALK THRU
the OLD
TESTAMENT

from
WALK THRU THE BIBLE

by
Kenneth Boa

Tyndale House Publishers, Inc.
Wheaton, Illinois

Scripture quotations are from the New American Standard Bible.
© The Lockman Foundation 1960, 1962, 1963, 1968, 1971, 1973, 1975.
Used by permission.

Library of Congress Catalog Card Number 80-52996.
ISBN 0-8423-6911-2, cloth.
Copyright © 1980 by Walk Thru the Bible Ministries, Inc.
Published by Tyndale House Publishers, Inc.
All rights reserved
Printed in the United States of America
First printing, September 1980

Acknowledgment

I am indebted to the Walk Thru the Bible team for their help and friendship during this project. Special thanks go to Max Anders, Ed Diaz, John Hoover, Bob Roland, Art Vander Veen, and Bruce Wilkinson. "Iron sharpens iron, so one man sharpens another" (Prov. 27:17).

K.B.

Dedication

To my wife Karen ("An excellent wife is the crown of her husband," Prov. 12:4a) and my daughter Heather ("Behold, children are a gift of the Lord," Ps. 127:3a).

Contents

FOREWORD

Talk Thru the Old Testament captures the heartbeat of Walk Thru the Bible's dynamic approach to biblical education.

Four years ago Walk Thru the Bible was founded to meet a felt need of Christians across America. For the vast majority of Christians (both new and old), the Bible resembles an enormous jigsaw puzzle with thousands of pieces: pieces of Genesis . . . Joshua . . . Job . . . Jeremiah . . . John. Week by week, through the media of personal Bible study, Christian books and magazines, pulpit messages, and Christian radio and television programs, the number of "pieces of the puzzle" increases.

But no one has ever taken the time to show how all those pieces fit together into an integrated whole. Most Christians have never seen the "box lid" of the Bible, and as a result, the pieces of the Bible remain largely a jumble of confusion.

Walk Thru the Bible exists to help people fit the diversified parts of their Bible into a complete, unified picture. Kenneth Boa's *Talk Thru the Old Testament* was written in that spirit and seeks to accomplish that goal. You cannot read this book without coming away with a fresh appreciation for the diversity and unity of the Old Testament . . . and for the infinite God Who gave it. The same vital messages and life-changing truths that spoke to God's men and women centuries ago are there to encourage and empower you today . . . as you *Talk Thru the Old Testament*.

Bruce H. Wilkinson, President
Walk Thru the Bible Ministries, Inc.
Atlanta, Georgia

Introduction to the
Old Testament

The Bible is the greatest work of literature, history, and theology ever written. In its production, preservation, proclamation, and product (changed history, changed lives), it stands as the most unique book in existence. It is a unity out of a diversity of authors, time span, and literary forms. The Old and New Testaments smoothly blend to create a bold sweep from eternity past to eternity future, from the heights of heaven to the depths of hell. In these 66 books we discover our past, understand our present, and attain hope for our future.

The Old Testament is a redemptive history that lays the foundation upon which the New Testament is built. There is a progressive revelation in the Scriptures, and what is anticipated in the Old Testament is unfolded in the New. The Old points ahead and the New points back to the central event in all history—the substitutionary death of the Messiah.

The Old Testament was originally divided into two sections: the Law and the Prophets (Matt. 7:12; Luke 16:16,29,31). This was later expanded into a threefold division of the Law, the Prophets, and the Writings (Luke 24:44). All 39 books in our Old Testament are contained in the 24 books of the Hebrew Bible.

The Greek translation of the Old Testament arranged the books in the four divisions that we use today: Law (5), History (12), Poetry (5), and Prophecy (17). The five books of the Law can be combined with the 12 historical books to get the following structure:

	Historical (17)	Poetical (5)	Prophetical (17)	
Pentateuch (5)	Genesis	Job	Isaiah	**Major (5)**
	Exodus	Psalms	Jeremiah	
	Leviticus	Proverbs	Lamentations	
	Numbers	Ecclesiastes	Ezekiel	
	Deuteronomy	Song of Solomon	Daniel	
Historical (12)	Joshua		Hosea	**Minor (12)**
	Judges		Joel	
	Ruth		Amos	
	1 Samuel		Obadiah	
	2 Samuel		Jonah	
	1 Kings		Micah	
	2 Kings		Nahum	
	1 Chronicles		Habakkuk	
	2 Chronicles		Zephaniah	
	Ezra		Haggai	
	Nehemiah		Zechariah	
	Esther		Malachi	

Events	Experience	Expectation
Past	Present	Future
God's Work	God's Ways	God's Will
Narrative	Poetry	Prophecy
Covenant People	Covenant Practice	Covenant Preachers

The 17 historical books trace the entire history of Israel from its inception to the time of the prophet Malachi. In the Pentateuch Israel was chosen, redeemed, disciplined, and instructed. The remaining 12 historical books record the conquest of the land, the period of the judges, the formation of a united kingdom, and the division of that kingdom into the North (Israel) and the South (Judah). Each kingdom was taken into captivity but many of the people eventually returned.

The five poetical books focus on a right relationship with God as the basis for a life of meaning, skill, and beauty.

The 17 prophetical books have a two-pronged message of condemnation (because of Israel's iniquity and idolatry) and consolation (future hope in spite of present judgment). Often at great personal cost these men refused to dilute God's strong words.

Introduction to the Pentateuch

The Five Books of Moses are variously known as the Law, the Torah (Hebrew for Law), the Law of Moses, the "five-fifths of the Law," and the Pentateuch. The word Pentateuch is derived from the Greek words *penta* (five) and *teuchos* (scroll or book).

Although there is much external and internal evidence that supports the Mosaic authorship of these five books, many critics in the last two centuries have challenged this. The usual scenario is that Israel's religion evolved through several stages and various literary strands appeared along the way. These were edited during the divided kingdom and after the Babylonian exile. These theories, however, are built upon assumptions that have since been proven false or remain unproven.

Is the Pentateuch Mosaic or is it a mosaic? These books show a clear continuity of content, theme, purpose, and style that point to a single author. They make up a unity, not a late and unreliable patchwork. Each book smoothly picks up where the previous book left off. There is a completeness about the Pentateuch not only in its consecutive history but also in its progressive spiritual development:

BOOK	KEY IDEA	THE NATION	THE PEOPLE	GOD'S CHARAC-TER	GOD'S ROLE	GOD'S COM-MAND
Genesis	Beginnings	Chosen	Prepared	Powerful Sovereign	Creator	"Let there be!"
Exodus	Redemp-tion	Delivered	Redeemed	Merciful	Deliverer	"Let My people go!"
Leviticus	Worship	Set Apart	Taught	Holy	Sanctifier	"Be holy!"
Numbers	Wandering	Directed	Tested	Just	Sustainer	"Go in!"
Deuter-onomy	Renewed Covenant	Made Ready	Retaught	Loving Lord	Rewarder	"Obey!"

Genesis — This book provides the foundation for the entire Bible in its history and theology. Its first 11 chapters give a sweeping survey of primeval events: God's work of creation, the fall of man, the judgment of the flood, and the spread of the nations. There is a sudden shift in chapter 12 as God singles out one man through whom He would bring salvation and bless all nations. The remainder of Genesis traces the story of Abraham and his descendants Isaac, Jacob, and Joseph.

Exodus — Jacob's descendants have moved from Canaan to Egypt and are suffering under the bondage of a new pharaoh. After a period of 400 years they cry to God for deliverance. God responds by empowering Moses to stand before Pharaoh and create the 10 devastating plagues. After their redemption in the Passover, the Israelites leave Egypt, cross the sea, and journey to Mt. Sinai. There God reveals His covenant law and gives them the pattern for the building of the tabernacle.

Leviticus — Now that the people have been redeemed and delivered, they must be set apart to God to live holy lives. God gives them instructions for the sacrificial system and the priesthood. The remainder of Leviticus teaches the people how to become ceremonially and morally pure. The emphasis is on sanctification, service, and obedience.

Numbers — Still at Mt. Sinai, the people receive additional directions before proceeding to the promised land of Canaan. When they are on the verge of entering the land, their faith crumbles and God disciplines them by making them wander in the wilderness until the disbelieving generation dies out. The new generation then reaches Moab, the doorway to the land of Canaan. It is here that God begins to instruct the people who are about to inherit the land.

Deuteronomy — Moses is at the end of his life and Joshua has been appointed as his successor. In his farewell messages to the generation that grew up in the wilderness, Moses reminds them of God's dealings in the past, reviews the need for righteousness and integrity in the present, and reveals what will happen in the near and distant future. Moses then blesses the people and views the promised land from Mt. Nebo before his death.

Genesis

"In the beginning God created the heavens and the earth."
Genesis 1:1

"And I will bless those who bless you, and the one who curses you I will curse. And in you all the families of the earth shall be blessed."
Genesis 12:3

Focus	Four Great Events				Four Great People			
	1			11	12			50
D I V I S I O N S	Creation	Fall	Flood	Nations (Babel)	Abraham	Isaac	Jacob	Joseph
	1 2	3 5	6 9	10 11	12 24	25 26	27 36	37 50
T O P I C S	Primeval History				Patriarchal History			
	Beginning of the Human Race				Beginning of the Hebrew Race			
Loca-tions	East (Eden to Ur)				West (Canaan to Egypt)			
Time	2,000 + Years (20% of Genesis)				About 286 Years (80% of Genesis)			

Talk Thru — Genesis contains the plot of the Bible in germinal form and holds the roots of every key biblical topic. It moves through a whole series of beginnings but has no finality. Genesis answers many of the basic questions of life: Where did everything come from? How did man get here? Why is there pain and evil in the world? Behind it all, God is assumed from the beginning.

This book is not a history of man so much as the first chapter in the history of the redemption of man. As such, Genesis is a highly selective spiritual interpretation of history. The 10-fold appearance of the phrase "the book of the generations" divides it into 10 sections, but its division into four great events (1-11) and four great people (12-50) is even more basic.

Four Great Events: Genesis 1-11 lays the foundation upon which the whole Bible is built. Because they are so crucial, these 11 chapters have been attacked more than any other section of Scripture. (1) *Creation:* God is the sovereign Creator of matter, energy, space, and time. Man is the pinnacle of the creation in Genesis 1-2. (2) *Fall:* Creation is followed by corruption. In the first sin man was separated from God, and in the second sin (Cain and Abel) man was separated from man. In spite of the devastating curse of the fall, God promised hope of redemption through the seed of the woman (Gen. 3:15). (3) *Flood:* As man multiplied, sin also multiplied until God was compelled to destroy humanity with the exception of Noah and his family. (4) *Nations:* Genesis teaches the unity of the human race—we are all children of Adam through Noah. Because of rebellion at the Tower of Babel, God fragmented the single culture and language of the post-flood world and scattered people over the face of the earth. These chapters portray darkness and spiritual hopelessness.

Four Great People: Now that the nations are scattered, God focuses on one man and his descendants through whom He would bless all nations (Genesis 12-50). (1) *Abraham:* The calling of Abraham in Genesis 12 is the pivotal point of the book. The three covenant promises God made to Abraham (land, descendants, and blessing) are foundational to His program of bringing salvation upon the earth. Abraham's greatest test of faith was the offering of Isaac, his divinely given heir. (2) *Isaac:* God established His covenant with Isaac as the spiritual link with Abraham. (3) *Jacob:* God transformed this man from selfishness to servanthood and changed his name to Israel, the father of the 12 tribes. (4) *Joseph:* Jacob's favorite son suffered at the hands of his brothers and became a slave in Egypt. After his meteoric rise to the rulership of Egypt, Joseph delivered his family from famine and brought them out of Canaan to Goshen.

Genesis ends on a dismal note of impending bondage with the death of Joseph. There is a great need for the redemption that is to follow in the book of Exodus.

Title — The Hebrew title is *bereshith,* "in the beginning." The Greek title is *Genesis,* a form of a word which means "origin, source, generation, birth." The third century B.C. Greek translation of the Old Testament called the *Septuagint* used this word in translating the phrase "the book of the generations." This phrase is the heading to the 10 divisions of Genesis (Gen. 2:4; 5:1; 6:9; 10:1; 11:10,27; 25:12,19; 36:1; 37:2). The Latin title is *Liber Genesis,* "the Book of Birth," taken from the Greek title. Genesis is indeed the book of beginnings (the universe, man, sin, sacrifice, etc.).

Author — Genesis ends some 300 years before Moses was born, but the evidence points to the Mosaic authorship of Genesis. Inspiration does not mean that all or even most of the content had to be given to Moses by direct revelation. Moses no doubt used earlier oral and possibly written material (it is conceivable that Abraham left some records). Moses evidently had access to his ancestors' family records (Gen. 5:1; 10:1; 25:19) that might have been brought down to Egypt by Jacob (Gen. 46). Whatever the sources, Moses was guided by the Holy Spirit as he put this book together (2 Pet. 1:21).

External Evidence: The earliest Jewish traditions as recorded in the Talmud attribute Genesis to Moses. Biblical passages like Deuteronomy 1:8; 2 Kings 13:23; and 1 Chronicles 1:1ff. allude to Genesis events as part of the Law of Moses. Our Lord often referred to the Law of Moses as a unit, and this Law was universally understood to include Genesis (Matt. 19:4-8; Luke 16:29-31; 24:27; John 5:46-47; 7:19,23).

Internal Evidence: Genesis is a literary unit in style and development, evidently written by a single hand. The appearance of Egyptian names (Gen. 37:36; 41:45; 46:20), words (Gen. 40:11), and customs shows an intimate acquaintance of its author with the ways of Egypt. Genesis connects well with the rest of the Pentateuch. It provides precisely the information needed to make Exodus intelligible. The genealogical line of Genesis 46 is resumed in Exodus 1:1ff. The end of Genesis is strikingly similar to the end of Deuteronomy. Moses is the only person who was qualified to write it. Unlike the rest of the Israelites, he was highly educated (Acts 7:22). As the author of Exodus to Deuteronomy, Moses would need to provide a systematic account of Israel's past (Genesis).

Date and Setting — Genesis may have been written by Moses in Egypt or Midian, but it is more likely that it was written after the exodus in the wilderness of Sinai. This would mean a date of composition shortly after 1445 B.C. (if the early date of the exodus is taken). It was written for the children of Israel who needed perspective on what God was doing with them and how this related to His covenant with them.

Theme and Purpose — The theme of Genesis is God's choice of a nation through whom He would bless all nations.

Over 2,000 years are covered in Genesis 1-11, but this represents only one-fifth of the book. By contrast, four-fifths of Genesis (12-50) cover less than 300 years. It is clear that Genesis is highly thematic, concentrating on the course of God's redemptive work. Genesis is not a complete or universal history.

Genesis was written to present the beginning of everything except God: the universe (1:1); man (1:27); the Sabbath (2:2-3); marriage (2:22-24); sin (3:1-7); sacrifice and salvation (3:15,21); the family (4:1-15); civilization (4:16-21); government (9:1-6); nations (11); Israel (12:1-3). It was also written to record God's choice of Israel and His covenant plan for the nation, so that the Israelites would have a spiritual perspective. Genesis shows how the sin of man is met by the intervention and redemption of God.

Contribution to the Bible — Genesis provides a historical perspective for the rest of the Bible by covering more

time than all the other biblical books combined. Its sweeping scope from Eden to Ur to Haran to Canaan to Egypt makes it the introduction not only to the Pentateuch but to the Scriptures as a whole. Genesis gives the foundation for all the great doctrines of the Bible. It shows how God overcomes man's failure under different conditions. Genesis is especially crucial to an understanding of Revelation, because the first and last three chapters of the Bible are so intimately related.

Christ in Genesis — Genesis moves from the general to the specific in its Messianic predictions: Christ is the seed of the woman (3:15), from the line of Seth (4:25), the son of Shem (9:27), the descendant of Abraham (12:3), of Isaac (21:12), of Jacob (25:23), and of the tribe of Judah (49:10).

Christ is also seen in people and events that serve as types (a type is a historical fact which illustrates a spiritual truth). Adam is "a type of Him who was to come" (Rom. 5:14). Both entered the world through a special act of God as sinless men. Adam was the head of the old creation: Christ is the Head of the new Creation. Abel's acceptable offering of a blood sacrifice points to Christ, and there is a parallel in his murder by Cain. Melchizedek ("righteous king") was "made like the Son of God" (Heb. 7:3). He was the king of Salem ("peace") who brought forth bread and wine and was the priest of the Most High God. Isaac and Joseph were also types of Christ. Joseph and Christ were both objects of special love by their fathers, both hated by their brethren, both rejected as rulers over their brethren, both conspired against and sold for silver, both condemned though innocent, and both raised from humiliation to glory by the power of God.

Exodus

"Say, therefore, to the sons of Israel, 'I am the LORD, and I will bring you out from under the burdens of the Egyptians, and I will deliver you from their bondage. I will also redeem you with an outstretched arm and with great judgments.' "

Exodus 6:6

"I am the LORD your God, who brought you out of the land of Egypt, out of house of slavery."

Exodus 20:2

Focus	Bondage		Deliverance				Revelation					
	1 6		7 18				19 40					
D I V I S I O N S	Bondage in Egypt	Call of Moses	Plagues	Passover	Red Sea Crossing	Journey to Mt. Sinai	Ten Commandments	Book of the Covenant	Plans for the Tabernacle	Priests and Levites	Golden Calf	Completion of the Tabernacle
	1 — 2	3 — 6	7 — 10	11 — 12	13 — 15	16 — 18	19 — 20	21 — 24	25 — 27	28 — 31	32 — 34	35 — 40
T O P I C S	Incubation of the Nation		Inception of the Nation				Infancy of the Nation					
	Preparation		Redemption				Instruction					
	People of God		Grace of God				Holiness of God					
Locations	Egypt		Wilderness				Mt. Sinai					
Time	430 Years (15% of Exodus)		2 Months (30% of Exodus)				10 Months (55% of Exodus)					

Talk Thru— Exodus abounds with God's powerful redemptive acts on behalf of His oppressed people. It begins in pain and ends in liberation: it moves from the groaning of the people to the glory of God. It is the continuation of the story that began in Genesis—the 70 descendants of Jacob that moved from Canaan to Egypt have multiplied under adverse conditions to a multitude of over 2½ million people. When the Israelites finally turned to God for deliverance from their bondage, God quickly responded by redeeming them "with an outstretched arm and with great judgments" (6:6). God faithfully fulfilled His promise made to Abraham centuries before (Gen. 15:13-14).

The book falls into three parts: (1) Bondage (1-6), (2) Deliverance (7-18), and (3) Revelation (19-40).

Bondage (1-6): After four centuries of slavery, the people of Israel cried to the God of Abraham, Isaac, and Jacob for deliverance. God had already prepared Moses for this purpose and commissioned him at the burning bush to stand before Pharaoh as the advocate for Israel. But Pharaoh hardened his heart: "Who is the LORD that I should obey His voice to let Israel go?" (5:2).

Deliverance (7-18): God soon revealed Himself to Pharaoh through a series of 10 "audio-visual" demonstrations (the 10 plagues). These plagues grew in severity until the 10th brought death to the firstborn of every household of Egypt. Israel averted this plague by means of the Passover lamb. Their faith in God at this point became the basis of their national redemption. As they left Egypt, God guided them by a pillar of fire and smoke and saved them from Egypt's pursuing army through the miraculous crossing of the sea. In the wilderness He protected and sustained them thoughout their journeys.

Revelation (19-40): Now that the people had experienced God's deliverance, guidance, and protection, they were ready to be taught what God expected of them. The redeemed people must now be set apart to walk with God. This is why the emphasis moves from narration in 1-18 to legislation in 19-40. On Mt. Sinai Moses received God's moral, civil, and ceremonial laws as well as the pattern for the tabernacle to be built in the wilderness. After God judged the people for their worship of the golden calf, the tabernacle was constructed and consecrated. It was a thing of beauty in a barren land and revealed much about the person of God and the way of Redemption.

Title — The Hebrew title is *we'elleh shemoth*, "and these are the names." This comes from the first phrase in 1:1. Exodus begins with "and" to show its continuity with Genesis. The Greek title is *Exodos*, "exit, departure, going out." The Septuagint used this word to describe the book by its key event (see 19:1, "gone out"). *Exodos* is translated "departure" in Luke 9:31 and 2 Peter 1:15, and in both places it speaks of physical death (Jesus and Peter). This fits well with Exodus' theme of redemption because it is accomplished through death. The Latin title is *Liber Exodus*, "the Book of Departure," taken from the Greek title.

Author — Critics have challenged the Mosaic authorship of Exodus in favor of a series of oral and written documents that were woven together by editors late in Israel's history. Their arguments are generally weak and far from conclusive, especially in view of the strong external and internal evidence that points to Moses as the author.

External Evidence: Exodus has been attributed to Moses since the time of Joshua (compare Exod. 20:25 with Josh. 8:30-32). Other biblical writers attribute Exodus to Moses: David (1 Kings 2:3), Ezra (Ezra 6:18), Daniel (Dan. 9:11), Malachi (Mal. 4:4), the disciples (John 1:45), and Paul (Rom. 10:5). This is also the testimony of Jesus (Mark 7:10; 12:26; Luke 20:37; John 5:46-47; 7:19,22,23). Jewish and Samaritan tradition consistently held the Mosaic authorship of Exodus.

Internal Evidence: Portions of Exodus are directly attributed to Moses (Exod. 15; 17:8-14; 20:1-17; 24:4,7,12; 31:18; 34:1-27). Moses' usual procedure was to record events soon after they occurred in the form of historical annals. It is clear from Exodus that the author must have been an eyewitness of the exodus and an educated man. He was acquainted with details about the customs and climate of Egypt and the plants, animals, and terrain of the wilderness. There is also a consistency of style and development that points to a single author. Its antiquity is supported by its frequent use of ancient literary constructions, words, and expressions.

Date and Setting — If the early date for the exodus (about 1445 B.C.) is assumed, this book was composed during the 40-year wilderness journey, between 1445 B.C. and 1405 B.C. Moses probably kept an account of God's work which he edited in the plains of Moab shortly before his death. Exodus covers the period from the arrival of Jacob in Egypt (about 1875 B.C.) to the erection of the tabernacle 431 years later in the wilderness (about 1445 B.C.).

Theme and Purpose — There are two basic themes in Exodus, and both tie in together. The first theme is redemption, portrayed in the Passover, and the second theme is deliverance, portrayed in the exodus from Egypt (Exod. 6:6; 15:13,16; Deut. 7:8). This redemption and deliverance was accomplished through the shedding of blood and by the power of God.

Exodus was written to portray the birth of Israel as the nation that would bring God's rule on earth. It records the story of Israel's redemption under the leadership of Moses. It also serves as an exposé of the falsehood of idolatry. Yahweh is revealed as infinitely superior to any so-called "gods." Exodus also teaches that obedience to God is necessary for a redeemed and set apart people.

Contribution to the Bible — Exodus accounts for many of the religious ceremonies and customs of Israel, the creation of the tabernacle, the formation of the priesthood, the Mosaic Law, and the sacrificial system. As such, Exodus is foundational for the following history of Israel. It describes how the Israelites escaped from Egypt, became the covenant people of God, and came to know His presence and His ways. Exodus stands at the heart of the Old Testament as the greatest example of the saving acts of God before Christ. It provides the framework for the rest of the Old Testament message. The Passover, the exodus, Moses, the Law, and the tabernacle dominated the thought of Israel for centuries to come.

Christ in Exodus — Exodus has no Messianic prophecies, but it is full of types and portraits of Christ. Here are seven: (1)

Moses: In dozens of ways Moses was a type of Christ (Deut. 18:15). Both Moses and Christ were prophets, priests, and kings; both were kinsman-redeemers; both were endangered in infancy; both voluntarily renounced power and wealth; both were deliverers, lawgivers, and mediators. (2) *The Passover:* John 1:29,36 and 1 Corinthians 5:7 make it clear that Christ is our slain Passover Lamb. There are many parallels between the Lamb of God and the Passover lamb. (3) *The seven feasts:* Each of these feasts portrays some aspect of the ministry of Christ. (4) *The exodus:* Paul relates the concept of baptism to the exodus event because baptism symbolizes death to the old and identification with the new (Rom. 6:2-3; 1 Cor. 10:1-2). (5) *The manna and water:* The New Testament applies both to Christ (John 6:31-35,48-63; 1 Cor. 10:3-4). (6) *The tabernacle:* In its materials, colors, furniture, and arrangement, the tabernacle clearly speaks of the person of Christ and the way of redemption. There is a progressive development from suffering, blood, and death to beauty, holiness, and the glory of God. The tabernacle is theology in object form. (7) *The high priest:* In several ways the high priest foreshadowed the ministry of Christ, our great High Priest (Heb. 4:14-16; 9:11-12,24-28).

Leviticus

"For the life of the flesh is in the blood, and I have given it to you on the altar to make atonement for your souls; for it is the blood by reason of the life that makes atonement."

Leviticus 17:11

"For I am the LORD, who brought you up from the land of Egypt, to be your God; thus you shall be holy for I am holy."

Leviticus 11:45 (cf. 19:2.)

Focus	Sacrifice			Sanctification					
	1 10			11 27					
D I V I S I O N S	Three Voluntary Offerings	Two Compulsory Offerings	Ministry of Priests in Offerings	Sanctification by Personal Purity	Sanctification by the Day of Atonement	Sanctification through Blood	Sanctification in Relationships	Sanctification by the Priests and Feasts	Sanctification in the Promised Land
	1 3	4 7	8 10	11 15	16	17	18 20	21 23	24 27
T O P I C S	How to Approach a Holy God			How to Walk with a Holy God					
	Worship			Practice					
	Access to God by Sacrifice			Fellowship with God by Obedience					
	"I the LORD your God am holy"			"You shall be holy"					
Loca-tion	Mt. Sinai								
Time	1 Month								

Talk Thru — It has been said that it took God only one night to get Israel out of Egypt, but it took 40 years to get Egypt out of Israel. The themes of Exodus were redemption and deliverance, but Leviticus focuses on sanctification and cleansing. In Exodus Israel was redeemed and established as a kingdom of priests and a holy nation. Leviticus carries on the story not only chronologically, but also logically, by showing how the children of Israel must fulfill their priestly call. They have been led out from the land of bondage in Exodus and into the sanctuary of God in Leviticus. They move from redemption to service, from deliverance to dedication.

At the end of Exodus the tabernacle had just been completed; Leviticus follows to show how it was to be used. This book served as a handbook for the Levitical priesthood, giving instructions and regulations for worship. Leviticus was used to guide a newly redeemed people into worship, service, and obedience to God. The historical narrative has come to a halt in this book because it emphasizes teaching and not time (only one month). It falls into two major sections: (1) Sacrifice (1-10), and (2) Sanctification (11-27).

Sacrifice (1-10): This section teaches that God must be approached by sacrificial offerings (1-7) and by the mediation of the priesthood (8-10). The blood sacrifices reminded the worshipers that the holy God required the costly gift of life (17:11). The blood of the innocent sacrificial animal became the substitute for the life of the guilty offerer: "without shedding of blood there is no forgiveness" (Heb. 9:22b). The first three sacrifices were voluntary and Godward; the last two were compulsory and manward. The former spoke of consecration, service, and fellowship, while the latter spoke of atonement and recompense.

Sanctification (11-27): The Israelites served a holy God (1-10) who required them to be holy as well (11-27). To be holy means to be "set apart" or "separated." They were to be separated *from* other nations *unto* God. In Leviticus the idea of holiness appears 87 times, sometimes meaning ceremonial holiness (ritual requirements), and at other times moral holiness (purity of life). This sanctification extended to purity of heart, body, and personal relationships. It was necessary to remove the defilement which separated the people from God so that they could have a walk of fellowship with their Redeemer.

The harsh laws and severe penalties in Leviticus revealed God's awesome holiness and intolerance of sin. The blessing of the people was based upon obedience (26:3-9,14-16).

Title — The Hebrew title is *wayyiqra*, "and he called" (Lev. 1:1). The Talmud refers to Leviticus as the "Law of the Priests," and the "Law of the Offerings." The Greek title used by the Septuagint is *Leuitikon*, "that which pertains to the Levites." The Latin Vulgate derived its name *Leviticus* from this work, and this was adopted as the English title. This title is slightly misleading because the book does not deal with the Levites as a whole but with the priests, a segment of the Levites.

Author — The kind of arguments used to support the Mosaic authorship of Genesis and Exodus apply to Leviticus because the Pentateuch is a literary unit. In addition to these arguments, here are others:

External Evidence: (1) There is a uniform ancient testimony to the Mosaic authorship of Leviticus. (2) There are ancient parallels to the Levitical system of trespass offerings in the Ras Shamra Tablets dating from about 1400 B.C. and found on the coast of northern Syria. (3) Christ ascribes the Pentateuch, which includes Leviticus, to Moses. More specifically, He alludes to Leviticus and attributes it to Moses (Matt. 8:2-4 and Lev. 14:1-4; Matt. 12:4 and Lev. 24:9; also see Luke 2:22).

Internal Evidence: (1) Leviticus states 56 times in its 27 chapters that Yahweh imparted these laws to Moses (see 1:1; 4:1; 6:1,24; 8:1). (2) The Levitical Code fits the time of Moses. Economic, civil, moral, and religious considerations show it to be ancient. Many of the laws are also related to a migratory lifestyle.

Date and Setting — No movement takes place in Leviticus—the children of Israel remain camped at the foot of Mt. Sinai (25:1-2; 26:46; 27:34). The new calendar of Israel began with the first Passover (Exod. 12:2), and according to Exodus 40:17 the tabernacle was completed exactly one year later. Leviticus picks up the story at this point and takes place in the first month of the second year. Numbers 1:1 opens at the beginning of the second month. Moses probably wrote much of

Leviticus during that first month. He may have put it in its final form shortly before his death in Moab, about 1405 B.C.

Theme and Purpose — The clear theme of Leviticus is holiness (11:45; 19:2). It teaches that one must approach a holy God on the basis of sacrifice and priestly mediation, and that one can only walk with a holy God on the basis of sanctification and obedience. God's chosen people must approach Him in a holy manner.

Leviticus was written to show Israel how to live as a priestly kingdom and a holy nation in fellowship with God. It provides a guide for worship, a law code, and a handbook on holiness for the priests. In Genesis man was ruined and Israel was born; in Exodus people were redeemed and Israel delivered; in Leviticus people were cleansed and Israel consecrated to the service of God.

Contribution to the Bible — For some readers Leviticus appears dull. It has no action or plot except for the death of Nadab and Abihu in chapter 10. It is heavy with rules, regulations and repetition. Its content seems outmoded and difficult to apply. But in reality Leviticus is rich in spiritual truth. It develops a number of doctrinal and practical themes centering on the questions of pardon for guilt and fellowship with God. It reveals how God in His grace accepts the death of a substitute as payment for the penalty of sin. And it has a number of types and portraits of the coming Messiah.

Leviticus is to Exodus what the Epistles are to the Gospels:

Exodus	Leviticus
pardon	purity
God's approach to man	man's approach to God
man's guilt	man's defilement
salvation	sanctification
a great act	a long process

The predictive types and symbols in this book are fulfilled in the New Testament, particularly in Hebrews.

Christ in Leviticus — (1) *The five offerings:* The *burnt offering* typifies Christ's total offering in submission to His

18

Father's will. The *meal offering* typifies Christ's sinless service. The *peace offering* typifies the fellowship believers have with God through the work of the cross. The *sin offering* typifies Christ as our guilt-bearer. The *trespass offering* typifies Christ's payment for the damage of sin. (2) *The high priest:* There are several comparisons and contrasts between Aaron, the first high priest and Christ, our eternal High Priest. (3) *The seven feasts: Passover* speaks of the substitutionary death of the Lamb of God. Christ died on the day of Passover. *Unleavened Bread* speaks of the holy walk of the believer (1 Cor. 5:6-8). *First Fruits* speaks of Christ's resurrection as the first fruits of the resurrection of all believers (1 Cor. 15:20-23). Christ rose on the day of the First Fruits. *Pentecost* speaks of the descent of the Holy Spirit after Christ's ascension. *Trumpets, the Day of Atonement*, and *Tabernacles* speak of events associated with the second advent of Christ. This may be why these three are separated by a long gap from the first four in Israel's year.

Numbers

"Surely all the men who have seen My glory and My signs, which I performed in Egypt and in the wilderness, yet have put Me to the test these ten times and have not listened to My voice, shall by no means see the land which I swore to their fathers, nor shall any of those who spurned Me see it."

Numbers 14:22-23

Focus	The Old Generation			The Tragic Transition			The New Generation			
	1 14			15 20			21 36			
D I V I S I O N S	Counting & Ordering of the People	Cleansing of the People	Complaints & Disbelief of the People	Instructions for Life in Canaan	The Rebellion of Korah	Aaron, the Levites, & Moses	Serpent of Brass & Story of Balaam	Second Census & Laws of Israel	Settling East of Jordan	Preparations for Settling in Canaan
	1 4	5 10:10	10:11 14	15	16	17 20	21 25	26 30	31 33	34 36
T O P I C S	Preparation			Postponement			Promise			
	Waiting			Wandering			Waiting			
	Census, Instruction, Travel			—			Travel, Census, Instruction			
Loca-tions	Sinai to Kadesh			Wilderness			Kadesh to Moab			
Time	About 2 Months (39% of Numbers)			38 Years (17% of Numbers)			A Few Months (44% of Numbers)			

Talk Thru — Israel as a nation was in its infancy at the outset of this book, only 13 months after its exodus from Egypt. In Numbers, the book of divine discipline, it became necessary for the nation to go through the painful process of maturation. God had to teach them the consequences of irresponsible decisions. The 40 years of wilderness experience transformed them from a rabble of ex-slaves into a nation ready to take the promised land. Numbers begins with the old generation (1-14), moves through a tragic transitional period (15-20), and ends with the new generation (21-36) at the doorway to the land of Canaan.

The Old Generation (1-14) -– The generation that witnessed God's miraculous acts of deliverance and preservation received further directions from God while they were still at the foot of Mt. Sinai (1-10:10). God's instructions were very explicit, reaching every aspect of their lives. He is the Author of order, not confusion, and this is seen in the way He organized the people around the tabernacle. Turning from the outward conditions of the camp (1-4) to the inward conditions (5-10), Numbers describes the spiritual preparation of the people.

Israel followed God step by step until Canaan was in sight. Then at the crucial moment they drew back in disbelief. Their murmurings had already become incessant ("Now the people became like those who complain of adversity in the hearing of the LORD," 11:1), but their disbelief after sending out the 12 spies at Kadesh-barnea was something God would not tolerate. Their rebellion here marks the pivotal point of the book. The generation of the exodus would not be the generation of the conquest.

The Tragic Transition (15-20) -– Disbelief brings discipline and hinders God's blessing. The old generation was doomed to literally kill time for 40 years of wilderness wanderings—one year for every day spent by the 12 spies in inspecting the land. They were judged by disinheritance and death as their journey changed from one of anticipation to one of aimlessness. Only Joshua and Caleb, the two spies who believed God, entered Canaan. Almost nothing is recorded about these transitional years of void.

The New Generation (21-36) -– When the transition to the new generation was complete, the people moved to the plains of Moab, directly east of the promised land (22:1). Before they could enter the land they had to wait until all was ready. Here they received new instructions, a new census was taken, Joshua was appointed as Moses' successor, and some of the people settled in the Transjordan.

Numbers records two generations (1-14 and 21-36), two numberings (1 and 26), two journeyings (10-14 and 21-27), and two sets of instructions (5-9 and 28-36). It illustrates both the kindness and severity of God (Rom. 11:22) and teaches that God's people can move forward only as far as they trust and depend on Him.

Title — The first word in the Hebrew text of Numbers is *wayyedabber*, "and he said." But Jewish writings usually refer to it by the fifth Hebrew word in 1:1, *bemidbar*, "in the wilderness." This relates better to the content of the book. The Greek title in the Septuagint is *Arithmoi*, "Numbers." The Latin Vulgate followed this title and translated it *Liber Numeri*, "the Book of Numbers." These titles are based on the two numberings: the generation of exodus (Num. 1) and the generation that grew up in the wilderness and conquered Canaan (Num. 26). Numbers has also been called the "Book of the Journeyings," the "Book of the Murmurings," and the "Fourth Book of Moses."

Author — The evidence that points to Moses as the author of Numbers is similar to that for the previous books of the Pentateuch. These five books form such a literary unit that they rise or fall together on the matter of authorship.

External Evidence: There is a universal ancient testimony to the Mosaic authorship of Numbers (Jews, Samaritans, the early church). There are also a number of New Testament passages that cite events from Numbers and associate them with Moses. These include John 3:14; Acts 7,13; 1 Corinthians 10:1-11; Hebrews 3-4; and Jude 11.

Internal Evidence: There are more than 80 claims that "the LORD spoke to Moses" (the first is 1:1). In addition, Numbers 33:2 makes this clear statement: "And Moses recorded their starting places according to their journeys by the command of the LORD..." Moses kept detailed records as an eyewitness of the events in this book. Moses, as the central character of Exodus to Deuteronomy, was better qualified than any other man to write these books.

Some have claimed that the third person references to Moses point to a different author. But this was a common practice in the ancient world (Caesar did the same in his writings).

Date and Setting — Leviticus covered only one month, but Numbers stretches over almost 39 years (about 1444 B.C. to 1405 B.C.). It records Israel's movement from the last 19 days at Mt. Sinai (1:1; 10:11) to the arrival in the plains of Moab in the 40th year (22:1; 26:3; 33:50; Deut. 1:3). Most of this time was spent wandering in and around Kadesh-barnea. Their tents occupied several square miles whenever they camped since there were over 2.5 million people (based on the census figures in Numbers 1 and 26). God miraculously fed and sustained them in the desert—He preserved their clothing and gave them manna, meat, water, leaders, and a promise.

Theme and Purpose — The theme of Numbers is the consequence of disbelief and disobedience to the holy God. The Lord disciplined His people but remained faithful to His covenant promises in spite of their fickleness. Numbers displays the patience, holiness, justice, mercy, and sovereignty of God toward His people. It teaches that there are no shortcuts to His blessings—He uses trials and tests for specific purposes.

Numbers was written to trace the history of Israel's wanderings from Sinai to Moab. But the fact that there is almost no record of the 38 years of wandering shows that Numbers is a very thematic history. It selects those events that are important to the development of God's redemptive program. The sins of the first generation were written as a reminder and a warning to the second generation. They must implicitly trust God before they can possess the land of blessing.

Contribution to the Bible — In Genesis God elected a people, in Exodus He redeemed them, in Leviticus He sanctified them, and in Numbers He directed them. Numbers takes up the story where Leviticus left off, on Mt. Sinai. Leviticus describes the believers' worship, Numbers their walk:

Leviticus	Numbers
sanctuary	wilderness
purity	pilgrimage
fellowship	faithlessness
legislative	narrative
ceremonial	historical

Numbers teaches the important lesson that biblical faith often requires trusting God against appearances (in this case, the prospect of annihilation by superior enemy forces). Two extensive New Testament passages turn to this wilderness experience for illustrations of spiritual truth. In 1 Corinthians 10:1-12 it illustrates the danger of self-indulgence and immorality, and in Hebrews 3:7-4:6 it illustrates the theme of entering God's rest through belief. "Now these things happened to them as an example, and they were written for our instruction, upon whom the ends of the ages have come" (1 Cor. 10:11).

Christ in Numbers — Perhaps the clearest portrait of Christ in Numbers is the bronze serpent on the stake, a picture of the crucifixion (21:4-9): "And as Moses lifted up the serpent in the wilderness, even so must the Son of Man be lifted up"(John 3:14). The rock that slaked the thirst of the multitudes was also a type of Christ: "...they were drinking from a spiritual rock which followed them; and the rock was Christ" (1 Cor. 10:4). The daily manna pictured the Bread of Life who came down from heaven (John 6:31-33).

In Numbers 24:17 Balaam foresaw the rulership of Christ: "I see him, but not now; I behold him, but not near; a star shall come forth from Jacob, and a scepter shall rise from Israel..." The guidance and presence of Christ is seen in the pillar of cloud and fire, and the sinner's refuge in Christ is portrayed in the six cities of refuge. The red heifer sacrifice (Num. 19) is also considered a type of Christ.

Deuteronomy

"And now, Israel, what does the LORD your God require from you, but to fear the LORD your God, to walk in all His ways and love Him, and to serve the LORD your God with all your heart and with all your soul, and to keep the LORD'S commandments and His statutes which I am commanding you today for your good?"

Deuteronomy 10:12-13

"I call heaven and earth to witness against you today, that I have set before you life and death, the blessing and the curse. So choose life in order that you may live, you and your descendants, by loving the LORD your God, by obeying His voice, and by holding fast to Him; for this is your life and the length of your days, that you may live in the land which the LORD swore to your fathers, to Abraham, Isaac, and Jacob, to give them."

Deuteronomy 30:19-20 (Also see 4:1; 5:29; 6:4-5.)

Focus	Remembering the Past	Reviewing the Present				Revealing the Future	Retirement of a Leader
	1 4	5 26				27 30	31 34
D I V I S I O N S	Historical Survey	Basic Commandments and Warnings	Ceremonial Laws	Civil Laws	Social Laws	Ratification of the Covenant	Farewell and Death of Moses
	1 4	5 11	12 16	17 20	21 26	27 30	31 34
T O P I C S	Moses' First Sermon	Moses' Second Sermon				Moses' Third Sermon	Moses' Parting Words
	Historical	Legal				Prophetical	Historical
	Retrospective	Introspective				Prospective	
Loca-tions	Moab						
Time	1 Month						

Talk Thru — Deuteronomy, Moses' "Upper Desert Discourse," consists of a series of farewell messages by Israel's 120-year-old leader to the new generation that is about to possess the land of promise. It is like Leviticus because of its vast legal material, but its emphasis is on the laymen rather than the priests and sacrifices. Moses reminds this second generation of their need for obedience in order to fulfill their divine calling: "He brought us out from there [Egypt] in order to bring us in [Canaan], to give us the land which He had sworn to our fathers" (6:23). Moses moves from a retrospective, to an introspective, and finally to a prospective look at God's dealings with Israel.

Remembering the Past (1-4) — Moses reaches into the past to remind the people of two undeniable facts in their history: (1) the moral judgment of God upon Israel's unbelief, and (2) the deliverance and provision of God during times of obedience. The simple lesson is that obedience brings blessing and disobedience, punishment.

Reviewing the Present (5-26) — This moral and legal section is the longest in the book because Israel's future as a nation in Canaan will depend upon a right relationship with God. These chapters sermonically review the three categories of the Law: (1) The testimonies (5-11). These are the moral duties — a restatement and expansion of the Ten Commandments plus an exhortation not to forget God's gracious deliverance. (2) The statutes (12-16). These are the ceremonial duties — sacrifices, tithes, and feasts. (3) The ordinances (17-26). These are the civil (17-20) and social (21-26) duties — the system of justice, criminal laws, and laws of warfare plus rules of property, personal and family morality, and social justice.

Revealing the Future (27-30) — In these chapters Moses wrote history in advance. He predicted what would befall Israel in the near future (blessings and cursings) and in the distant future (dispersion among the nations and eventual return). Moses listed the terms of the covenant that was about to be ratified by the people.

Retirement of a Leader (31-34) — Because Moses was not allowed to enter the land, he appointed Joshua as his successor and delivered a farewell address to the multitude. God Himself buried Moses in an unknown place (perhaps to prevent idolatry). Moses finally entered the promised land when he appeared with Christ on the Mount of Transfiguration (Matt. 17:3). The last three verses of the Pentateuch (34:10-12) give an appropriate epitaph to this great man.

Title — The Hebrew title of Deuteronomy is *haddebharim*, "the words," taken from the opening phrase in 1:1, "These are the words." The parting words of Moses to the new generation were given in oral and written form so that they would endure to all generations. It has been called "five-fifths of the Law" since it completes the five books of Moses. The Jewish people have also called it *mishneh hattorah*, "repetition of the Law," and the "Book of Admonitions." The Septuagint mistranslated 17:18, "a copy of this law" as *to deuteronomion touto*, "this second law." Deuteronomy, however, is not a second law but an adaptation and expansion of much of the original law given on Mt. Sinai. The English title comes from the Greek title *Deuteronomion*, "Second Law." Deuteronomy has also been well called the "Book of Remembrance."

Author — The Mosaic authorship of Deuteronomy has been vigorously attacked by critics who claim that Moses was only the traditional originator of these laws. Some critics grant that part of Deuteronomy may have come from Mosaic times through oral tradition. The usual argument is that it was anonymously written not long before 621 B.C. and used by King Josiah to bring about his reform in that year (2 Kings 22-23). There are several reasons why these arguments are not valid.

External Evidence — (1) The Old Testament attributes Deuteronomy and the rest of the Pentateuch to Moses (see Josh. 1:7; Judg. 3:4; 1 Kings 2:3; 2 Kings 14:6; Ezra 3:2; Neh. 1:7; Ps. 103:7; Dan. 9:11; Mal. 4:4). (2) There is evidence from Joshua and 1 Samuel that these laws existed in the form of codified written statutes and exerted an influence on the Israelites in Canaan. (3) Christ quoted it as God's Word in turning back Satan's three temptations (Matt. 4:4,7,10) and attributed it directly to Moses (Matt. 19:7-9; Mark 7:10; Luke 20:28; John 5:45-47). (4) Deuteronomy is cited more than 80 times in 17 of the 27 New Testament books. These citations support the Mosaic authorship (see Acts 3:22; Rom. 10:19). (5) Jewish and Samaritan tradition points to Moses.

Internal Evidence: (1) Deuteronomy makes about 40 claims that Moses wrote it. Read 31:24-26 (also see 1:1-5; 4:44-46; 29:1; 31:9). (2) Deuteronomy fits the time of Moses, not Josiah: Canaan is viewed from the outside, the Canaanite religion is seen as a future menace, it assumes the hearers remember Egypt and the wilderness, Israel is described as living in tents, there is no evidence of a divided kingdom. (3) There would be a serious problem of misrepresentation and literary forgery if written in the 7th century B.C. (4) Geographical and historical details show a firsthand knowledge. (5) It follows the treaty form used in the 15th and 14th centuries B.C. (6) Moses' obituary in 34 was probably written by Joshua.

Date and Setting — Like Leviticus, Deuteronomy is a stationary book. It takes place entirely on the plain of Moab due east of Jericho and the Jordan River (1:1; 29:1; Josh. 1:2). It covers about one month (combine 1:3; 34:8 with Josh. 5:6-12). The book was written at the end of the 40-year period in the wilderness (about 1405 B.C.) when the new generation was on the verge of entering Canaan. Moses wrote it to encourage the people to believe and obey God in order to receive God's blessings.

Theme and Purpose — "Beware lest you forget" is a key theme in Deuteronomy. Moses emphasizes the danger of forgetfulness because it leads to arrogance and disobedience. They must remember two things: (1) when they prosper, it is God who has caused it, and (2) when they disobey God, He will discipline them as He did when the previous generation failed to believe Him at Kadesh-barnea. Deuteronomy is a call to obedience as a condition to blessing. God has always been faithful to His covenant and He now extends it to the new generation. Deuteronomy is a covenant renewal document that uses the same format as Near Eastern treaties in the time of Moses. These treaties had the following elements: (1) a preamble (a list of the parties making the treaty; 1:1-5), (2) a historical prologue (the benevolent dealings of the king in the past; 1:6-4:43), (3) stipulations (conditions of the covenant; 4:44-26:19), (4) ratification (blessings and cursings; 27-30), and (5) continuity (provisions for maintaining the covenant; 31-34). There is an emphasis on choice, and the people are urged to choose life rather than death (30:19-20). They are told to "hear" (50 times)

and "do," "keep," "observe" (177 times) God's commands out of a heart of "love" (21 times).

Contribution to the Bible — Deuteronomy is a supplementary book to the rest of the Pentateuch and fills a role similar to that of the Gospel of John compared to the synoptic gospels. It fills in missing elements and gives the spiritual significance of the history found in the other books of Moses. Genesis to Numbers portray God's ways, Deuteronomy reveals God's love:

Genesis to Numbers	Deuteronomy
development of Israel's history	philosophy of Israel's history
divine performances	divine principles
God speaks to Moses	Moses speaks to the people

The emphasis on God's love in this book (4:37; 7:7-8; 10:15; 23:5) was a crucial step for Israel's understanding.

Deuteronomy was perhaps Christ's favorite book. He quoted from it often: Matthew 4:4,7,10; 22:37,38; Mark 7:10; 10:19; 12:29,30.

Christ in Deuteronomy — The most obvious portrait of Christ is found in 18:15: "The LORD your God will raise up for you a prophet like me from among you, from your countrymen, you shall listen to him" (also 18:16-19; Acts 7:37). As mentioned before under Exodus, Moses was a type of Christ in many ways. He was the only biblical figure other than Christ to fill the three offices of prophet (34:10-12), priest (Exod. 32:31-35), and king (33:4-5). Both were in danger of death during childhood, both were saviors, intercessors, and deliverers, both were rejected by their brethren. Moses was one of the greatest men who ever lived, combining not just one or two memorable virtues but many.

The Feasts of Israel

			The First Coming of Christ		
Month	Day(s)	Feast	Look Back On . . .	Looks Ahead To . . .	Scripture
1st	14	Passover	Redemption of Firstborn	Christ's Redeeming Death	1 Corinthians 5 1 Peter 1:18-19
1st	15-21	Un-leavened Bread	Separation from Other Nations	Holy Walk of Believers	1 Corinthians 5:7 Galatians 5:9,16-
1st	16	First Fruits	Harvest in the Land	Resurrection of Christ Revelation 1:5	1 Corinthians 15:20-23
3rd	6	Pentecost	Completion of Harvest	Sending of the Holy Spirit	Acts 2:1-47 1 Corinthians 12:

The Summer Gap (John 4:35)

			The Second Coming of Christ		
7th	1	Trumpets	Israel's New Year	Israel's Regathering	Isaiah 27:12-13 Matthew 24:21-31
7th	10	Day of Atonement	Israel's National Sin	Israel's National Conversion	Zechariah 12:10 Romans 11:26-27
7th	15-22	Tabernacles	Israel in the Wilderness	Israel in the Kingdom	Zechariah 14:4-16 Revelation 7:9-17

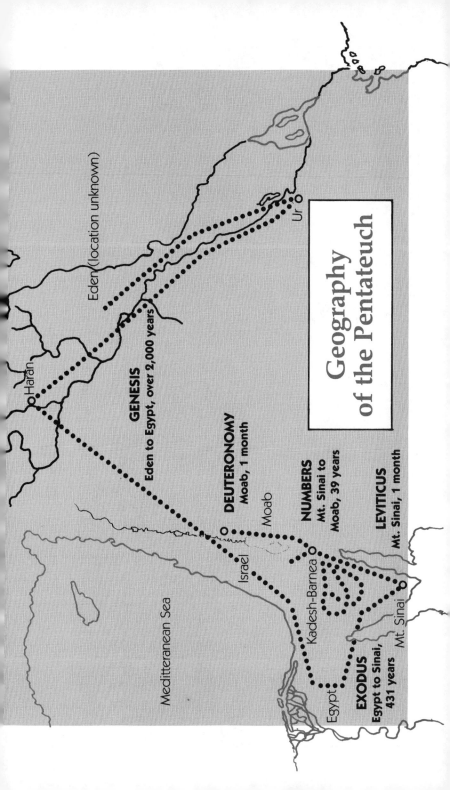

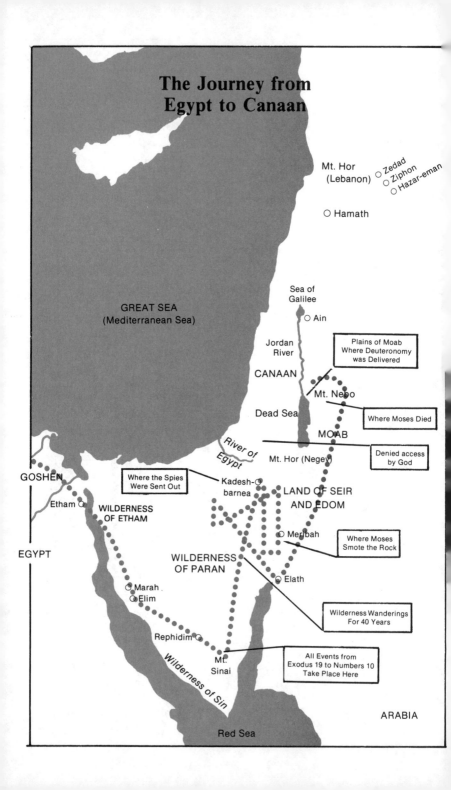

Introduction to the Historical Books

The 12 historical books pick up the story of Israel where it left off at the end of Deuteronomy. These books describe the occupation and settlement of Israel in the promised land, the transition from judges to the monarchy, the division and decline of the kingdom, the captivities of the northern and southern kingdom, and the return of the remnant.

The historical books break into three divisions: (1) the theocratic books (Joshua, Judges, Ruth), (2) the monarchical books (Samuel, Kings, Chronicles), and (3) the restoration books (Ezra, Nehemiah, Esther).

The Theocratic Books

These books cover the conquest and settlement of Canaan and life during the time of the judges. During these years (1405-1043 B.C.), Israel was a nation ruled by God (a theocracy).

Joshua: The first half of Joshua describes the seven-year conquest of the land of promise through faith and obedience on the part of Joshua and the people. After their spiritual and physical preparation, the Israelites took the land in three campaigns: central, southern, and northern. The last half of the book details the partitioning of the land among the 12 tribes and closes with Joshua's challenge to the people.

Judges: The disobedience in Judges stands in contrast to the faithful obedience found in Joshua. The Israelites did not drive out all the Canaanites and began to take part in their idolatry.

Judges records seven cycles of foreign oppression, repentance, and deliverance. The people failed to learn from these cycles, and the book ends with two illustrations of idolatry and immorality.

Ruth: This little book sheds a ray of light in an otherwise dark period. The story of Ruth occurred in the days of the judges, but it is a powerful illustration of righteousness, love, and faithfulness to the Lord.

The Monarchical Books

These six books trace the history of Israel's monarchy from its inception in 1043 B.C. to its destruction in 586 B.C.

1 Samuel: The prophet Samuel carried Israel across the transition from the judges to the monarchy. The people clamored for a king and God told Samuel to anoint Saul. Saul began well but soon degenerated into an ungodly tyrant. David became God's king-elect but he was pursued by the jealous Saul whose murderous intentions were checked only by death.

2 Samuel: Upon the demise of Saul, David reigned for seven years over Judah and another 33 years over the 12 reunited tribes. His reign was characterized by great blessing until he committed adultery and murder. From that point until his death he was plagued by personal, family, and national struggles.

1 Kings: Solomon brought the kingdom to its political and economic zenith, but this wisest of men played the fool in his multiple marriages with foreign women. After his death in 931 B.C., the kingdom was tragically divided when the 10 northern tribes of Israel set up their own king. Only the southern kingdom of Judah (two tribes) remained subject to the Davidic dynasty.

2 Kings: The story of the divided kingdom continues in 2 Kings as it carries Israel and Judah to their bitter ends. None of the 19 kings of Israel did what was right in the sight of God, and their corruption led to captivity at the hands of the Assyrians in 722 B.C. Judah lasted longer because eight of its 20 rulers followed the Lord. But Judah also fell in judgment and was carried away by the Babylonians between 605 B.C. and 586 B.C.

1 Chronicles: The books of Chronicles give a divine perspective on the history of Israel from the time of David to the two captivities. The first book begins with a nine-chapter genealogy from Adam to the family of Saul, followed by a spiritually-oriented account of the life of David.

2 Chronicles: This book continues the narrative with the life of Solomon, and focuses on the construction and dedication of the temple. It then traces the history of the kings of Judah only, giving the spiritual and moral reasons for its ultimate downfall.

The Restoration Books

The last three historical books describe the return of a remnant of the Jews to their homeland after 70 years (605-536 B.C.) of captivity. They were led in the period from 536-420 B.C. by Zerubbabel Ezra, and Nehemiah.

Ezra: Babylon was conquered by Persia in 539 B.C. and Cyrus issued a decree in 536 B.C. that allowed the Jews to return to Palestine. Zerubbabel led about 50,000 to Jerusalem to rebuild the temple, and years later (458 B.C.), Ezra the priest returned with almost 2,000 Jews.

Nehemiah: The temple was built, but the wall of Jerusalem still lay in ruins. Nehemiah obtained permission, supplies, and money from the king of Persia to rebuild the walls (444 B.C.). After the walls were built, Ezra and Nehemiah led the people in revival and reforms.

Esther: The story of Esther took place between chapters 6 and 7 of Ezra. Most of the Jews chose to remain in Persia, but their lives were in danger because of a plot to exterminate them. God sovereignly intervened and used Esther and Mordecai to deliver the people.

Joshua

"So Joshua took the whole land, according to all that the LORD
had spoken to Moses, and Joshua gave it for an inheritance to
Israel according to their divisions by their tribes. Thus the land
had rest from war."

Joshua 11:23
(Also see 21:43-45.)

Focus	Conquest			Settlement		
	1 — 12			13 — 24		
D I V I S I O N S	Preparation of the People for War	The Central Campaign at Jericho and Ai	The Southern and Northern Campaigns	Allocations for Five Tribes and Caleb	Allocations for Seven Tribes and Levites	Joshua's Challenge to the Leaders and the People
	1 — 5	6 — 8	9 — 12	13 — 17	18 — 21	22 — 24
T O P I C S	Entering the Land	Conquering the Land		Dividing the Land		
	Possessing Canaan			Partitioning Canaan		
	Action			Allocation		
Loca-tions	9½ Tribes on the West Side of the Jordan — CANAAN 2½ Tribes on the East Side of the Jordan — TRANSJORDAN					
Time	7 Years (50% of Joshua)			About 18 Years (50% of Joshua)		

Talk Thru — Joshua, the first of the 12 historical books, forges a link between the Pentateuch and the remainder of Israel's history. It picks up the story where Deuteronomy left off and takes Israel from the wilderness to the promised land of Canaan. Israel has now reached its climactic point of fulfilling the centuries-old promise in Genesis of a homeland. The vision is now a venture; anticipation has become actuality. Moses was called to lead Israel out of bondage, but Joshua was called to bring Israel into blessing. The whole Pentateuch was a preparation for the consummation in Joshua. This book stresses that the victory of the people was based on faith and obedience (1 John 5:4). The first half (1-12) describes the seven-year conquest of the land, and the second half (13-24) gives the details of the partitioning and settlement of the land.

Conquest (1-12): The first five chapters record the spiritual, moral, and physical preparation of Joshua and the people for the impending conquest of Canaan. Joshua was given a charge by God to complete the task begun by Moses (1:2). After being encouraged by God, Joshua sent out two spies who came back with a favorable report (in contrast to the spies of the previous generation). Obedience and faith were united in the miraculous crossing of the Jordan River (3-4).

Joshua's campaign in central Canaan (6-8) drove a strategic wedge between the northern and southern cities that prevented a massive Canaanite alliance against Israel. This divide-and-conquer strategy proved effective, but God's directions for taking the first city (Jericho) sounded like foolishness from a military point of view. The Lord used this to test the people and teach them that Israel's success in battle would always be by His power and not their own might or cleverness. Sin had to be dealt with at once because it brought severe consequences and defeat (7).

The southern and northern campaigns (9-12) were also successful, but an unwise oath made to the deceptive Gibeonites forced Israel to protect them and disobey God's command to eliminate the Canaanites.

Settlement (13-24): Joshua was growing old and God told him to divide the land among the 12 tribes. Much remained to be won, and the tribes were to continue the conquest by faith after Joshua's death. Chapters 13-21 describe the allocation of the land to the various tribes as well as the inheritance of Caleb (14-

15) and the Levites (21). The last chapters (22-24) record a near civil war (22) and Joshua's final challenge to the leaders who must keep the law of God (23) and to the people who must serve the Lord (24). Possessing the land would not be enough—God also wanted the people to be blessed in the land, and this would require unity and obedience.

Title — This book is appropriately named after its central figure. Joshua's original name was *Hoshea*, "salvation" (Num. 13:8,16; Deut. 32:44), but Moses evidently changed it to *Yehoshua*, "Yahweh is salvation." He was also called *Yeshua*, a shortened form of *Yehoshua*. This is the Hebrew equivalent of the Greek name *Iesous* (Jesus). Thus the Greek title given to the book in the Septuagint was *Iesous Naus*, "Joshua the Son of Nun." The Latin title was *Liber Josue*, the "Book of Joshua."

Author — Although it cannot be proven, Jewish tradition seems correct in assigning the authorship of this book to Joshua himself. There are three small portions, however, that must have been added after Joshua's death. These are: (1) Othniel's capture of Kiriath-sepher (15:13-19; compare Judg. 1:9-15), (2) Dan's migration to the north (19:47; cf. Judg. 18:27-29), and (3) Joshua's death and burial (24:29-33). These may have been inserted early in the time of the judges by Eleazer the priest and his son Phineas (24:33).

Joshua 24:26 makes this clear statement: "And Joshua wrote these words in the book of the law of God . . ." This refers at least to Joshua's farewell charge if not to the book as a whole (also see 18:9). Joshua was the best qualified person to write the book as Israel's leader and an eyewitness of most of the events. He even uses the first person in one place (5:6, "us"; "we" appears in some manuscripts of 5:1). The book was written soon after the events happened: Rahab was still alive (6:25). Other evidences for early authorship are the detailed information about Israel's campaigns and the use of the ancient names of the Canaanite cities.

The unity of style and organization suggests a single authorship for the bulk of the book. But a number of critics support the same late document theory for Joshua that they use for the Pentateuch. In fact they often make it one with the Pentateuch, thus forming a "Hexateuch." The claim is that several sources were combined and edited centuries after the events took place. But there is no historical or textual basis for these theories.

Joshua was born a slave in Egypt but became a conqueror in Canaan. He served as personal attendant to Moses, one of the 12 spies (only he and Caleb believed God), and Moses' successor. His outstanding qualities were obedient faith, courageousness, and dedication to God and His Word.

Date and Setting — The conquest took place about 1405 B.C. (The late date of the exodus would mean a conquest around 1240 B.C. According to 13:2-3, the Philistines were not a threat or a dominant power in Joshua's time, but they were by 1200 B.C. A 1240 B.C. conquest would have meant a powerful Philistine force rather than the confused situation Joshua found.) Joshua died about 1380 B.C. at the age of 110, so the book covers events from 1405-1380 B.C.

The Canaanites at that time were morally and spiritually degraded and politically weak. Tablets from Ras Shamra reveal their brutality, corruption, infant sacrifice, serpent worship, and male and female prostitution. God used Israel as His rod of judgment against them because their iniquity was now "complete" (Gen. 15:16).

Theme and Purpose — The theme of Joshua is Israel's possession of the promised land and enjoyment of God's blessings through obedient faith.

Joshua's historical purpose is to document the conquest of Canaan by the Israelites under Joshua's leadership. As such, Joshua joins the 11 out of 17 historical books that carry on the geographical and chronological story of Israel from the time of Abraham to Malachi. The other 10 are: Genesis, Exodus, Numbers, Judges, 1 and 2 Samuel, 1 and 2 Kings, Ezra, and Nehemiah. The remaining six—Leviticus, Deuteronomy, Ruth, 1 and 2 Chronicles, and Esther—are supplementary in nature. Out of the list of 11, only Joshua does *not* record a massive failure by Israel or its leadership (the sin in chapter 7 was quickly remedied).

Theologically, Joshua teaches that victory and blessing come through obedience and trust in God. Active faith leads to obedience which in turn brings blessing. God required the people to attempt the impossible in submission to His directions before He made it possible for them to succeed. The book emphasizes God's covenant faithfulness to His promises regarding a land for Israel, and God's holiness in bringing judgment upon the immoral Canaanites.

Contribution to the Bible — Joshua acts as a historical link that continues the story left off in the Pentateuch. It is a theological history that teaches moral and spiritual lessons as it brings Israel from the wilderness up to the time of the judges. In Genesis God's people were prepared, in Exodus they were redeemed, in Leviticus they were taught, and in Numbers they failed God's test at Kadesh-barnea. The new generation was taught in Deuteronomy and tested in Joshua (Jericho). This time they passed the test of belief and received God's blessings. Israel moved from prospect to possession, from vision to venture. One of the key concepts in Joshua is the importance of the written Word of God (1:8; 8:32-35; 23:6-16; 24:26-27).

Christ in Joshua — Like Moses, Joshua is a type of Christ. His name *Yeshua* ("Yahweh is salvation") is the Hebrew equivalent of the name *Jesus.* In his role of triumphantly leading his people into their possessions, he foreshadowed the One who brought "many sons to glory" (Heb. 2:10). "But thanks be to God, who always leads us in His triumph in Christ" (2 Cor. 2:14; see Rom. 8:37). Joshua succeeded Moses and won the victory unreached by Moses. Christ succeeded the Mosaic law and won the victory that could not be reached by the law (John 1:17; Rom. 8:2-4; Gal. 3:23-25; Heb. 7:18-19).

The "captain of the host of the LORD" (5:13-16) met by Joshua was evidently a preincarnate appearance of Christ (compare 5:15 with Exod. 3:2).

Rahab's scarlet cord portrays safety through the blood (Heb. 9:19-22). This Gentile harlot is found in Christ's genealogy (Matt. 1:5) because of her faith (Heb 11:31).

Judges

"And they forsook the LORD, the God of their fathers, who had brought them out of the land of Egypt, and followed other gods from among the gods of the peoples who were around them and bowed themselves down to them; thus they provoked the LORD to anger."

Judges 2:12

"In those days there was no king in Israel; everyone did what was right in his own eyes."

Judges 21:25

Focus	Deter-ioration	Deliverances				Depravity
	1 2	3 16				17 21
DIVISIONS	Transition and Introduction	Five Judges (Cycles 1,2,3)	Gideon—The Hesitant Hero (Cycle 4)	Abimelech and Six Judges (Cycles 5,6)	Samson—The Carnal Champion (Cycle 7)	Idolatry and Immorality During the Judges
	1 2	3 5	6 8	9 12	13 16	17 21
TOPICS	Causes of the Cycles	Course of the Cycles				Conditions During the Cycles
	Expla-nation	Manifestation				Illustration
	Prologue	Narrative				Epilogue
Locations	Canaan and Transjordan					
Time	About 335 Years					

41

Talk Thru— The book of Judges stands in stark contrast to Joshua. There, an obedient people conquered the land through trust in the person and power of God. But in Judges, a disobedient and idolatrous people were frequently defeated because of their rejection of the person and power of God. Following the death of Joshua, Israel plunged into a 350-year spiritual Dark Ages. After Joshua and the generation of the conquest passed on, "there arose another generation after them who did not know the LORD, nor yet the work which He had done for Israel" (2:10; see 2:7-10 and Josh. 24:31). Judges opens with a description of Israel's deterioration, continues with seven cycles of oppression and deliverance, and concludes with two illustrations of Israel's depravity.

Deterioration (1-2): Judges begins with short-lived military successes after Joshua's death, but quickly turns to the repeated failure by all the tribes to drive out their enemies. The people felt the lack of a unified central leader, but the primary reason for their failure was a lack of faith and obedience to God (2:1-3). Compromise led to conflict and chaos. Israel "did not drive out the inhabitants" (1:21, 27, 29, 30)—instead of removing the moral cancer spread by the inhabitants of Canaan, they contracted the disease. The Canaanite gods literally became a snare to them (2:3). Judges 2:11-23 is a microcosm of the pattern found in Judges 3-16.

Deliverances (3-16): This section describes seven apostasies (falling away from God), seven servitudes, and seven deliverances. Each of the seven cycles has five steps: sin, servitude, supplication, salvation, and silence. These are also described by rebellion, retribution, repentance, restoration, and rest. The seven cycles connect together as a descending spiral of sin (2:19). Israel vascillated between obedience and apostasy as the people failed to learn from their mistakes. Apostasy grew, but the rebellion was not continual. The times of rest and peace were longer than the times of bondage. The monotony in Israel's sins can be contrasted with the creativity in God's methods of deliverance.

The judges were military and civil leaders during this period of loose confederacy. Thirteen are mentioned in this book and four more are found in 1 Samuel (Eli, Samuel, Joel, and Abijah).

Cycle	Oppressor	Years of Oppression	Deliverer	Years of Peace
1 (3:7-11)	Mesopotamians	8	Othniel	40
2 (3:12-30)	Moabites	18	Ehud	80
Parenthesis (3:31)	Philistines	—	Shagmar	—
3 (4:1-5:31)	Canaanites	20	Deborah/ Barak	40
4 (6:1-8:32)	Midianites	7	Gideon	40
5 (8:33-10:5)	Abimelech	3	Tola/Jair	45
6 (10:6-12:15)	Ammonites	18	Jepthah/Ibzan/ Elon/Abdon	6,7,10,8
7 (13:1-16:31)	Philistines	40	Samson	20

Depravity (17-21): These chapters illustrate (1) religious apostasy (17-18), and (2) social and moral depravity (19-21) during the period of the judges. Chapters 19-21 contain one of the worst tales of degradation in the Bible. Judges closes with a key to understanding the period: ". . . everyone did what was right in his own eyes" (21:25). The people didn't do what was *wrong* in their own eyes, but what was "evil in the sight of the LORD."

Title — The Hebrew title is the word for the leaders, *shophetim* ("judges, rulers, deliverers, saviors"). *Shophet* not only carries the idea of maintaining justice and settling disputes, but it is also used of liberating and delivering. First the judges delivered the people, then they ruled and administered justice. The Septuagint used the Greek equivalent of this word, *Kritai* ("Judges"). The Latin Vulgate called it *Liber Judicum,* the "Book of Judges." This book could also be appropriately titled The Book of Failure.

Author — The author of Judges is anonymous, but it may have been written by Samuel or one of his prophetic students. Jewish tradition (the Talmud) attributes Judges to Samuel, and certainly he was the crucial tie between the period of judges and the period of kings.

It is clear from 18:31 and 20:27 that the book was written after the ark was removed from Shiloh (1 Sam. 4:3-11). The repeated phrase "In those days there was no king in Israel"

(17:6; 18:1; 19:1; 21:25) shows that Judges was also written after the commencement of Saul's reign but before the divided kingdom. The fact that the Jebusites were dwelling in Jerusalem "to this day" (1:21) means that it was written before 1004 B.C. when David dispossessed the Jebusites (2 Sam. 5:5-9). Thus, the book was written during the time of Samuel, and it is likely that Samuel compiled this book from oral and written source material. His prophetic ministry clearly fits the moral commentary of Judges, and the consistent style and orderly scheme of Judges support a single compiler.

Judges 18:30 has a phrase that poses a problem to this early date of composition: ". . . until the day of the captivity of the land." If this refers to the 722 B.C. Assyrian captivity of Israel it could have been inserted by a later editor. It is more likely a reference to the Philistine captivity of the land during the time of the judges. This event is described by "captivity" in Psalm 78:61.

Date and Setting — If Judges was not written by Samuel, it was at least written by a contemporary of Samuel between 1043 B.C. (the beginning of Saul's reign) and 1004 B.C. (David's capture of Jerusalem).

Joshua's seven-year conquest was general in nature; much of the land remained to be possessed (Josh. 13:1). There were still important Canaanite strongholds that had to be taken by the individual tribes. Some of the nations were left "to test Israel" (3:1,4). During this time the Egyptians had strong control along the coastal routes, but they were not interested in the hill country where Israel was primarily established.

The events covered in Judges range from about 1380-1045 B.C. (about 335 years). But the period of the judges extends another 30 years since it includes the life of Samuel (1 Sam. 1:1-25:1). There are overlappings in the rules of some of the judges because not all of them ruled over the entire land. Judges describes the cycles of apostasy, oppression, and deliverance in the southern region (3:7-31), the northern region (4:1-5:31), the central region (6:1-10:5), the eastern region (10:6-12:15), and the western region (13:1-16:31). The spread of apostasy covered the whole land.

Theme and Purpose — The historical purpose of Judges

is to carry the story of Israel from the death of Joshua to the time of Samuel and the beginning of the united kingdom. It was written during the reign of Saul (1043-1011 B.C.) or during the first seven years of David's reign (1011-1004 B.C.), and it gives an explanation and defense of Israel's monarchy (17:6; 18:1; 19:1; 21:25). The nation needed to be unified under a righteous king.

Like the other historical books of the Bible, Judges presents the historical facts in a very selective and thematic way. For example, 17-21 actually preceded most of 3-16, but these chapters appear at the end of the book to illustrate the moral conditions that were prevailing during the period. Judges gives a geographical survey of apostasy to illustrate its spread and a chronological survey to illustrate its growing intensity. The book reaches a climax in 17-21 with the last verse as a fitting summary.

Theologically, Judges makes a clear contrast between the idolatry, immorality, and violence of Israel and Yahweh's covenant faithfulness and gracious deliverance of the people. In His patient love, God forgave the people every single time they repented. Israel often acted in foolishness, ingratitude, stubbornness, and rebellion, and this led to defeat. Sin always leads to suffering, and repentance always leads to deliverance.

Contribution to the Bible — Judges records the failure of the theocracy due to lack of faith and obedience. They were disloyal to their divine King and would later find it easier to follow an earthly king. Judges stands in bold opposition to Joshua:

Joshua	Judges
Freedom	Bondage
Progress	Decline
Conquest through belief	Defeat through disbelief
"Far be it from us that we should forsake the LORD to serve other gods" (24:16)	"And the sons of Israel did what was evil in the sight of the LORD, and forgot the LORD their God, and served the Baals and the Asheroth" (3:7)
Israel served God (24:31)	Israel served self (21:25)
Israel knew the person of God and the power of God (24:16-18,31)	Israel knew neither the person of God nor the power of God (2:10)
Objective morality	Subjective morality
Israel pressing onward	Israel spiralling downward
Sin judged	Sin tolerated
Faith and obedience	Lack of both

Christ in Judges — Each judge was a savior and a ruler, a spiritual and political deliverer. Thus, the judges portray the role of Christ as the Savior-King of His people. The book of Judges also illustrates the need for a Righteous King.

Looking ahead to 1 Samuel, 17 judges are mentioned altogether. Some were warrior-rulers (e.g., Othniel, Gideon), one was a priest (Eli), and one was a prophet (Samuel). This gives a cumulative picture of the three offices of Christ (prophet, priest, and king).

Ruth

"But Ruth said, 'Do not urge me to leave you or turn back from following you; for where you go, I will go, and where you lodge, I will lodge. Your people shall be my people, and your God, my God. Where you die, I will die, and there I will be buried. Thus may the LORD do to me, and worse, if anything but death parts you and me."

Ruth 1:16-17

Focus	Ruth's Love Demonstrated		Ruth's Love Rewarded	
DIVISIONS	Ruth's Decision	Ruth's Devotion	Ruth's Redeemer	Ruth's Reward
TOPICS	Ruth and Naomi		Ruth and Boaz	
	Discourage-ment	Discovery	Decision	Development
	Choice	Labor	Claim	Reward
Loca-tions	Moab	Bethlehem in Judah		
Time	About 30 Years			

Talk Thru — Ruth is the story of a woman who lived above the norm of her day. It was written during the time of David, but the events took place during the time of the judges. This was generally a desert of rebellion and immorality in Israel's history, but the story of Ruth stands in contrast as an oasis of integrity and righteousness.

Ruth was "a woman of excellence" (3:11) who showed loyal love to her mother-in-law Naomi and her near-kinsman Boaz. In both relationships, goodness and love were clearly manifested. Her love was demonstrated in 1-2 and rewarded in 3-4.

Ruth's Love Demonstrated (1-2): The story begins with a famine in Israel, a sign of disobedience and apostasy (Deut. 28-30). An Israelite named Elimelech ("my God is king") in a desperate act moved from Bethlehem ("house of bread"—note the irony) to Moab. He sought life in that land, but he and his two sons Mahlon ("sick") and Chilion ("pining") only found death. The deceased sons left two Moabite widows, Orpah ("stubborness") and Ruth ("friendship"). Naomi heard that the famine in Israel was over and decided to return, no longer as Naomi ("pleasant") but as Mara ("bitter"). She told her daughters-in-law to remain in Moab and remarry since there was no security for an unmarried woman in those days. Orpah chose to leave Naomi and is never mentioned again. Ruth resolved to cling to Naomi and follow Yahweh, the God of Israel. She gave up her culture, people, and language because of her love.

Naomi's misfortune led her to think that Yahweh was her enemy, but He had plans she didn't know about. In her plight she had to let Ruth glean at the edge of a field. This was a humiliating and dangerous task because of the character of the reapers. But God's providential care brought her to the field of Boaz, Naomi's kinsman. Boaz ("in him is strength") began to love, protect, and provide for her.

Ruth's Love Rewarded (3-4): Boaz took no further steps, so Naomi devised a dangerous plan that would force him to make a decision about Ruth. In 3:10-13 Boaz revealed why he took no action: he was older than Ruth (he was perhaps 20 years her senior), and he was not the nearest kinsman. Nevertheless, God rewarded Ruth's devotion by giving her Boaz as a husband and providing her with a son, the grandfather of David.

All throughout the book several things could have prevented the happy ending, but God sovereignly and subtly guided the circumstances to accomplish His gracious plan. The book began with death and bereaving but ends with life and rejoicing. Ruth came to know Yahweh and Naomi came to know His ways. Ruth began as a heathen but ended as a member of the royal Messianic line.

Title — *Ruth* is the Hebrew title of this book. This name may be a Moabite modification of the Hebrew word *reiut*, "friendship, association." The Septuagint entitled the book *Routh*, the Greek equivalent of the Hebrew name. The Latin title is *Ruth*, a transliteration of *Routh*.

Author — The author of Ruth is unknown, but Talmudic tradition attributes it to Samuel. However, this is unlikely because he died before David's coronation (1 Sam. 25:1), and Ruth was probably written during David's reign. The anonymity of the book does not detract from its spiritual value or literary beauty.

Date and Setting — Ruth 4:18-22 gives a genealogy from Perez to Boaz to David. If it was written after David's reign, it probably would have included Solomon. David reigned from 1011-971 B.C., and Ruth was probably written around 1000 B.C. (Samuel lived from about 1105 B.C. to about 1015 B.C.).

Apart from the closing genealogy, the book of Ruth covers the period from about 1150 B.C. to 1120 B.C. This means a date of composition approximately 120 years after the date of the content, enough time to require an explanation of a custom no longer practiced in Israel (4:7-8).

Ruth 1:1 sets the scene: "Now it came about in the days when the judges governed...." This was a general time of apostasy, warfare, decline, violence, moral decay, and anarchy. These years were often characterized by political, moral, and social chaos. There were rivalries among the tribes and periods of foreign oppression. Ruth provides a cameo of the other side of the story. Not all of the people were corrupt during this turbulent time. Many lived godly lives in these difficult years.

Moab was a region northeast of the Dead Sea whose inhabitants were descendants of Lot. The Moabites worshiped Chemosh among other gods, and the Scriptures record two times when they fought against Israel (Judg. 3:12-30 and 1 Sam.

14:47). Ruth takes place about two centuries after the first war and about 80 years before the second.

This book was appropriately read during Israel's harvest festival (Pentecost).

Theme and Purpose — Judges 17-21 is an appendix to that book, offering two illustrations of unrighteousness during the time of the judges. Ruth serves as a third illustration of life during this time, but it is an illustration of godliness. It is a positive picture of real faith and obedience (1:16-17; 3:10) that leads to blessing (4:13,17). Ruth also teaches that Gentiles could believe in the true God (three out of the four women mentioned in Christ's genealogy in Matt. 1 were Gentiles—Tamar, Rahab, and Ruth). Ruth explains how a Gentile woman could become a member of the royal lineage of David and shows the divine origin of the Davidic dynasty (4:18-22).

The theme of Ruth is redemption, especially as it relates to the kinsman-redeemer. It reveals Yahweh's gracious character and sovereign care for His people (2:12). It stresses God's providential rewards for faithfulness. Not all was lost during this chaotic period—there was always a faithful remnant of those who did what was right in the sight of the Lord.

Contribution to the Bible — (1) Literary—Ruth is a book of simplicity but profundity. It is one of literature's best examples of filial love and piety. (2) Historical—Ruth provides a bridge between the judges and the monarchy (its last word is "David"). It illustrates faithfulness amid infidelity. (3) Doctrinal—Ruth teaches that the Gentiles are not outside the scope of redemption. (4) Moral—Ruth communicates high ideals of integrity in relationships and marriage.

Ruth is one of the two biblical books named after a woman:

Ruth	Esther
A Gentile woman	A Jewish woman
Lived among the Jews	Lived among the Gentiles
Married a Jewish man in the royal line of David	Married a Gentile man who ruled an empire
A story of faith and blessing	A story of faith and blessing

The book of Ruth contrasts with Judges in several ways:

Ruth	Judges
Fidelity, righteousness, purity	Immorality
Following the true God	Idolatry
Devotion	Decline, debasement, disloyalty
Love	Lust
Peace	War
Kindness	Cruelty
Obedient faith leads to blessing	Disobedience leads to sorrow
Spiritual light	Spiritual darkness

Christ in Ruth — The concept of the kinsman-redeemer or *goel* (3:9, "close relative") is an important portrayal of the work of Christ. The *goel* must: (1) be related by blood to those he redeems (Deut. 25:5, 7-10; John 1:14; Rom. 1:3; Phil. 2:5-8; Heb. 2:14-15); (2) be able to pay the price of redemption (2:1; 1 Pet. 1:18-19); (3) be willing to redeem (3:11; Matt. 20:28; John 10:15,18; Heb. 10:7); (4) be free himself (Christ was free from the curse of sin). The word *goel* is used 13 times in this short book, and it is a clear picture of the mediatorial work of Christ.

1 Samuel

"And Samuel said, 'Has the LORD as much delight in burnt offerings and sacrifices as in obeying the voice of the LORD? Behold, to obey is better than sacrifice, and to heed than the fat of rams. For rebellion is as the sin of divination, and insubordination is as iniquity and idolatry. Because you have rejected the word of the LORD, He has also rejected you from being king.' "

1 Samuel 15:22-23
(Also see 1 Samuel 8:5-9,12-22.)

Focus	Samuel		Saul		Saul and David			
	1 8		9 15		16 31			
D I V I S I O N S	Early Life and Call of Samuel	Defeat, Revival, and Warning	The Selection of Saul	The Disobedience and Rejection of Saul	David in the Court of Saul	David's Escape and Flight from Saul	David's Encounters with Saul in the Wilderness	Saul's Final Downfall and Death
	1 3	4 8	9 12	13 15	16 19	20 23	24 26	27 31
T O P I C S	The Last Judge		The First King		The King-Elect			
	Transition from Judges to Kings		The Rise of Saul		The Decline of Saul and Rise of David			
Loca-tion	Israel in Canaan							
Time	About 94 Years							

52

Talk Thru — First Samuel records the crucial transition from the theocracy under the judges to the monarchy under the kings. Its three key characters are Samuel (1-8), Saul (9-31), and David (16-31).

Samuel (1-8): Samuel's story began late in the turbulent time of the judges when Eli was the judge-priest of Israel. His birth and early call by Yahweh are found in chapters 1-3. Because of his responsiveness to God (3:19), he was confirmed as a prophet (3:20-21) at a time when "word from the LORD was rare . . . visions were infrequent" (3:1).

Corruption at Shiloh (e.g., Eli's notoriously wicked sons) led to Israel's defeat in the crucial battle of Aphek (4:1-11). The ark of the covenant, God's "throne" among the people, was lost to the Philistines, the priesthood was disrupted with the death of Eli and his sons, and the glory of God departed from the tabernacle (Ichabod, "no glory," 4:21). Samuel began to function as the last of the judges and the first in the order of the prophets (Acts 3:24). His prophetic ministry (7:3-17) led to a revival in Israel, the return of the ark, and the defeat of the Philistines. When Samuel was old and his sons were unjust judges, the people wrongly cried out for a king. They wanted a visible military and judicial ruler so they could be "like all the nations" (8:5,20).

Saul (9-15): In their impatient demand for a king, the people chose less than God's best. Their motive (8:5) and criteria (9:2) were wrong. Saul started well (9-11), but his good characteristics soon degenerated. In spite of Samuel's solemn prophetic warning (12), Saul and the people began to act wickedly. Saul presumptuously assumed the role of a priest (compare 2 Chron. 26:18) and offered up sacrifices (13). He made a foolish vow (14) and disobeyed God's command to destroy the Amalekites (15). Samuel's powerful words in 15:22-23 evoked a pathetic response in 15:24-31.

Saul and David (16-31): Now that Saul was rejected by God, Samuel was commissioned to anoint David, Israel's next king. God's king-elect served in Saul's court (16:14-23) and defeated the Philistine Goliath (17). Jonathan's devotion to David led him to sacrifice the throne as Saul's son (20:30-31) in acknowledgment of David's divine right to the throne (18). David became a growing threat to the insanely jealous Saul, but he was protected from Saul's wrath by Jonathan, Michal, and Samuel (19).

Saul's open rebellion against God was manifest in his refusal to give up what God said could not be his. David was protected again by Jonathan from Saul's murderous intent (20), but Saul became more active in his pursuit of David. The future king fled to a Philistine city where he feigned insanity (21), and fled again to Adullam where a band of men formed around him (22).

David continued to escape from the hand of Saul and on two occasions spared Saul's life when he had the opportunity to take it (24-26). David again sought refuge among the Philistines, but was not allowed to fight on their side against Israel. Saul, afraid of impending battle against the Philistines, foolishly consulted a medium at Endor to hear the deceased Samuel's advice (28). The Lord rebuked Saul and pronounced his doom; he and his sons were killed by the Philistines on Mount Gilboa (31).

Title — The books of 1 and 2 Samuel were originally one book in the Hebrew Bible, known as the "Book of Samuel" or simply "Samuel." This name has been variously translated "the name of God," "his name is God," "heard of God," and "asked of God." The Septuagint divided Samuel into two books even though it is one continuous account. This division artificially breaks up the history of David. The Greek (Septuagint) title was *Bibloi Basileion*, "Books of Kingdoms," referring to the later kingdoms of Israel and Judah. First Samuel was called *Basileion Alpha*, "I Kingdoms." Second Samuel and 1 and 2 Kings were called "II, III, and IV Kingdoms." The Latin Vulgate originally called the books of Samuel and Kings *Libri Regum*, "Books of the Kings," listing them as "I, II, III, and IV Kings." Later the Latin Bible combined the Hebrew and Greek titles for the first of these books to get *Liber I Samuelis*, the "First Book of Samuel," or simply "I Samuel."

Author — The author of Samuel (1 and 2 Sam.) is anonymous, but Jewish Talmudic tradition says that it was written by Samuel. Samuel may have written the first portion of the book, but his death in 1 Samuel 25:1 makes it clear that he did not write all of 1 and 2 Samuel. Samuel did write a book (10:25), and written records were available. As the head of a company of prophets (10:5; 19:20), Samuel would be a logical candidate for biblical authorship. The Jews came to esteem Samuel second only to Moses among their leaders.

First Chronicles 29:29 refers to "the chronicles of Samuel the seer," "the chronicles of Nathan the prophet," and "the chronicles of Gad the seer" that record the acts of David from first to last. All three men evidently contributed to these two books which were originally one. It is very possible that a single compiler, perhaps a member of the prophetic school, used these chronicles to put the book of Samuel together. This is suggested by the unity of plan and purpose and by the smooth transitions between sections.

Date and Setting — If Samuel wrote the material in the first 24 chapters, it would have been soon before his death (about 1015 B.C.). He was born around 1105 B.C. and ministered as a judge and prophet in Israel between 1067 B.C. and c. 1015 B.C. The books of Samuel end in the last days of David, so they must have been compiled after 971 B.C. The reference in 1 Samuel 27:6 to the divided monarchy in which Judah was separate from Israel indicates a compilation date after Solomon's death in 931 B.C. But there is no mention of the Assyrian captivity of Israel in 722 B.C., and this probably means that Samuel was written before this key event.

First Samuel covers the 94-year period from the birth of Samuel to the death of Saul (c. 1105-1011 B.C.) The Philistines strongly oppressed Israel from 1087 B.C. until the battle of Ebenezer in 1047 B.C. (7:10-14). But even after this time they had military and economic control. The Philistines lived in the coastal plains, and the hill country of the Israelites kept them from being completely subdued. Israel needed to unify under a central monarchy in order to expand.

Theme and Purpose — The books of Samuel give a prophetically-oriented history of Israel's early monarchy. The first of these books picks up the story of Israel left off in Judges 16:31. Samuel followed Samson, and he too had to deal with the Philistines since Samson did not accomplish a permanent victory. First Samuel traces the transition of leadership in Israel from judges to kings, from a theocracy to a monarchy. The monarchy brought greater stability because the people found it easier to follow an earthly king. Samuel was the kingmaker who anointed the first two rulers of the united kingdom. Saul quickly

disobeyed God and became a tyrant. David became the first real theocratic king—he allowed God to rule through him.

In their actions during the period of the judges, the people rejected Yahweh as their King. The clamor for an earthly king in 1 Samuel was the natural outcome of this practical rejection (see 8:7). God had intended to give Israel a king (Gen. 49:10; Deut. 17:14-20), but the people insisted on the king of their choice instead of waiting for God's king. Nevertheless, this book teaches the sovereign control of Yahweh who establishes and removes kings. Saul was rejected by the Lord because he failed to learn the truth that "to obey is better than sacrifice" (15:22). He became characterized by mental imbalance, raging jealousy, foolishness, and immorality. David illustrated the principle that "God sees not as man sees" (16:7). The Lord established the Davidic dynasty because of David's obedience, wisdom, and dependence on God.

Samuel also reveals the critical role of the prophets in their divinely commissioned exhortations to the kings and the people or Israel.

Contribution to the Bible — Historically, 1 Samuel provides the crucial link from the judges to the monarchy. It is a fast-moving narrative that gives a spiritual perspective on three very different personalities whose lives were interwoven: Samuel, Saul, and David.

This is the first book to use the word Messiah ("anointed," 2:10). It is also the first to call God the "LORD of hosts" (e.g., 1:3). The well-known words Ichabod ("no glory," 4:21) and Ebenezer ("stone of help," 7:12) come from this book. Our Lord alluded to 1 Samuel on at least two occasions: Matthew 12:3,4 (21:6), and Luke 16:15 (16:7).

Christ in 1 Samuel — Samuel is a type of Christ in that he was a prophet, priest, and judge. He was highly revered by the people and brought in a new age.

David is one of the primary Old Testament portrayals of the person of Christ. He was born in Bethlehem, worked as a shepherd, and ruled as the king of Israel. He was the anointed king who became the forerunner of the Messianic King. His typical Messianic psalms came out of his years of rejection and danger (see Ps.22). God enabled David, who walked "after His own heart" (13:14), to become Israel's greatest king. The New Testament specifically calls Christ the "descendant of David according to the flesh" (Rom. 1:3) and "the root and the offspring of David" (Rev. 22:16).

2 Samuel

"Now therefore, O LORD God, the word that Thou hast spoken
concerning Thy servant and his house, confirm it forever, and
do as Thou hast spoken, that Thy name may be magnified
forever, by saying, 'The LORD of hosts is God over Israel'; and
may the house of Thy servant David be established before
Thee."

2 Samuel 7:25-26
(Also see 5:12.)

Focus	David's Triumphs			David's Transgressions	David's Troubles		
	1 10			11 14	15 24		
D I V I S I O N S	David's Reign in a Divided Nation	David's Reign Over a United Nation	David's Reign Over an Expanding Nation	David's Sin and God's Judgment	Absalom's Attempt to Overthrow David	Continuing Unrest and Violence	David's Final Words and Acts
	1 4	5 7	8 10	11 14	15 18	19 20	21 24
T O P I C S	Success			Failure	Trials		
	Civil War, Coronation, Conquests			Crimes	Conflicts		
	Obedience brings God's		blessing	Disobedience	brings God's judgment		
	1 7		8 10	11 12	24		
Locations	David in Hebron	David in Jerusalem					
Time	7½ Years	33 Years					

Talk Thru — Second Samuel continues the account of the life of David left off at the end of 1 Samuel. Soon after the death of Saul, the king-elect became the king enthroned, first over Judah when he reigned in Hebron for 7½ years, and finally over all Israel when he reigned in Jerusalem for 33 years. This book reviews the key events in the 40-year reign of the man who became the halfway point between Abraham and Christ. It can be surveyed in the three divisions of David's Triumphs (1-10), David's Transgressions (11-14), and David's Troubles (15-24).

David's Triumphs (1-10): Chapters 1-4 record the seven-year reign of David over the territory of Judah. Even though Saul was David's murderous pursuer, David did not rejoice in his death because he recognized that Saul had been divinely anointed as king. Saul's son Ishbosheth was installed by Abner as a puppet king over the northern tribes of Israel. David's allies led by Joab defeated Abner and Israel (2:17; 3:1). Abner defected and arranged to unite Israel and Judah under David but he was killed by Joab out of revenge. The powerless Ishbosheth was murdered by his own men and David was made king of Israel (5:3). David soon captured and fortified Jerusalem and made it the civil and religious center of the now united kingdom. Under David's rule the nation prospered militarily, economically, and spiritually. David brought the ark to Jerusalem and sought to build a house for God (7). His obedience in placing the Lord at the center of his rule led to great national blessing (8-10). "And the LORD helped David wherever he went" (8:14).

David's Transgressions (11-14): David's crimes of adultery and murder (11) mark the pivotal point of the book. Because of these transgressions, David's victories and successes are changed to the personal, family, and national troubles which are recorded throughout the rest of 2 Samuel. The disobedience of the king produced chastisement and confusion on every level (12-24). David's glory and fame faded, and it was never the same again. Nevertheless, David confessed his guilt when confronted by Nathan the prophet and was restored by God. A sword remained in David's house as a consequence of the sin; the baby died, his son Ammon committed incest, and his son Absalom murdered Ammon.

David's Troubles (15-24): The consequences continued with Absalom's rebellion against his father. He shrewdly "stole away the hearts of the men of Israel" (15:6). David was forced to flee from Jerusalem, and Absalom set himself up as king. David would have been finished, but God kept Absalom from pursuing him until David had time to regather his forces. Absalom's army was defeated by David's, and Joab killed Absalom in spite of David's orders to have him spared.

David sought to amalgamate the kingdom, but conflict broke out between the 10 northern tribes of Israel and the two southern tribes of Judah and Benjamin. Israel decided to follow a man named Sheba in a revolt against David, but Judah remained faithful to him. This led to war, and Joab defeated the rebels.

The closing chapters (21-24) are really an appendix to the book because they categorically enumerate David's words and deeds. They show how intimately the affairs of the people as a whole were tied to the spiritual and moral condition of the king. The nation enjoyed God's blessing when David was obedient to the LORD and suffered hardship when David disobeyed God.

Title

Title — See 1 Samuel, Title for details on the titles of the books of Samuel. The Hebrew title for both books (originally one) is *Samuel*. The Greek title for 2 Samuel is *Basileion Beta*, "II Kingdoms." The Latin title is *Liber II Samuelis*, the "Second Book of Samuel," or simply "II Samuel."

Author

Author — Since 1 and 2 Samuel were one Hebrew book, the authorship of both was discussed under 1 Samuel, Author. Second Samuel was probably compiled by one man who combined the written chronicles of Nathan the prophet and Gad the seer (1 Chron. 29:29). In addition to these written sources, the compiler evidently used another source called "the book of Jashar" (1:18).

Date and Setting

Date and Setting — Under 1 Samuel, Date and Setting, the composition date for these books was shown to be sometime after the death of Solomon (931 B.C.) but before the Assyrian captivity of the northern kingdom (722 B.C.). It is likely that Samuel was composed early in the divided kingdom, perhaps around 900 B.C.

The story of David begins in 1 Samuel 16 and ends in 1 Kings 2. Second Samuel records the major events of David's 40-year rule. His reign in Hebron began in 1011 B.C. and ended in 1004

B.C. (5:5). His 33-year reign over the united Judah and Israel went from 1004 B.C. to 971 B.C. After Jerusalem became the seat of the monarchy, Israel became a powerful and expanding force. David took a kingdom that was on the brink of ruin under the heel of the Philistines and transformed it into a formidable empire. But he never enjoyed a path of ease—danger dogged him and the kingdom until the end of his days.

Theme and Purpose

Theme and Purpose — There is no real break in the narrative between 1 Samuel 31:13 and 2 Samuel 1:1. The two books of Samuel were originally one book written to provide a divine perspective on the establishment of the united kingdom under Saul and its expansion under David. These books repeatedly illustrate the hostility between the 10 northern and two southern tribes and the difficulty of keeping them united. The final split between Israel and Judah that occurred after the death of Solomon in 931 B.C. comes as no surprise in light of 1 and 2 Samuel.

The book of 2 Samuel offers a very candid portrait of the strengths and weaknesses of David's 40-year reign. God is no respecter of persons, and the heroes of the Bible like David are not glorified to the neglect of their sin. This balanced presentation of the life of Israel's greatest king reveals the origin of a perpetual dynasty (7:16).

Several spiritual truths are reinforced and illustrated in the life of David. The most obvious of these is the cause and effect principle stressed in every book since Genesis: obedience (1-7) brings God's blessings (8-10), and disobedience (11) leads to God's judgment (12-24). The consequences of sin cannot be avoided; "when sin is accomplished, it brings forth death" (Jas. 1:15), in this case, many.

Contribution to the Bible

Contribution to the Bible — First Samuel reveals how the kingdom was established and 2 Samuel shows how it was consolidated. This book tells us how the nation was unified, how it obtained Jerusalem as its royal capital, how it subdued its enemies and extended its boundaries, and how it achieved economic prosperity. It records the beginning of an endless dynasty and the life of a man about whom more is known than any other individual in the Old Testament.

Christ in 2 Samuel — As seen under 1 Samuel, David is one of the most important types of Christ in the Old Testament. In spite of his sins, he remained a man after God's own heart because of his responsive and faithful attitude toward Yahweh. He sometimes failed in his personal life but he never flagged in his relationship to the Lord Unlike all successive kings, idolatry never became a problem during his reign. He was a true servant of Yahweh, obedient to His law, and an ideal king. His rule was usually characterized by justice, wisdom, integrity, courage, and compassion. He conquered Jerusalem and sat upon the throne of Melchizedek, the "righteous king" (Gen. 14:18). David was the standard by which all subsequent kings were measured.

Of course, David's life in chapters 1-10 is a far greater portrayal of the future Messiah than his life in 11-24. Sin mars potential. The closest way in which he foreshadowed the coming King can be seen in the important covenant God made with him in 7:4-17. David wanted to make a house for Yahweh, but Yahweh made a house for David. The same three promises of an eternal kingdom, throne, and seed were also made of Christ in Luke 1:32-33. There were nine different dynasties in the northern kingdom of Israel but there was only one dynasty in Judah. The promise of a permanent dynasty is fulfilled in Christ, the "son of David" (Matt. 21:9; 22:45), who will sit upon the throne of David (Isa. 9:7; Luke 1:32).

1 Kings

"And as for you, if you will walk before Me as your father David walked, in integrity of heart and uprightness, doing according to all that I have commanded you and will keep My statutes and My ordinances, then I will establish the throne of your kingdom over Israel forever, just as I promised to your father David, saying, 'You shall not lack a man on the throne of Israel.'"

1 Kings 9:4-5

"So the LORD said to Solomon, 'Because you have done this, and you have not kept My covenant and My statutes, which I have commanded you, I will surely tear the kingdom from you, and will give it to your servant.'"

1 Kings 11:11

Focus	United Kingdom			Divided Kingdom		
	1 11			12 22		
D I V I S I O N S	Solomon's Rise to Power	Solomon's Temple Built and Dedicated	Solomon's Fame, Fortune, and Failure	A Nation Torn in Two	Ministry of Elijah	Final Days of Ahab
	1 4	5 8	9 11	12 16	17 19	20 22
T O P I C S	Solomon			Split	Elijah and Ahab	
	Expansion and Glorification			Division and Decline		
	One King			Many Kings		
Loca- tions	Jerusalem Capital of United Kingdom			10 Northern Tribes (Israel)— Samaria Capital 2 Southern Tribes (Judah)— Jerusalem Capital		
Time	40 Years			78 Years		

63

Talk Thru — The first half of 1 Kings concerns the life of one of the most amazing men who ever lived. More than any man before or since, he knew how to amass and creatively use great wealth. With the sole exception of Jesus Christ, Solomon was the wisest man in human history. He brought Israel to the peak of its size and glory, and yet the kingdom was disrupted soon after his death, torn in two by civil strife. This book divides clearly into two sections: United Kingdom (1-11) and Divided Kingdom (12-22).

United Kingdom (1-11): These chapters give an account of Solomon's attainment of the throne, wisdom, architectural achievements, fame, wealth, and tragic unfaithfulness. Solomon's half-brother Adonijah attempted to take the throne as David's death was nearing, but Nathan the prophet alerted David who quickly directed the coronation of Solomon as coregent (1). Solomon still had to consolidate his power and deal with those who opposed his rule. Only when this was done was the kingdom "established in the hands of Solomon" (2:46). Solomon's ungodly marriages (cf. 3:1) would eventually turn his heart from the Lord, but he began well with a genuine love for Yahweh and a desire for wisdom. This wisdom led to the expansion of Israel and the zenith of its power. Solomon's empire stretched from the border of Egypt to the border of Babylonia, and peace prevailed.

From a theocratic perspective, Solomon's greatest achievement was the building of the temple. The ark was placed in this exquisite building and the glory of God filled it. Solomon prayed a magnificent prayer of dedication and bound the people with an oath to remain faithful to Yahweh (8).

Solomon continued to grow in fame, power, and wealth, for the Lord was with him. But his wealth later became a source of trouble as he began to purchase forbidden items. He acquired many foreign wives who led him into idolatry; it is an irony of history that this wisest of men acted as a fool in his old age. God pronounced judgment and foretold that Solomon's son would rule only a fraction of the kingdom (Judah).

Divided Kingdom (12-22): Upon Solomon's death, God's words came to pass. Solomon's son Rehoboam chose the foolish course of promising more severe taxation. Jeroboam, an officer in Solomon's army, led the 10 northern tribes in revolt. They made him their king, leaving only Judah and Benjamin in the south under Rehoboam. This was the beginning of a chaotic period with two nations and two sets of kings. There was continual enmity and strife between the northern and southern kingdoms. There was also apostasy in the north (Jeroboam set up a false system of worship) and in the south (idolatry). Of all the northern and southern kings listed in this book, only Asa (15:9-24) and Jehoshaphat (22:41-50) "did what was right in the sight of the LORD" (15:11; 22:43). Apart from them, there is no relief from the wickedness of these kings—they were idolaters, usurpers, and murderers.

Ahab brought a measure of cooperation between the northern and southern kingdoms, but he reached new depths of wickedness as a king. He was the man who introduced Jezebel's Baal worship to Israel. The prophet Elijah ministered during this low period in Israel's history, providing a ray of light and witness of the word and power of God. But Ahab's encounter with Elijah never brought him to turn from his false gods to Yahweh. Ahab's treachery in the matter of Naboth's vineyard (21) brought a prophetic rebuke from Elijah. Ahab repented (21:29) but later died in battle with the Arameans because of his refusal to heed the words of Micaiah, another prophet of God.

Title — Like the two books of Samuel, the two books of Kings were originally one in the Hebrew Bible. The original title was *melechim*, "kings," taken from the first word in 1:1, *vehamelech*, "Now King . . ." The Septuagint artificially divided the book of Kings in the middle of the story of Ahaziah into two books. It called the books of Samuel "I and II Kingdoms" and the books of Kings "III and IV Kingdoms." The Septuagint may have divided Samuel, Kings, and Chronicles into two books each because the Greek required a greater amount of scroll space than the Hebrew. The Latin title for these books was *Liber Regum Tertius et Quartus,* the "Third and Fourth Book of Kings."

Author — The author of 1 and 2 Kings is unknown, but there is evidence that supports the tradition in the Talmud that Kings was written by the prophet Jeremiah. The author was clearly a prophet-historian as seen in the prophetic exposé of apostasy. There is an emphasis in 1 and 2 Kings on the righteous judgment of God on idolatry and immorality. The style of these books is also similar to that found in Jeremiah. The phrase "to this day" in 8:8 and 12:19 indicates a time of authorship prior to the Babylonian captivity (586 B.C.). But the last two chapters of 2 Kings were written after the captivity, probably by a Jewish captive in Babylon.

Evidently, the bulk of 1 and 2 Kings was written before 586 B.C. by a compiler who had access to several historical documents. Some of these are mentioned: "the book of the acts of Solomon" (11:41), "the Book of the Chronicles of the Kings of Israel" (14:19), and "the Book of the Chronicles of the Kings of Judah" (14:29; 15:7). These books may have been a part of the official court records (see 2 Kings 18:18). In addition, Isaiah 36-39 was probably used as a source (compare with 2 Kings 18-20).

Date and Setting — The book of Kings was written to the remaining kingdom of Judah before and after its Babylonian exile. The majority was compiled by a contemporary of Jeremiah if not by Jeremiah himself (c. 646-570 B.C.). It is a record of disobedience, idolatry, and ungodliness which serves as an explanation for the Assyrian captivity of Israel (722 B.C.) and the Babylonian captivity of Judah (586 B.C.). First Kings covers the 118 years from the beginning of Solomon's reign in 971 B.C. to the beginning of Ahaziah's reign in 853 B.C. The key date is 931 B.C., the year in which the kingdom was divided:

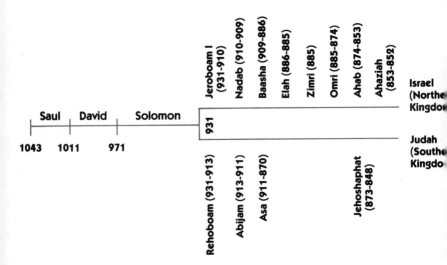

Theme and Purpose — The theme of 1 Kings is that the welfare of Israel and Judah depended upon the covenant faithfulness of the people and their king. Historically, it was written to give an account of the reigns of the kings from Solomon to Jehoshaphat (Judah) and Ahaziah (Israel). The two books of Kings as a whole trace the monarchy from the point of its greatest prosperity under Solomon to its demise and destruction in the Assyrian and Babylonian captivities.

Theologically, 1 Kings provides a prophetically-oriented evaluation of the spiritual and moral causes that led to political and economic effects in the two kingdoms. The material is too selective to be considered a biography of the kings. For example, Omri was one of Israel's most important rulers from a political point of view, but because of his moral corruption, his achievements are dismissed in eight verses. The lives of these kings are used to teach several basic principles: (1) man cannot properly rule himself without conscious dependence on the help of God; (2) the kings had great responsibility as God's administrators, because the circumstances of the nation depended in large part upon their faithfulness to Yahweh; (3) the kings were illustrations of the people as a whole—just as they disregarded God's prophets, so did the people; and (4) observance of God's law produces blessing, but apostasy is rewarded by judgment.

Contribution to the Bible — In 1 Samuel the kingdom was established, and in 2 Samuel it was consolidated. First Kings brings the kingdom from the height of its glory to a sudden abyss of division and decline. This book begins a set pattern in its portrayal of each king that is carried on in 2 Kings. The account shifts between the kings of Israel and Judah in a way that synchronizes the two monarchies. The accession year of every king is dated in terms of its overlap with the ruler of the other kingdom. Introductory and concluding formulas are used, and a theological verdict on the reign of each king is passed. The life and reign of David is the standard by which the kings of Judah are judged.

First Kings also shows how the prophetic ministry came into its maturity at the end of the united kingdom and throughout the divided kingdom. This book describes the ministries of several of God's prophets.

Christ in 1 Kings — Solomon typifies Christ in a number of ways. His fabled wisdom pointed ahead to "Christ Jesus, who became to us wisdom from God" (1 Cor. 1:30). His fame, glory, wealth, and honor foreshadow Christ in His kingdom. Solomon's rulership brought knowledge, peace, and worship. But with all of Solomon's splendor, the Son of Man said of His coming, "something greater than Solomon is here" (Matt. 12:42).

The prophet Elijah was more a type of John the Baptist than of Christ, but his prophetic ministry and miraculous works illustrate aspects of the life of Christ.

2 Kings

"And the sons of Israel walked in all the sins of Jeroboam which he did; they did not depart from them, until the LORD removed Israel from His sight, as He spoke through all His servants the prophets. So Israel was carried away into exile from their own land to Assyria until this day."

2 Kings 17:22-23

"And the LORD said, 'I will remove Judah also from My sight, as I have removed Israel. And I will cast off Jerusalem, this city which I have chosen, and the temple of which I said, "My name shall be there." ' "

2 Kings 23:27

Focus	Divided Kingdom				Surviving Kingdom	
	1 17				18 25	
D I V I S I O N S	Elisha Replaces Elijah	Elisha's Miraculous Ministry	Destruction of Ahab and Preservation of Joash	Final Countdown for the Northern Kingdom	Hezekiah's Righteous Reign	Final Countdown for the Southern Kingdom
	1 3	4 8	9 12	13 17	18 20	21 25
T O P I C S	Israel's Corruption and Captivity				Judah's Corruption and Captivity	
	Elisha		Kings of Israel and Judah		Kings of Judah	
Loca-tions	Israel and Judah				Judah	
Time	131 Years (853-722 B.C.)				155 Years (715-560 B.C.)	

Talk Thru — Second Kings continues without interruption the story left off in 1 Kings. The twin kingdoms of Israel and Judah pursue a collision course with captivity as the glory of the once united kingdom becomes increasingly remote. Division has led to decline and now ends in double deportation: Israel captured by Assyria and Judah by Babylonia. This book traces the history of the divided kingdom in 1-17 and the history of the surviving kingdom in 18-25.

Divided Kingdom (1-17): These chapters record the story of Israel's corruption in a relentless succession of bad kings from Ahaziah to Hoshea. The situation in Judah during this time (Jehoram to Ahaz) is somewhat better, but far from ideal. This depressing period in the northern kingdom of Israel is interrupted only by the ministries of godly prophets like Elijah and Elisha. At the end of Elijah's miraculous ministry, Elisha was installed and authenticated as his successor. He was a force of righteousness in a nation that never served the true God or worshiped at the temple in Jerusalem. Elisha's ministry was characterized by miraculous provisions of sustenance and life. Through him God demonstrated His gracious care for the nation and His concern for any person who would come to Him. But like his forerunner Elijah, Elisha was basically rejected by Israel's leadership.

Elisha instructed one of his prophetic assistants to anoint Jehu king over Israel. Jehu fulfilled the prophecies concerning Ahab's descendants by putting them to death. He killed Ahab's wife Jezebel and his sons. Jehu also killed the priests of Baal and eliminated Baal worship (established by Ahab) in Israel. But he did not depart from the calf worship originally set up by Jeroboam. The loss of the house of Ahab meant the alienation of Israel and Judah and the weakening of both. Israel's enemies began to get the upper hand. Meanwhile in Judah, Jezebel's daughter Athaliah killed all the descendants of David except for Joash and usurped the throne. But Jehoiada the priest eventually removed her from the throne and placed Joash in power. Joash restored the temple and served God.

Syria gained virtual control over Israel but there was no response to God's chastisement—the kings and people refused to repent. Nevertheless, there was a period of restoration under Jeroboam II, but the continuing series of wicked kings in Israel led to its overthrow by Assyria.

Surviving Kingdom (18-25): Of Israel's 19 kings, none did what was right in God's sight. All but one of its nine dynasties were created by murdering the previous king. In Judah there was only one dynasty, and eight out of its 20 rulers did what was right before God. But Judah's collapse finally came, and it was just as devastating as Israel's, resulting in the Babylonian exile. The account in 18-25 reads more easily than 1-17 because there is no more alternating between northern and southern kingdoms—only Judah is left.

Six years before the overthrow of Israel's capital in Samaria, Hezekiah became king of Judah. Because of his exemplary faith and reforms, God spared Jerusalem from Assyria and brought in a measure of prosperity to Judah. But Hezekiah's son Manasseh was so idolatrous that his long reign led to the downfall of Judah. Even Josiah's later reforms could not stem the tide of evil, and the four kings that succeeded him were as wicked as ever. Judgment came with three deportations to Babylonia. The third occurred in 586 B.C. when Nebuchadnezzar destroyed Jerusalem and the temple. Still, the book ends on a note of hope as God preserved a remnant for Himself.

Title — The books of Kings were originally a single Hebrew book (see 1 Kings, Title). The Hebrew title of *melechim*, "Kings" was changed by the Septuagint which combined the books of Samuel and Kings into "I, II, III, IV Kingdoms." The original Latin title for Kings was III and IV Kings, but when I and II Kings was changed to I and II Samuel, III and IV Kings was changed to I and II Kings.

Author — The authorship of Kings was discussed under 1 Kings, Author. If this now divided book was not written by Jeremiah, it was probably written by a prophetic contemporary of his. The bulk of 2 Kings was written before the Babylonian captivity (see "to this day" in 17:34,41).

The literary style of 2 Kings is similar to the book of Jeremiah, and it has been argued that the omission of Jeremiah's ministry in the account of King Josiah and his successors would be glaring if Kings was not written by Jeremiah himself. However, the last two chapters were evidently added to the book after the Babylonian captivity and written by someone other than Jeremiah. The prophet Jeremiah was exiled to Egypt (Jer.

43:1-8), not to Babylonia. It is interesting that 2 Kings 24:18-25:30 is almost the same as Jeremiah 52. Both passages probably came from a more complete source.

Date and Setting — The last recorded event in 2 Kings is the release of Jehoiachin (25:27-30) which took place in 560 B.C. Most of 1-2 Kings was probably written just prior to 586 B.C., but chapters 24-25 were written after Jehoiachin's release, perhaps around 550 B.C.

Chapters 1-17 cover the 131 years from 853 B.C. (King Ahaziah of Israel) to 722 B.C. (the Assyrian captivity of Israel). Chapters 18-25 cover the 155 years from the beginning of Hezekiah's reign in 715 B.C. to the release of Jehoiachin in Babylonia in 560 B.C. The united kingdom lasted for 112 years (1043-931 B.C.), the northern kingdom of Israel existed for another 209 years (931-722 B.C.), and the southern kingdom of Judah continued for another 136 years beyond that (722-586 B.C.). During this 457-year kingdom period, there were great shifts of world power. Egyptian and Assyrian control over Palestine fluctuated; Assyria rose to preeminence, declined, and was finally conquered by Babylonia.

The books of Kings show that judgment came to the kingdoms of Israel and Judah because of idolatry, immorality, and disunity. Judah lasted 136 years longer than Israel because of the relative good of eight out of its 20 kings. Israel never broke away from Jeroboam's calf worship, but Judah at least had periods of revival in the worship of Yahweh. It was during these years that God sent many of His prophets. In the northern kingdom there were Elijah, Elisha, Amos, and Hosea. In the southern kingdom there were Obadiah, Joel, Isaiah, Micah, Nahum, Zephaniah, Jeremiah, and Habakkuk.

Theme and Purpose — The two books of Kings were artificially divided in the middle of the reign of King Ahaziah of Israel. Because both books were originally one, they share the same theme and purpose (see 1 Kings). They record the pivotal events in the careers of the kings of Israel and Judah and show how disobedience and rebellion against God led to the failure and overthrow of the monarchy. Kings was written selectively, not exhaustively, from a prophetic viewpoint to teach that the decline and collapse of the two kingdoms occurred because of failure on the part of the rulers and people to heed the warnings of God's messengers. The spiritual climate of the nation determined its political and economic conditions.

The prophets of Yahweh play a prominent role in 1 and 2 Kings as God uses them to remind the kings of their covenant responsibilities as His theocratic administrators. When the king kept the covenant, he and the nation would be richly blessed. But judgment consistently fell upon those who refused to obey God's law. God is seen in Kings as the controller of history who reveals His plan and purpose to His people. Tragically, the people were concerned more with their own plans, and their rejection of God's rule led to exile at the hands of the Assyrians and Babylonians.

Contribution to the Bible — Second Kings continues and completes the history of Israel and Judah as nations. The kingdom was established in 1 Samuel and consolidated in 2 Samuel. First Kings records its division and decline, and 2 Kings its deterioration and destruction.

1 Kings	2 Kings
Opens with David, King of Israel	Closes with Nebuchadnezzar, King of Babylonia
Solomon's glory	Jehoiachin's shame
The temple built and consecrated	The temple violated and destroyed
Begins with blessings for obedience	Ends with judgment for disobedience
The growth of apostasy	The consequences of apostasy
The united kingdom is divided	The two kingdoms are destroyed

Theologically, Kings stresses that God is the sovereign Lord over the history of Israel and the other nations. He predicts and controls history and uses various nations as His instruments of judgment for Israel's failure to keep the covenant. The king was to act as the servant of God by leading the nation into righteousness and fellowship with the Lord, but most of the kings perverted the purpose of their office because of their moral and spiritual rebellion.

Christ in 2 Kings — Unlike the nine different dynasties in the northern kingdom, the kings of Judah reigned as one continuous dynasty. In spite of Queen Athaliah's attempt to destroy the house of David, God remained faithful to His covenant with David (2 Sam. 7) by preserving his lineage. Jesus the Messiah is his direct descendant.

While Elijah was a type of John the Baptist (Matt. 11:14; 17:10-12; Luke 1:17), Elisha was a type of Christ. Elijah generally lived apart from the people and stressed law, judgment, and repentance. Elisha lived among the people and emphasized grace, life, and hope.

1 Chronicles

"Thine, O LORD, is the greatness and the power and the glory and the victory and the majesty, indeed everything that is in the heavens and the earth; Thine is the dominion, O LORD, and Thou dost exalt Thyself as head over all. Both riches and honor come from Thee, and Thou dost rule over all, and in Thy hand is power and might; and it lies in Thy hand to make great, and to strengthen everyone."

1 Chronicles 29:11-12

Focus	Royal Line of David		Reign of David			
	1　　　　9	10				29
D I V I S I O N S	Genealogies of David and Israel	The Anointing of David, and the Ark of God	David's Covenant and Expanding Kingdom	David's Preparations for the Temple and its Worship	David's Final Words	
	1　　　　9	10　　16	17　　21	22　　27	28　　29	
T O P I C S	Ancestry	Activity	Anticipation		Advice	
	Genealogies	History				
	A Priestly View of David's Reign					
Loca-tion	Judah					
Time	Thousands of Years	40 Years				

Talk Thru — The books of 1 and 2 Chronicles cover the same period of Jewish history described in 2 Samuel through 2 Kings. But the perspective of Chronicles is quite different from that of Samuel and Kings, and this raises it above the level of repetition or supplement. While 2 Samuel and Kings give a political history of Israel and Judah, Chronicles gives a religious history of the Davidic dynasty (Judah). The former books were written with a prophetic and moral orientation, but Chronicles was written from a priestly and spiritual vantage point. First Chronicles parallels 2 Samuel, and 2 Chronicles parallels 1 and 2 Kings.

Because of the opening genealogy, Chronicles retraces the whole story of Israel's history up to the return from captivity in order to give the returned remnant a divine perspective on the developments of their past. The whole book of 1 Chronicles, like 2 Samuel, is dedicated to the life of David. It begins with the royal line of David (1-9) before surveying key events of the reign of David (10-29).

Royal Line of David (1-9): These nine chapters are the most comprehensive genealogical tables in the Bible. They trace the family tree of David and Israel as a whole, but in a highly selective manner. The genealogies place a disproportionate emphasis on the tribes of Judah and Benjamin because Chronicles is not concerned with the northern kingdom but with the southern kingdom and the Davidic dynasty. They show God at work in selecting and preserving a people for Himself from the beginning of human history to the period after the Babylonian exile. The genealogies move from the patriarchal period (Adam to Jacob: 1:1-2:2) to the national period (Judah, Levi, and the other tribes of Israel; 2:3-9:44). They demonstrate God's keeping of His covenant promises in maintaining the Davidic line through the centuries. The priestly perspective of Chronicles is evident in the special attention given to the tribe of Levi.

Reign of David (10-29): Compared with 2 Samuel, David's life in 1 Chronicles is seen in an entirely different light. This is clear from both the omissions and the additions. Chronicles completely *omits* David's struggles with Saul, his seven-year reign in Hebron, his various wives, and Absalom's rebellion. It also omits the event in 2 Samuel which hurt the rest of his life—his sin with Bathsheba. Chronicles is written from a more positive perspective that emphasizes God's grace and forgiveness in order to encourage the Jews who have just returned from captivity. Chronicles *adds* events not found in 2 Samuel like David's preparations for the temple and its worship.

Only one chapter is given to Saul's reign (10) because his heart was not right with God. David's story begins with his coronation over all Israel after he had already reigned for seven years as king over Judah. Chronicles stresses his deep spiritual commitment, courageousness, and integrity. It emphasizes his concern for the things of the LORD including his return of the ark and his desire to build a temple for God. God established His crucial covenant with David (17), and the kingdom was strengthened and expanded under his reign (18-20). His sin in numbering the people is recorded to teach the consequences of disobeying God's law. The rest of the book (22-29) is concerned with David's preparations for the building of the temple and the worship associated with it. The priestly perspective of Chronicles can be seen in the disproportionate space given to the temple and the priests. David was not allowed to build the temple (28:3), but he designed the plans, gathered the materials, prepared the site, and arranged for the Levites, priests, choirs, porters, soldiers, and stewards. The book closes with his beautiful public prayer of praise and the accession of Solomon.

Title
— The books of 1 and 2 Chronicles were originally one continuous work in the Hebrew. The title was *hayyamim*, meaning "the words (accounts, events) of the days." The equivalent meaning today would be "the events of the times." Chronicles was divided into two parts in the third century B.C. Greek translation of the Hebrew Bible (the Septuagint). At that time it was given the name *Paraleipomenon*, "(of) things omitted," referring to the things omitted from Samuel and Kings. Some copies add the phrase, *Basileon Iouda*, "concerning the kings of Judah." The first book of Chronicles was called *Paraleipomenon primus*, "the first book of things omitted." The name "Chronicles" comes from Jerome in his Latin Vulgate Bible (A.D. 385-405): *Chronicorum Liber.* He meant his title in the sense of "the chronicles of the whole of sacred history."

Author
— Although the text does not identify the author, there are several facts that seem to support the tradition in the Jewish Talmud that Ezra the priest was the author. The content points to a priestly authorship because of the emphasis on the

temple, the priesthood, and the theocratic line of David in the southern kingdom of Judah. The content also indicates that Chronicles was at least written by a contemporary of Ezra. Stylistically, Chronicles is quite similar to the book of Ezra, and both share a priestly perspective: genealogies, temple worship, ministry of the priesthood, and obedience to the law of God. In addition, the closing verses of 2 Chronicles (36:22-23) are repeated with minor changes as the opening verses of Ezra (1:1-3a). Thus, Chronicles and Ezra may have been one consecutive history like Luke and Acts.

Ezra was an educated scribe (Ezra 7:6), and according to 2 Maccabees 2:13-15, Nehemiah collected an extensive library which was available to Ezra for his use in compiling Chronicles. Many of these documents and sources are listed in the book (see 2 Chronicles, Author). Scholars of Israel accumulated and compared historical material, and the author of Chronicles was really a compiler who drew from many sources under the guidance of the Holy Spirit.

Date and Setting — The genealogies in 1-9 cover the time from Adam to David, and chapters 10-29 focus on the 33 years of David's rule over the united kingdoms of Israel and Judah (1004-971 B.C.). However, the genealogies extend to about 500 B.C. because they mention Zerubbabel, grandson of King Jeconiah, who led the first return of the Jews from exile in 538 B.C., and also Zerubbabel's two grandsons Pelatiah and Jeshaiah (3:21). Ezra probably completed Chronicles between 450 and 430 B.C. and addressed it to the returned remnant. Ezra led some of the exiles to Jerusalem in 457 B.C. and ministered to the people as their spiritual leader. During Ezra's time, Nehemiah was the political leader and Malachi was the moral leader. The book was written to the people of Israel's "Second Commonwealth" to encourage and remind them that they remain the covenant people of God. Chronicles spends a disproportionate time on the reigns of David and Solomon because they brought the kingdom to its pinnacle. This would remind the Jews of their spiritual heritage and identity during the difficult times they were facing.

Theme and Purpose — Chronicles was written to provide a spiritual perspective on the historical events from the time of David to Cyrus' decree in 538 B.C. It traces Israel's lineage back to the dawn of the human race and forward to the end of the Babylonian captivity to reveal God's faithfulness and continuing purpose for His people. Because it was written to the returning remnant, Chronicles has a more positive thrust than Samuel or Kings. It does not deny failures but concentrates on the Messianic line, the temple, and spiritual reforms. The readers needed encouragement in rebuilding their heritage. Chronicles teaches that Yahweh is still with them—He brought them back and enabled them to rebuild the temple. All is not lost; though the glory has departed and they are under the control of Gentile powers, God still has a future for them. The throne of David was gone but the line of David still stood.

Chronicles emphasizes the role of the law, the priesthood, and the temple. Although Solomon's temple was gone, the second temple could be regarded as the remnant's link to the first. This book also taught that the past was pregnant with lessons for their present. Apostasy, idolatry, intermarriage with Gentiles, and lack of unity were the reasons for their recent ruin. It is significant that after the exile, Israel never again worshiped foreign gods.

Contribution to the Bible — What Deuteronomy is to the rest of the Pentateuch and John is to the synoptic gospels, Chronicles is to Israel's history in Samuel and Kings. Although there is overlap between Chronicles and the earlier kingdom books, the following table emphasizes some of the differences:

Samuel and Kings	Chronicles
The continuation of Israel's history from the united kingdom to the two captivities	Focuses on the southern kingdom and the Davidic line
Political history	Religious history
Prophetic authorship: emphasizes the prophetic ministry and moral concerns	Priestly authorship: emphasizes the priestly ministry and spiritual concerns
Written by authors soon after the events	Written by Ezra many years after the events
More negative—rebellion and tragedy	More positive—apostasy, but hope in spite of tragedy
Message of judgment	Message of hope
Man's failings	God's faithfulness
Emphasizes kings and prophets	Emphasizes the temple and the priests

The English Bible follows the arrangement of the Septuagint by placing Chronicles after Kings. But Chronicles appears at the end of the Hebrew Bible. Thus, "Abel to . . . Zechariah" in Matthew 23:35 and Luke 11:51 is like saying "Genesis to Chronicles," the equivalent of our saying "Genesis to Malachi."

Christ in 1 Chronicles — See Christ in 1 and 2 Samuel for a description of David as a portrait of Christ. The Davidic covenant of 2 Samuel 7 is found again in 1 Chronicles 17:11-14. Solomon fulfilled part, but the promise of the eternality of David's throne could only point to the coming of Israel's Messiah.

The tribe of Judah was placed first in the national genealogy in 1 Chronicles because the monarchy, temple, and Messiah (Gen 49:10) would come out of this tribe. Since Chronicles was the last book of the Hebrew Bible, the genealogies in chapters 1-9 in effect lead into the genealogy of Christ in the first book of the New Testament.

2 Chronicles

"For the eyes of the LORD move to and fro throughout the earth that He may strongly support those whose heart is completely His."

2 Chronicles 16:9a

"Listen to me, O Judah and inhabitants of Jerusalem, put your trust in the LORD your God, and you will be established. Put your trust in His prophets and succeed."

2 Chronicles 20:20b
(Also see 7:13-14.)

Focus	Solomon's Glory		Judah's Decline and Deportation							
	1　　　　　　9		10　　　　　　　　　　　　　　　　　　　　　　　　36							
D I V I S I O N S	Solomon's Magnificent Temple	Solomon's Worship and Works	Rebellion Against Rehoboam	Reigns of Abijah and Asa	Reform under Jehoshaphat	Reigns of Jehoram to Amaziah	Reigns of Uzziah to Ahaz	Reform under Hezekiah	Reigns of Judah's Last Kings	
	1　　　5	6　　　9	10　　12	13　　16	17　　20	21　　25	26　　28	29　　32	33　　36	
T O P I C S	The Temple Constructed and Consecrated		The Temple Desecrated and Destroyed							
	The Reign of Solomon (Splendor)		The Ruin of Judah (Degeneration and Disaster)							
	A Priestly View of Judah's History									
Locations	Judah									Babylonia
Time	40 Years		393 Years							

81

Talk Thru — Second Chronicles continues the spiritual commentary on Israel's kingdom period begun in 1 Chronicles. It parallels 1 and 2 Kings but virtually ignores the northern kingdom because of its false worship and refusal to acknowledge the temple in Jerusalem. Chronicles focuses on the fortunes of the southern kingdom of Judah, and in particular on those kings who did that which is right in the sight of the Lord. It devotes considerable space to the spiritual reformations under Asa (14-15), Jehoshaphat (17-20), Joash (23:16-24:16), Hezekiah (29-32), and Josiah (34-35). This book repeatedly teaches that whenever God's people forsake Him, He withdraws His blessings, but trust and obedience to the Lord bring victory for Judah. Everything in Chronicles is related to the temple, and it is no accident that it concludes with Cyrus' edict to rebuild it. Solomon's glory is seen in 1-9, and Judah's decline and deportation in 10-36.

Solomon's Glory (1-9): The reign of Solomon brought in Israel's golden age of peace, prosperity, and temple worship. The kingdom was united and its boundaries extended to their greatest point. Solomon's wealth, wisdom, palace, and temple became legendary. His mighty spiritual, political, and architectural feats raised Israel to her zenith. But it is in keeping with the purpose of Chronicles that six out of these nine chapters concern the construction and dedication of the temple.

Judah's Decline and Deportation (10-36): The glory was unfortunately short-lived: soon after Solomon's death the nation was divided, and both kingdoms began a downward spiral that could only be delayed by the religious reforms, but not stopped. The nation generally forsook the temple and the worship of Yahweh, and was soon torn by warfare and unrest. The reformation efforts on the part of some of Judah's kings were valiant, but never lasted beyond one generation. Nevertheless, about 70% of chapters 10-36 deals with the eight good kings, leaving only 30% to cover the 12 evil rulers. Each king is seen with respect to his relationship to the temple as the center of worship and spiritual strength. When the king served Yahweh, Judah was blessed with political and economic prosperity.

Here is a *brief* survey of Judah's 20 rulers: (1) Rehoboam—Not righteous, but he humbled himself before God and averted His wrath (12:12). (2) Abijah—A short and evil reign, but he conquered Israel because the "sons of Judah . . . trusted in the Lord" (13:18). (3) Asa—Destroyed foreign altars and idols, conquered Ethiopians against great odds through his trust in God, and restored the altar of the Lord. But he failed to trust God when threatened by Israel. (4) Jehoshaphat—Brought in a great revival; "he took great pride in the ways of the Lord" (17:6). Overthrew idols, taught God's Word to the people, and trusted in Him before battle. (5) Jehoram—A wicked king who followed the ways of Ahab and married his daughter. He led Judah into idolatry and when he died in pain, "he departed with no one's regret" (21:20). (6-7) Ahaziah and Athaliah—He was as wicked as his father and so was his mother Athaliah. Both were murdered. (8) Joash—Repaired the temple and restored the worship of God. But when Jehoiada the priest died, he allowed the people to abandon the temple and return to idolatry. (9) Amaziah—Mixed in his relationship to God, he later forsook the Lord for the gods of Edom. He was defeated by Israel and later murdered. (10) Uzziah—He started well with the Lord and was blessed with military victories. But when he was strong, he became proud and presumptuously played the role of a priest by offering incense in the temple. He was struck with leprosy because of this. (11) Jotham—Rebuilt the gate of the temple and revered God. The Lord blessed him with prosperity and victory. (12) Ahaz—A wicked king and idolater. He was oppressed by his enemies and forced to give tribute to the Assyrians out of the temple treasures. (13) Hezekiah—Judah's greatest king. He repaired and reopened the temple and put away the altars and idols set up by his father Ahaz. Judah was spared destruction by Assyria because of his righteousness. His reforms were given only a few verses in Kings but three chapters in Chronicles. (14-15) Manasseh and Amon—Manasseh was Judah's most wicked king. He set up idols and altars all over the land. But he repented when he was carried away by Assyria. God brought him back to Judah and he made a half-way reform, but it was too late. Amon followed in his father's wickedness. Both kings were murdered. (16) Josiah—He led in reforms and spiritual revival. He centered worship around the temple, found the law and obeyed it, and reinstituted the Passover. (17-19) Jehoahaz, Jehoiakim, Jehoiachin—Their relentless evil finally brought the downfall of Judah. The temple was ravaged in each of their reigns. (20) Zedekiah—

Judah's last king was also wicked. Jerusalem and the temple were destroyed and the captivity began. Chronicles nevertheless ends on a note of hope at the end of the captivity with Cyrus' decree for them to return: "Whoever there is among you of all His people, may the LORD his God be with him, and let him go up!" (36:23).

Title — See 1 Chronicles, Title for more detail. Hebrew title: *hayyamim*, "the events of the days." Greek title: *Paraleipomenon secundus*, "the second book of things omitted." Latin title: *Chronicorum Liber*, the "Book of Chronicles."

Author — Here are the listed sources of 1 and 2 Chronicles (see 1 Chronicles, Author). These include official and prophetic records: (1) The Book of the Kings of Israel and Judah (or Judah and Israel) (1C 9:1; 2C 16:11; 20:34; 25:26; 27:7; 28:26; 32:32; 35:27; 36:8), (2) A Commentary on the Book of the Kings (2C 24:27), (3) Chronicles of Samuel the Seer (1C 29:29), (4) Chronicles of Nathan the Prophet (1C 29:29; 2C 9:29), (5) Chronicles of Gad the Seer (1C 29:29), (6) The prophecy of Ahijah the Shilonite (2C 9:29), (7) The Visions of Iddo the Seer (2C 9:29; 12:15; 13:22), (8) Records of Shemaiah the Prophet (2C 12:15), (9) Records of Iddo the Prophet on genealogies (2C 12:15), (10) Treatise of the Prophet Iddo (2C 13:22), (11) The Annals of Jehu the son of Hanani (2C 20:34), (12) The Acts of Uzziah by Isaiah the Prophet (2C 26:22), (13) The Vision of Isaiah the Prophet (2C 32:32), (14) The Records of the Hozai (2C 33:19), (15) The Account of the Chronicles of King David (1C 27:24), (16) The Writing of David and his son Solomon (2C 35:4). In addition to these, the author/compiler had genealogical lists and documents like the message and letters of Sennacherib (2C 32:10-17).

Date and Setting — See 1 Chronicles, Date and Setting for the background of 1 and 2 Chronicles. Chapters 1-9 cover the 40 years from 971-931 B.C., and chapters 10-36 cover the 393 years from 931-538 B.C. Jeremiah's prediction of a 70-year captivity in Babylonia (36:21; Jer. 29:10) was fulfilled in two ways: (1) a political captivity in which Jerusalem was overcome from 605 B.C. to 536 B.C., and (2) a religious captivity involving the destruction of the temple in 586 B.C. and the rebuilding of the new temple in 516/515 B.C.

Theme and Purpose — The book of 2 Chronicles provides a topical history of the end of the united kingdom (Solomon) and the kingdom of Judah. Chronicles is more than historical annals; it is a divine editorial on the spiritual character-istics of the Davidic dynasty. This is why it focuses on the southern rather than the northern kingdom. Most of the kings failed to realize that apart from its true mission as a covenant nation called to bring others to Yahweh, Judah had no calling, no destiny, and no hope of becoming great on its own. Only what was done in accordance with God's will had any lasting value. Chronicles concentrates on the kings who were con-cerned with maintaining the proper service of God and the times of spiritual reform. But growing apostasy inevitably led to judgment.

The temple in Jerusalem is the unifying theme of 1 and 2 Chronicles. Much of the material found in 2 Samuel to 2 Kings was omitted in Chronicles because it does not develop this theme. In 1 Chronicles 11-29, the central message is David's preparation for the construction and service of the temple. Most of 2 Chronicles 1-9 is devoted to the building and consecration of the temple. Chapters 10-36 omit the kings of Israel in the north because they had no ties with the temple. Prominence is given to the reigns of Judah's temple restorers (Asa, Jehoshaphat, Joash, Hezekiah, and Josiah). The temple symbolically stood for God's presence among His people and their high calling. It was the spiritual link between their past and future. Thus, Ezra wrote this book to encourage the people to accept the new temple raised on the site of the old and to remind them of their true calling and God's faithfulness in spite of their low circum-stances. The Davidic line, temple, and priesthood were still theirs.

Contribution to the Bible — Chronicles begins with Adam and ends with the decree of Cyrus (538 B.C.). In this respect Chronicles touches upon more history than any other Old Testament book. It focuses on the period from David to the captivity of Judah and looks at the reigns of 21 kings and one queen. At the time it was written it taught lessons from the past, illustrated God's faithfulness in the present (the return from captivity and the new temple), and anticipated the fulfillment of God's promises in the future (the Messianic line).

As a chronicle of the temple, the book surveys its conception (David), construction and consecration (Solomon), corruption and cleansing (the kings of Judah), and conflagration (Nebuchadnezzar).

Christ in 2 Chronicles — The throne of David was destroyed but the line of David remained fast. Murders, treachery, battles, and captivity all threatened the Messianic line but it remained clear and unbroken from Adam to Zerubbabel. The fulfillment in Christ can be seen in the genealogies of Matthew 1 and Luke 3.

The temple also pointed ahead to Christ. When He came, He said "something greater than the temple is here" (Matt. 12:6). He also likened His body to the temple: "Destroy this temple, and in three days I will raise it up" (John 2:19). In Revelation 21:22 He replaces the temple: "And I saw no temple in it, for the Lord God, the Almighty, and the Lamb, are its temple."

Ezra

"Whoever there is among you of all His people, may his God be
with him! Let him go up to Jerusalem which is in Judah, and
rebuild the house of the LORD, the God of Israel; He is the God
who is in Jerusalem."

Ezra 1:3

"For Ezra had set his heart to study the law of the LORD, and to
practice it, and to teach His statutes and ordinances in Israel."

Ezra 7:10
(Also see 6:14)

Focus	Rebuilding the Temple		(Book of Esther)	Rebuilding the People	
	1	6		7	10
D I V I S I O N S	Commission of the Temple Builders	Completion of the Temple Project		Commission of the Spiritual Leaders	Completion of the Spiritual Reforms
	1 · 2	3 · 6		7 · 8	9 · 10
T O P I C S	The Return under Zerubbabel		5 8 Y E A R G A P	The Return under Ezra	
	Restoration			Reformation	
	Decree and Journey	Work		Decree and Journey	Work
Loca-tions	Persia to Jerusalem			Persia to Jerusalem	
Time	23 Years (538-515 B.C.) (60% of Ezra)			1 Year (457 B.C.) (40% of Ezra)	

Talk Thru — Ezra continues the story exactly where it left off at the end of 2 Chronicles. This book shows how God's promise in Jeremiah 29:10-14 to bring His people back into their land was fulfilled. Israel's second exodus, this time from Babylonia, was less impressive than the first because only a remnant chose to leave. But God was with these people, and although their days of glory seemed over, their spiritual heritage still remained and God's rich promises would yet be fulfilled. Ezra relates the story of the first two returns from Babylonia, the first led by Zerubbabel and the second led decades later by Ezra. Its two divisions are Rebuilding the Temple (1-6) and Rebuilding the People (7-10), and they are separated by a 58-year gap during which the story of Esther took place.

Rebuilding the Temple (1-6): King Cyrus of Persia overthrew Babylonia in 539 B.C. and issued a decree in 538 B.C. that allowed the exiled Jews to return to their homeland. Isaiah prophesied about two centuries before that the temple would be rebuilt, and actually named Cyrus as the one who would bring it about (Isa. 44:28-45:4). Cyrus may have read and responded to this passage. Out of a total Jewish population of perhaps 2-3 million, only 49,897 chose to take advantage of this offer. Only the most committed would be willing to leave a life of relative comfort in Babylonia, endure a 900-mile trek, and face further hardship by rebuilding a destroyed temple and city. Zerubbabel, a "prince" of Judah (he was a direct descendant of King David), led the faithful remnant back to Jerusalem. Those who returned were from the tribes of Judah, Benjamin, and Levi, but it is evident that representatives from the other 10 tribes eventually returned as well. The 10 "lost tribes" were not entirely lost. Zerubbabel's priorities were in the right place: he first restored the altar and the religious feasts before beginning work on the temple itself. The foundation of the temple was laid in 536 B.C., but opposition arose and the work ceased from 534-520 B.C. While Ezra 4:1-5,24 concerns Zerubbabel, 4:6-23 concerns opposition to the building of the wall of Jerusalem some time between 464 and 444 B.C. These verses were probably placed here to illustrate the antagonism to the work of rebuilding. The prophets Haggai and Zechariah exhorted the people to get back to building the temple (5:1-2), and the work started again under Zerubbabel and Joshua the high priest. Tattenai, a Persian governor, protested to King Darius I about the temple building and challenged their authority to continue. King Darius found the decree of Cyrus and confirmed it, even forcing Tattenai to provide whatever was needed to complete the work. It was finished in 515 B.C.

Rebuilding the People (7-10): A smaller return under Ezra took place in 457 B.C., 81 years after the first return under Zerubbabel. Ezra the priest was given authority by King Artaxerxes I to bring people and contributions for the temple in Jerusalem. God protected this band of less than 2,000 (males) and they safely reached Jerusalem with their valuable gifts from Persia. Many priests but few Levites returned with Zerubbabel and Ezra (2:36-42; 8:15-19). God used Ezra to rebuild the people spiritually and morally. When he discovered that the people and the priests had intermarried with foreign women, Ezra identified with the sin of his people and offered a great intercessory prayer on their behalf. During the 58-year gap between Ezra 6 and 7, the people fell into a confused spiritual state and Ezra was alarmed. They quickly responded to Ezra's confession and weeping by making a covenant to put away their foreign wives and live their lives in accordance with God's law. This confession and response to the Word of God brought about a great revival and changed lifestyles.

Title
— Ezra is the Aramaic form of the Hebrew word *'ezer,* "help," perhaps meaning "Yahweh helps." Ezra and Nehemiah were originally bound together as one book because Chronicles, Ezra, and Nehemiah were viewed as one continuous history. The Septuagint called Ezra-Nehemiah *Esdras deuteron,* "Second Esdras." First Esdras was the name of the apocryphal book of Esdras. The Latin title was *Liber primus Esdrae,* the "First Book of Ezra." In the Latin Bible, Ezra was called 1 Ezra and Nehemiah was called 2 Ezra.

Author
— Although Ezra is not specifically mentioned as the author, he is certainly the best candidate. Jewish tradition (the Talmud) attributes the book to Ezra, and portions of the book (7:28-9:15) are written in the first person, from Ezra's point of view. The vividness of the details and descriptions favors an author who was an eyewitness of the later events of the book. As in Chronicles, there is a strong priestly emphasis, and Ezra was a direct priestly descendant of Aaron through Eleazar,

Phineas, and Zadok (7:1-5). He studied, practiced, and taught the law of the Lord as an educated scribe (7:10-12). He also had access to the library of written documents gathered by Nehemiah according to 2 Maccabees 2:13-15. Ezra no doubt used this material in writing Ezra 1-6 as he did in writing Chronicles. Some think that Ezra composed Nehemiah as well by making use of Nehemiah's personal diary.

Ezra was a godly man marked by strong trust in the Lord, moral integrity, and grief over sin. He was a contemporary of Nehemiah (Neh. 8:1-9; 12:36) who arrived in Jerusalem in 444 B.C. Tradition holds that Ezra was the founder of the Great Synagogue where the canon of Old Testament Scripture was settled. There is also a tradition that he collected the biblical books into a unit and that he originated the synagogue form of worship.

Some arguments have been forwarded to refute the authenticity and early date of Ezra and Nehemiah by pushing their authorship into the Greek period. There are some problems with certain names but these are far from conclusive. The weight of evidence points to a fifth century B.C. authorship.

Date and Setting — The following table shows the chronological relationship of the books of Ezra, Nehemiah, and Esther:

538-515	483-473	457	444-c.425
Zerubbabel	Esther	Ezra	Nehemiah
Ezra 1-6	Book of Esther	Ezra 7-10	Book of Nehemiah
First Return	—	Second Return	Third Return

These books fit against the background of these Persian kings:

Cyrus	Cambyses	Smerdis	Darius I	Xerxes	Artaxerxes I
(559-530)	(530-522)	(522)	(521-486)	(486-464)	(464-423)

Cyrus overthrew Babylonia in October, 539 B.C. and issued his decree allowing the Jews to return in 538 B.C. The temple was begun in 536 B.C. The exile lasted only 50 years after 586 B.C., but the 70-year figure for the captivity comes from a beginning date of 606 B.C. when the first deportation to

Babylonia took place. The work on the temple was discontinued in 534 B.C., resumed in 520 B.C., and completed in 515 B.C. It was started under Cyrus and finished under Darius I. The two intervening kings, Cambyses and Smerdis, are not mentioned in any of these books. The prophets Haggai and Zechariah ministered during Zerubbabel's time, around 520 B.C. and later. Esther's story fits entirely in the reign of Xerxes, and Ezra ministered during the reign of Artaxerxes I as did Nehemiah. There were three waves of deportation to Babylonia (606, 597, 586) and three returns from Babylonia: 538 (Zerubbabel), 457 (Ezra), and 444 (Nehemiah).

Ezra probably wrote this book between 457 B.C. (the events of 7-10) and 444 B.C. (Nehemiah's arrival in Jerusalem). During the period covered by the book of Ezra, Gautama Buddha (560-480) was in India, Confucius (551-479) was in China, and Socrates (470-399) was in Greece.

Theme and Purpose

Theme and Purpose — The basic theme of Ezra is the spiritual, moral, and social restoration of the returned remnant in Jerusalem under the leadership of Zerubbabel and Ezra. Israel's worship was revitalized and its people were purified. God's faithfulness is seen in the way He sovereignly protected His people by a powerful empire while they were in captivity. They prospered in their exile and God raised up pagan kings who were sympathetic to their cause and encouraged them to rebuild their homeland. God also provided zealous and capable spiritual leaders who directed the return and the rebuilding. He kept the promise He made in Jeremiah 29:14: " 'And I will be found by you,' declares the LORD, 'and I will restore your fortunes and will gather you from all the nations and from all the places where I have driven you,' declares the LORD, 'and I will bring you back to the place from where I sent you into exile.' "

Contribution to the Bible

Contribution to the Bible — Ezra fills in the history of the first two returns from the Babylonian captivity, and Nehemiah covers the third. This book forcefully emphasizes the power of the Word of God and the crucial need to obey it on every level of life (1:1; 3:2; 6:14,18; 7:6,10,14; 9:4; 10:3,5). Ezra follows 2 Chronicles in the English Bible because it carries the story on from that point. But in the Hebrew Bible it appears with

Nehemiah as one book just preceding Chronicles, the last book.

Christs in Ezra — Ezra reveals God's continued fulfillment of His promise to David to keep his descendants alive. Zerubbabel himself was part of the Messianic line as the grandson of Jeconiah (Jehoiachin, 1 Chron. 3:17-19). See Matthew 1:12-13. There is a positive note of hope in Ezra and Nehemiah because the remnant has returned to the land of promise. It was in this land that the Messianic promises would be fulfilled, because they were connected with places like Bethlehem, Jerusalem, and Zion. Christ would be born in Bethlehem (Mic. 5:2), not in Babylonia.

The book of Ezra as a whole also typifies Christ's work of forgiveness and restoration.

Nehemiah

"Then I said to them, 'You see the bad situation we are in, that Jerusalem is desolate and its gates burned by fire. Come, let us rebuild the wall of Jerusalem that we may no longer be a reproach.' "

Nehemiah 2:17

"So we built the wall and the whole wall was joined together to half its height, for the people had a mind to work."

Nehemiah 4:6

Focus	Rebuilding			Revival	Reform
	1 7	8 10	11 13		
D I V I S I O N S	Conception of the Walls	Construction of the Walls	Completion of the Walls	Repentance and Revival of the People	Repopulation and Reform of the People
	1 2	3 4	5 7	8 10	11 13
T O P I C S	Renewed Walls			Renewed Covenant	Renewed Nation
	Civil Reform			Religious Reform	Political Reform
	Construction of the City			Instruction of the People	
Location	Jerusalem				
Time	About 19 Years				

Talk Thru — Nehemiah was closely associated with the ministry of Ezra, his contemporary. Ezra was a priest who brought spiritual revival; Nehemiah was a governor who brought physical and political reconstruction and led the people in moral reform. They combined to make an effective team in comprehensively building up the post-exilic remnant. The last Old Testament prophet Malachi also ministered during this time to provide additional moral and spiritual direction. The book of Nehemiah takes us to the end of the historical story line in the Old Testament, about 400 years before the birth of the promised Messiah. Its three divisions are: Rebuilding (1-7), Revival (8-10), and Reform (11-13).

Rebuilding (1-7): Nehemiah's great concern for his people and the welfare of Jerusalem led him to take bold action. The walls of Jerusalem were destroyed by Nebuchadnezzar in 586 B.C., but evidently they were almost rebuilt after 464 B.C. when Artaxerxes I took the throne of Persia (see Ezra 3:6-23). When he heard that opposition led to their destruction, Nehemiah first prayed on behalf of his people and then secured Artaxerxes' permission, provision, and protection for the massive project of rebuilding the walls. The return under Nehemiah in 444 B.C. took place 13 years after the return led by Ezra and 94 years after the return led by Zerubbabel. Nehemiah inspected the walls and challenged the people to "arise and build" (2:18). Work began immediately on the wall and its gates with people building portions corresponding to where they were living. But opposition quickly arose, first in the form of mockery, then in the form of conspiracy when the work was progressing at an alarming rate. Nehemiah overcame threats of force by setting half of the people on military watch and half on construction. While the external opposition continued to mount, internal opposition also surfaced. The wealthier Jews were abusing and extorting from those who were forced to mortgage their property and sell their children into slavery. Nehemiah again dealt with the problem by the twin means of prayer and action. He also led by example when he sacrificed his governor's salary. In spite of deceit, slander, and treachery, Nehemiah continued to trust in God and press on with singleness of mind until the work was completed. The task was accomplished in an incredible 52 days, and even the enemies recognized that it could only have been accomplished with the help of God (6:16).

Revival (8-10): The construction of the walls was followed by consecration and consolidation of the people. Ezra the priest was the leader of the spiritual revival in chapters 8-10, and this is reminiscent of the reforms he led 13 years earlier (Ezra 9-10). Ezra stood on a special wooden podium after the completion of the walls and gave the people a marathon reading of the law, translating from the Hebrew into Aramaic so they could understand. They responded with weeping, confession, obedience, and rejoicing. The Levites and priests led them in a great prayer that surveyed God's past work of deliverance and loyalty on behalf of His people, and magnified God's attributes of holiness, justice, mercy, and love. The covenant was then renewed with God as the people committed themselves to separate from the Gentiles in marriage and obey God's commandments.

Reform (11-13): Lots were drawn to determine who would remain in Jerusalem and who would return to the cities of their inheritance. One tenth were required to stay in Jerusalem, and the rest of the land was resettled by the people and priests. The walls of Jerusalem were dedicated to the Lord in a joyful ceremony accompanied by instrumental and vocal music.

Ezra's revival in 8-10 was unfortunately short-lived, and Nehemiah, who had returned to Persia in 432 B.C. (13:6), made a second trip to Jerusalem around 425 B.C. to reform the people. He cleansed the temple, enforced the Sabbath, and required the people to put away all foreign wives.

Title — The Hebrew for Nehemiah is *nehemyah*, "comfort of Yahweh." The book is of course named after its chief character whose name appears in the opening verse. The combined book of Ezra-Nehemiah was given the Greek title *Esdras deuteron*, "Second Esdras" (see Ezra, Title) in the Septuagint. The Latin title of Nehemiah was *Liber secundus Esdrae*, the "Second Book of Ezra" (Ezra was the first). At this point it was considered a separate book from Ezra and later called *Liber Nehemiae*, the "Book of Nehemiah."

Author — It is clear that much of this book came from Nehemiah's personal memoirs. The reporting is remarkably candid and vivid. Certainly 1:1-7:5; 12:27-43; 13:4-31 are the "words of Nehemiah" (1:1). Some think that Nehemiah composed those portions and compiled the rest. Others think that

Ezra wrote 7:6-12:26; 12:44-13:3 and compiled the rest, making use of Nehemiah's diary. A third view that neither wrote it seems least likely from the evidence. Nehemiah 7:5-73 is almost the same as Ezra 2:1-70, and both lists may have been taken from the same document.

An argument has been made from the appearance of the name Jaddua (12:11,22) in the list of priests and Levites that Nehemiah must be dated after the time of Ezra or Nehemiah. Jaddua was high priest from 351-331 B.C. during the time of Alexander the Great. But this name may have been added later, or it may be that Nehemiah lived to see the young Jaddua.

As cupbearer to Artaxerxes I, Nehemiah held a position of great responsibility. His role of tasting the king's wine to prevent him from poisoning put him in a place of trust and confidence as one of the king's advisors. As governor of Jerusalem from 444-432 B.C. (5:14; 8:9; 10:1; 13:6), Nehemiah demonstrated courage, compassion for the oppressed, integrity, godliness, and selflessness. He was willing to give up the luxury and ease of the palace to help his people. He was a dedicated layman who had the right priorities and was concerned for God's work, able to encourage and rebuke at the right times, strong in prayer, and gave all glory and credit to God.

Date and Setting — See Ezra, Date and Setting because both books share the same historical background. The book of Nehemiah fits within the reign of Artaxerxes I of Persia (464-423 B.C.). Esther was Artaxerxes' stepmother, and it is possible that she was instrumental in Nehemiah's appointment as the king's cupbearer. Nehemiah left Persia in the 20th year of Artaxerxes (444 B.C., 2:1), returned to Persia in the 32nd year of Artaxerxes (432 B.C., 13:6), and left again for Jerusalem "after some time" (13:6), perhaps around 425 B.C. This book could not have been completed until after his second visit to Jerusalem.

The historical reliability of this book has been supported by the Elephantine Papyri. These documents mention Sanballat (2:19) and Jehohanan (6:18; 12:23) and indicate that Bigvai replaced Nehemiah as governor of Judah by 410 B.C.

Malachi lived and ministered during Nehemiah's time, and a comparison of the books shows that many of the evils encountered by Nehemiah were specifically denounced by Malachi. The coldhearted indifference toward God described in both books remained a problem in Israel during the 400 silent years before Christ.

Theme and Purpose — While Ezra deals primarily with the religious restoration of Judah, Nehemiah is concerned with Judah's political and geographical restoration. The first seven chapters are devoted to the rebuilding of Jerusalem's walls because Jerusalem was the spiritual and political center of Judah. Without walls, Jerusalem could hardly be considered a city at all. As governor, Nehemiah also established firm civil authority. Ezra and Nehemiah worked together to build the people spiritually and morally so that the restoration would be complete. Thus, Nehemiah functions as the natural sequel to the book of Ezra, and it is not surprising that the two books were regarded as a unit for centuries.

Nehemiah was also written to show the obvious hand of God in the establishment of His people in their homeland in the years after their exile. Under the leadership of Nehemiah, they accomplished in 52 days what had not been done in the 94 years since the first return under Zerubbabel. By obedient faith they were able to overcome what appeared to be insurmountable opposition.

Contribution to the Bible — Nehemiah fills in our understanding of a period that would otherwise be unclear. Along with Ezra it provides the background for the post-exilic period and the three post-exilic prophets (Haggai, Zechariah, and Malachi).

Ezra 1-6	Esther	Ezra 7-10		Nehemiah
Restoration under Zerubbabel	5 8	Reformation under Ezra	1 3	Reconstruction under Nehemiah
538-515	Y e a r	457	Y e a r	444-c.425
Temple		People		Walls
Haggai, Zechariah	G a P	—	G a P	Malachi
First Return (about 50,000)		Second Return (about 2,000)		Third Return

The role of prayer in the life of Nehemiah is striking. It is instructive to study the series of problems, reactions, and prayers of Nehemiah presented in this book (see 1:5-11; 2:1-4,19-20; 4:1-6,7-10,11-14; 6:9,14). Nehemiah demonstrated a balanced blend of dependence and discipline, prayer and planning. His prayers were generally short but fervent. Chapters 1-7 are filled with leadership principles, 8-10 with spiritual principles, and 11-13 with moral and social principles.

Christ in Nehemiah — Like Ezra, Nehemiah portrays Christ in His ministry of restoration. Nehemiah illustrates Christ in that he gave up a high position to identify with the plight of his people; he came with a specific mission and fulfilled it; and his life was characterized by prayerful dependence upon God.

In this book, everything was restored except the king. The temple was rebuilt, Jerusalem was reconstructed, the covenant was renewed, and the people were reformed. The Messianic line was intact, but the King was yet to come. The decree of Artaxerxes in his 20th year (444 B.C., 2:2) marked the beginning point of Daniel's prophecy of the 70 weeks (see Dan. 9:25-27). "So you are to know and discern that from the issuing of a decree to restore and rebuild Jerusalem until Messiah the Prince there will be seven weeks and sixty-two weeks; it will be built again, with plaza and moat, even in times of distress" (Dan. 9:25). Messiah would come at the end of the 69 weeks, and this was exactly fulfilled in A.D. 33 (see Christ in Daniel).

Esther

"For if you remain silent at this time, relief and deliverance will arise for the Jews from another place and you and your father's house will perish. And who knows whether you have not attained royalty for such a time as this?"

Esther 4:14

Focus	Grave Danger		Great Deliverance	
	1 4	5 10		
D I V I S I O N S	Esther Replaces Vashti as Queen	Haman Plots to Destroy the Jews	Haman's Hate, Humiliation, and Hanging	The Jews' Conquest and Commemoration
	1 2	3 4	5 7	8 10
T O P I C S	Plotting Destruction		Preventing Destruction	
	Conflict	Cunning	Courage	Conquest
	Exaltation	Persecution	Preservation	Commemoration
	Feast of Ahasuerus	Fast of Mordecai	Feasts of Esther	Feast of Purim
Location	Persia			
Time	10 Years			

Talk Thru — The story of Esther fits between chapters 6 and 7 of Ezra, between the first return led by Zerubbabel and the second return led by Ezra. It provides the only biblical portrait of the vast majority of Jews who chose to remain in Persia rather than return to Palestine. God's guiding and protective hand on behalf of His people is evident throughout this book even though His name does not appear once. The clearly emerging message is that God uses ordinary men and women to overcome impossible circumstances to accomplish His gracious purposes. Chapters 1-4 describe the grave danger to the Jews, and chapters 5-10 describe their great deliverance by God.

Grave Danger (1-4): The story begins in Ahasuerus' winter palace at Susa. The king gave a lavish banquet and display of royal glory for the people of Susa and proudly sought to make queen Vashti's beauty a part of the program. There was fear when she refused that other women would become insolent if Vashti went unpunished, and the king was counseled to depose her and seek another queen. Esther later found favor in the eyes of Ahasuerus and won the royal "beauty pageant." At her uncle Mordecai's instructions, she did not reveal that she was Jewish. Through her, Mordecai was able to warn the king of an assassination plot, and his deed was recorded in the palace records. Meanwhile, Haman became captain of the princes but Mordecai refused to bow to him. When he learned that Mordecai was Jewish, Haman plotted for a year to eliminate all Jews as his rage and hatred grew. He cast lots *(purim)* daily during this period until he determined the best day to have them massacred. Through bribery and lies he convinced Ahasuerus to issue an edict that all Jews in the empire would be slain 11 months hence in a single day. Haman conceived his plot out of envy and vengeance and executed it with malicious craft. The decree created a state of confusion, and Mordecai asked Esther to appeal to the king to spare the Jews. At the peril of her life, Esther decided she would see the king and reveal her nationality in a desperate attempt to dissuade Ahasuerus. Mordecai convinced her that she was called to her high position for this purpose.

Great Deliverance (5-10): After fasting, Esther appeared before the king and wisely invited him to a banquet along with Haman. At the banquet she requested them to attend a second banquet, waiting for the right moment to divulge her request.

Haman was flattered but later enraged when he saw Mordecai. He took his wife's suggestion of building a large gallows for Mordecai (he couldn't wait the 11 months for Mordecai to be slain). That night Ahasuerus decided to treat his insomnia by reading the palace records. When he read about Mordecai's deed, he wanted him to be honored. Haman, thinking the king wanted to honor him, told him how it should be done and then found out it was for Mordecai. He was humbled and infuriated by being forced to honor the man he loathed. At Esther's second banquet Ahasuerus offered her up to half of his kingdom for the third time. She then made her plea for her people and accused Haman of his treachery. The infuriated king had Haman hanged on the gallows he had built for Mordecai. The 75-foot height of the gallows was designed to make Mordecai's downfall a city-wide spectacle, but it ironically provided Haman with unexpected public attention . . . posthumously.

Persian law sealed with the king's ring (3:12) could not be revoked, but at Esther's request the king issued a new decree to all the provinces that the Jews could assemble and defend themselves on the day when they were to be attacked by their enemies. This decree changed the outcome intended by the first and produced great joy. Mordecai was also elevated and set over the house of Haman. When the fateful day of the two decrees came, the Jews defeated their enemies in their cities throughout the Persian provinces, but did not take the plunder. The next day became a day of celebration and an annual Jewish holiday called the Feast of Purim. The word was derived from the Assyrian *puru*, meaning "lot," referring to the lots cast by Haman to determine the day of the Jewish extermination. The story closes with the advance of Mordecai to a position second only to the king. Esther's qualities of maturity, faith, courage, charm, and discretion contributed to the joyful ending reminiscent of a fairy tale.

Title — Esther's Hebrew name was *Hadassah*, "myrtle" (2:7), but her Persian name *'ester* was derived from the Persian word for "star" *(stara)*. The Greek title for this book is *Esther*, and the Latin title is *Hester*.

Author — There is no indication of the author in the text, but the evident knowledge of Persian etiquette and customs, the palace in Susa, and details of the events in the reign of Aha-suerus indicate that the author lived in Persia during this period. The obvious Jewish nationalism and knowledge of Jewish customs further suggest that the author was Jewish. If this Persian Jew was not an eyewitness, he probably knew those who were. The book must have been written soon after the death of King Ahasuerus (464 B.C.), because 10:2-3 speaks of his reign in the past tense. Some writers suggest that Mordecai himself wrote the book, but this seems unlikely, for although Mordecai did keep records (9:20), 10:2-3 implies that his career was already over. But the author certainly made use of Mordecai's records and may have had access to the Book of the Chronicles of the Kings of Media and Persia (2:23; 10:2). Ezra and Nehemiah have also been suggested for authorship, but the vocabulary and style of Esther is dissimilar to that found in their books. It seems most likely that a younger contemporary of Mordecai composed the book.

Date and Setting — Ahasuerus was the Hebrew name and Xerxes the Greek name of Khshayarsha, king of Persia in 486-464 B.C. According to 1:3, the feast of Xerxes took place in his third year, or 483 B.C. The historian Herodotus referred to this banquet as the occasion of Xerxes' planning for a military campaign against Greece. But in 479 B.C. he was defeated by the Greeks at Salamis, and Herodotus tells us that he sought consolation in his harem. This corresponds to the time when he held a "contest" and crowned Esther queen of Persia (2:16-17). It was in 473 B.C. that the events of the rest of the book took place (3:7-12), so the chronological span is 10 years (483-473 B.C.). The probable time of authorship was between 464 B.C. (the end of Xerxes' reign; see 10:2-3) and c.435 B.C. (the palace at Susa was destroyed by fire around that time, and such an event would probably have been mentioned). The historical and linguistic features of Esther do not support a date later than 400 B.C.; there is no trace of Greek influence.

Xerxes was a boisterous man of emotional extremes whose actions were often strange and contradictory. This fact sheds light on his ability to sign a decree for the extermination of the Jews and two months later sign a second decree allowing them to overthrow their enemies.

Esther was addressed to the many Jews who did not return

to their homeland. Not all the godly people left—some did not return for legitimate reasons. But most were disobedient in staying in Persia. Nevertheless, God continued to care for His people in voluntary exile.

Theme and Purpose — The book of Esther was written to show how the Jewish people were protected and preserved by the gracious hand of God from the threat of annihilation. Although God disciplined His covenant people, He never abandoned them. The God of Israel is the sovereign controller of history, and His providential care can be seen all throughout this book: He raised a Jewish girl out of obscurity to become the queen of the most powerful empire in the world; He ensured that Mordecai's loyal deed was recorded in the palace records; He guided Esther's intrusion into the king's court; He superintended the timing of Esther's two feasts; He was involved in Ahasuerus' insomnia and the cure he used for it; He saw that Haman's gallows would be utilized in an unexpected way; He gave Esther great favor in the sight of the king; and He brought about the new decree and the eventual victory of the Jews. No miracles were involved, but the events meshed together with obvious purpose—a slight change would have affected the whole outcome. Even in Persia the words of Genesis 12:3 rang true: "And I will bless those who bless you, and the one who curses you I will curse."

Esther was also written to provide the historical basis and background for the Feast of Purim. To this day this book perpetuates the memory of God's deliverance of His people from certain destruction.

Contribution to the Bible — Ezra deals primarily with the restoration of the Jewish people after the exile, Nehemiah deals with their physical and spiritual reconstruction, and Esther deals with their preservation. Esther is more like a drama than any other portion of Scripture with its unexpected and ironic plot twists. Because of its unusual nature, Esther hopped from place to place in the canon of Scripture. The Septuagint even sandwiched it between two apocryphal books, the Wisdom of Sirach and Judith. It was found in the "Writings" section of the Hebrew Bible as one of the five rolls *(Megilloth)*. The other four are Song of Solomon, Ruth, Lamentations, and Ecclesiastes. These books are read on Jewish holidays, and Esther is still read on the Feast of Purim.

There has been opposition to acceptance of Esther as divinely inspired, especially because no form of the name of God is used, and yet there are 187 references to the Persian king. Nor is there any mention of the law, the offerings and sacrifices, prayer, or anything supernatural. Objections also appeared early in the Christian community because it is never quoted in the New Testament and because Esther gives the historical background for a nationalistic Jewish festival which has no connection with later Christian truth. It has also been challenged because of the bloodthirsty spirit of chapter 9. The Jews tried to overcome embarrassment by creating an apocryphal book called *Additions to Esther* which is full of references to God. Here are some reasons that combine to explain the omission of God: (1) The book was written in Persia and would be censored or profaned by substitution of a pagan god's name. (2) The general disobedience of the Jews in preferring the comfort of Persia to the hardships of rebuilding their homeland may be another factor. (3) The silence was intentional to illustrate the hidden but providential care of God in spite of outward appearances. This is a subtle form of revelation that shows the hand of God behind every event. (4) The name of Yahweh (YHWH) does appear in acrostic form four times in the Hebrew text (1:20; 5:4,13; 7:7). Incidentally, the word "Jews" appears 43 times in the plural and eight times in the singular. It was derived from "Judah" because of the predominance of this tribe. The term was applied to all descendants of Jacob.

Christ in Esther — Esther, like Christ, put herself in the place of death for her people but received the approval of the King. She also portrays Christ's work as Advocate on our behalf. This book reveals another Satanic threat to destroy the Jewish people and thus, the Messianic line. God continued to preserve His people in spite of opposition and danger, and nothing could prevent the coming of Messiah.

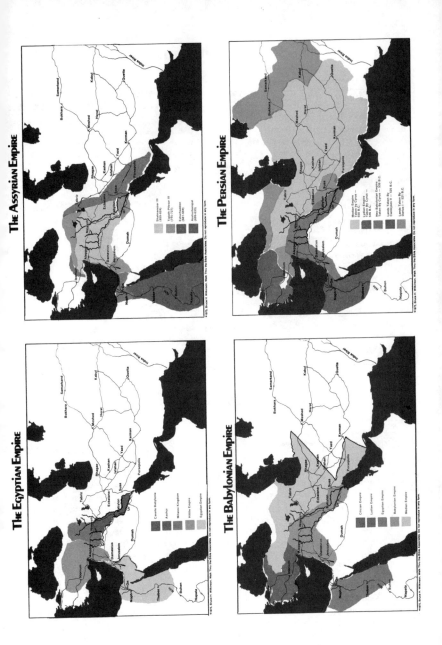

The Egyptian Empire

The Assyrian Empire

The Babylonian Empire

The Persian Empire

Kings of Israel

Dynasty		Name (Character)	Length of Reign*	Relation to Predecessor	End of Reign	1 & 2 Kings	2 Chronicles
I	1	Jeroboam I (Bad)	931/30 - 910/09 = 22		Stricken by God	1 Kings 11:26-14:20	2 Chr. 9:29-13:22
	2	Nadab (Bad)	910/09 - 909/08 = 2	Son	Murdered by Baasha	1 Kings 15:25-28	
II	3	Baasha (Bad)	909/08 - 886/85 = 24		Died	1 Kings 15:27-16:7	2 Chr. 16:1-6
	4	Elah (Bad)	886/85 - 885/84 = 2	Son	Murdered by Zimri	1 Kings 16:6-14	
III	5	Zimri (Bad)	885/84 = 7 days	Captain of Chariots	Suicide by fire	1 Kings 16:9-20	
IV	6	Omri** (Bad)	885/84 - 874/73† = 12	Captain of Army	Died	1 Kings 16:15-28	
	7	Ahab (Bad)	874/73 - 853 = 21	Son	Wounded in battle	1 Kings 16:28-22:40	2 Chr. 18:1-34
	8	Ahaziah (Bad)	853 - 852 = 1	Son	Fell through lattice	1 Kings 22:40-2 Kings 1:18	2 Chr. 20:35-37
	9	Jehoram ☆ (Bad)	852 - 841 = 11	Brother	Murdered by Jehu	2 Kings 3:1-9:25	2 Chr. 22:5-7
V	10	Jehu (Bad)	841 - 814/13 = 28		Died	2 Kings 9:1-10:36	2 Chr. 22:7-12
	11	Jehoahaz (Bad)	814/13 - 798 = 16	Son	Died	2 Kings 13:1-9	
	12	Jehoash‡ (Bad)	798 - 782/81 = 16	Son	Died	2 Kings 13:10-14:16	2 Chr. 25:17-24
	13	Jeroboam II (Bad)	793/92 - 753† = 40	Son	Died	2 Kings 14:23-29	
	14	Zechariah (Bad)	753 - 752 = 6 months	Son	Murdered by Shallum	2 Kings 14:29-15:12	
VI	15	Shallum (Bad)	752 = 1 month		Murdered by Menahem	2 Kings 15:10-15	
VII	16	Menahem (Bad)	752 - 742/41 = 10		Died	2 Kings 15:14-22	
	17	Pekahiah (Bad)	742/41 - 740/39 = 2	Son	Murdered by Pekah	2 Kings 15:22-26	
VIII	18	Pekah (Bad)	752 - 732/31† = 20	Captain of Army	Murdered by Hoshea	2 Kings 15:27-31	2 Chr. 28:5-8
IX	19	Hoshea (Bad)	732/31 - 723/22 = 9		Deposed to Assyria	2 Kings 15:30-17:6	

*According to Edwin R. Thiele. **Tibni coregency unsuccessful. †Overlapping/coregency.
☆Also Joram. ‡Also Joash.

Kings of Judah

Dynasty	Name (Character)	Length of Reign*	Relation to Predecessor	End of Reign	1 & 2 Kings	2 Chronicles
1	Rehoboam (Bad)	931/30 - 913 = 17	Son	Died	1 Kings 11:42-14:31	2 Chr. 9:31-12:16
2	Abijam (Bad)	913 - 911/10 = 3	Son	Died	1 Kings 14:31-15:8	2 Chr. 13:1-22
3	Asa (Good)	911/10 - 870/69 = 41	Son	Died	1 Kings 15:8-24	2 Chr. 14:1-16:14
4	Jehoshaphat (Good)	873/72 - 848* = 25	Son	Died	1 Kings 22:41-50	2 Chr. 17:1-20:37
5	Jehoram (Bad)	853-841* = 8	Son	Stricken by God (Bowels)	2 Kings 8:16-24	2 Chr. 21:1-20
6	Ahaziah (Bad)	841 = 1	Son	Murdered by Jehu	2 Kings 8:24-9:29	2 Chr. 22:1-9
7	Athaliah (Bad)	841 - 835 = 6	Mother	Murdered by Army	2 Kings 11:1-20	2 Chr. 22:1-23:21
8	Joash (Good)	835 - 796 = 40	Grandson	Murdered by servants	2 Kings 11:1-12:21	2 Chr. 22:10-24:27
9	Amaziah (Good)	796 - 767 = 29	Son	Murdered by court members	2 Kings 14:1-20	2 Chr. 25:1-28
10	Azariah⁰ (Good)	792/91 - 740/39* = 52	Son	Stricken by God (Leprosy)	2 Kings 15:1-7	2 Chr. 26:1-23
11	Jotham (Good)	750 - 732/31* = 18	Son	Died	2 Kings 15:32-38	2 Chr. 27:1-9
12	Ahaz (Bad)	735 - 716/15* = 19	Son	Died	2 Kings 16:1-20	2 Chr. 28:1-27
13	Hezekiah (Good)	716/15 - 687/86 = 29	Son	Died	2 Kings 18:1-20:21	2 Chr. 29:1-32:33
14	Manasseh (Bad)	697/96 - 643/42* = 55	Son	Died	2 Kings 21:1-18	2 Chr. 33:1-20
15	Amon (Bad)	643/42 - 641/40 = 2	Son	Murdered by servants	2 Kings 21:19-26	2 Chr. 33:21-25
16	Josiah (Good)	641/40 - 609 = 31	Son	Wounded in battle	2 Kings 22:1-23:30	2 Chr. 34:1-35:27
17	Johoahaz (Bad)	609 = 3 months	Son	Deposed to Egypt	2 Kings 23:31-33	2 Chr. 36:1-4
18	Jehoiakim (Bad)	609 - 598 = 11	Brother	Died in Babylonian Siege?	2 Kings 23:34-24:5	2 Chr. 36:5-7
19	Johoiachin (Bad)	598 - 597 = 3 months	Son	Deposed to Babylon	2 Kings 24:6-16	2 Chr. 36:8-10
20	Zedekiah (Bad)	597 - 586 = 11	Uncle	Deposed to Babylon	2 Kings 24:17-25:30	2 Chr. 36:11-21

☆Also Uzziah.
* According to Edwin R. Thiele. Some overlapping/coregencies.
These are biblical numbers and do not always reflect coregencies.

Introduction to the Poetical Books

Until recently, not many people knew that fully one-third of the Hebrew Bible was written in poetry. This became more obvious when poetic sections were set off from prose sections in some English translations. In fact, there are only five Old Testament books that appear to have no poetry: Leviticus, Ruth, Ezra, Haggai, and Malachi. The five books now known as the poetical books serve as a hinge which links the past of the historical books to the future of the prophetical books. These books explore the experiential present and emphasize a lifestyle of godliness. Unlike the Pentateuch and 12 historical books, the poetical books do not advance the story of the nation Israel. Instead, they delve deeply into crucial questions about pain, God, wisdom, life, and love—all in the present tense.

Job: Job was a righteous man who was suddenly embroiled in an intense ordeal of every kind of suffering. He went through three cycles of debate with his friends who insisted that his misfortune must have been caused by sin. When God finally revealed Himself in His majesty and power to Job, it became obvious that the real issue was not Job's suffering but God's sovereignty. Job's questions were never answered but he willingly submitted to the wisdom and righteousness of God.

Psalms: The five books of psalms span the centuries from Moses to the post-exilic period and cover the full range of human emotions and experiences. The wide variety of psalms (lament, thanksgiving, praise, enthronement, pilgrimage, etc.)

suited them for service as the temple hymnal for the people of Israel. The psalms were set to music and focused on worship.

Proverbs: The book of Proverbs was designed to equip the reader in practical wisdom, discernment, discipline, and discretion. These maxims emphasize the development of skill in all the details of life so that beauty and righteousness will replace foolishness and evil as one walks in dependence upon God.

Ecclesiastes: The Preacher of Ecclesiastes applied his great mind and considerable resources to the quest for purpose and satisfaction in life under the sun. He found that wisdom, wealth, works, pleasure, and power all led to futility and striving after wind. The problem was compounded by the injustices and uncertainties of life and apparent absurdity of death. The only source of ultimate meaning and fulfillment is God Himself. One should therefore acknowledge his inability to understand all the ways of God, trust and obey Him, and enjoy His gifts.

Song of Solomon: This beautiful song portrays the intimate love relationship between Solomon and his Shulammite bride. It magnifies the virtues of physical and emotional love in marriage.

Hebrew Poetry — The five poetical books illustrate three kinds of poetry: (1) lyric poetry—originally accompanied by music on the lyre, this poetry often has strong emotional elements (most of Psalms); (2) didactic poetry—teaches principles about life by means of maxims (Proverbs, Ecclesiastes); (3) dramatic poetry—dialogue in poetic form (Job, Song of Solomon).

Hebrew poetry is not based on assonance (rhyme) or meter. It has some rhythm which is produced by tonal stress, but this is not prominent. The real key to this kind of poetry is *parallelism,* which involves the "rhyming" of ideas through careful arrangement of parallel thoughts. At least six kinds of parallelism have been distinguished in Hebrew poetry: (1) *Synonymous parallelism.* Here the second line reinforces the thought of the first by using similar words and concepts (see Job 38:7; Ps. 3:1; 25:4; 49:1; Prov. 11:7,25; 12:28). (2) *Synthetic parallelism.* The second line adds to or completes the idea of the first line (see Ps. 1:1-2;

23:1,5; 95:3; Prov. 4:23). (3) *Antithetic parallelism.* The thought of the first line is contrasted in the second line (see Ps. 1:6; 18:27; Prov. 10:1; 14:34; 15:1). (4) *Emblematic parallelism.* The first line uses a figure of speech to illuminate the main point conveyed by the second line (Ps. 42:1; Prov. 11:22; 25:25; 27:17). (5) *Climactic parallelism.* The second line repeats the first with the exception of the last term (see Ps. 29:1; Prov. 31:4). (6) *Formal parallelism.* The lines are joined solely by metric considerations (see Ps. 2:6). Parallelism is found not only in couplets (two lines), but also in triplets and quatrains (three and four lines), and sometimes in whole stanzas.

Hebrew poetry is also characterized by vivid figures of speech: (1) *Simile.* A comparison between two things that resemble one another in some way (see Ps. 1:3,4; 5:12; 17:8; 131:2). (2) *Metaphor.* A comparison in which one thing is declared to be another (see Ps. 23:1; 84:11; 91:4). (3) *Implication.* An implied comparison between two things in which the name of one thing is used in place of the other (see Ps. 22:16; Jer. 4:7). (4) *Hyperbole.* The use of exaggeration to emphasize a point (see Ps. 6:6; 78:27; 107:26). (5) *Rhetorical question.* The use of a question to confirm or deny a fact (see Ps. 35:10; 56:8; 94:6; 106:2). (6) *Metonymy.* One noun used in place of another because of some relationship between the two (see Ps. 5:9; 18:2; 57:9; 73:9). (7) *Anthropomorphism.* Assigning an appropriate part of the human body to God's Person to convey some truth about God (see Ps. 11:4; 18:15; 31:2; 32:8). (8) *Zoomorphism.* Assigning an appropriate part of an animal to God's Person to convey some truth about God (see Ps. 17:8; 36:7; 63:7; 91:4). (9) *Personification.* Assigning the characteristics of a human to lifeless objects (see Ps. 35:10; 77:16; 96:11; 104:19). (10) *Apostrophe.* Addressing lifeless objects (see Ps. 114:5). (11) *Synecdoche.* Representation of the whole by a part or a part by the whole (see Ps. 91:5). Visual imagery is clearly predominant in the poets.

Another technique in Hebrew poetry is the alphabetic acrostic—the first Hebrew letter in a line is the first letter of the alphabet, the second is the second letter of the alphabet, and so on. There are several variations on this technique (e.g. Ps. 119 and each chapter in Lamentations).

There are also three books of wisdom within the poets: Job, Proverbs, and Ecclesiastes. These books are denoted as such by the content, not the form. It is likely that there were schools of wisdom in Israel (1 Sam. 24:13; 1 Kings 4:29-34). These wise men were practical observers of life who gave right answers in critical situations.

Job

"Though He slay me, I will hope in Him. Nevertheless I will argue my ways before Him."

Job 13:15

"But He knows the way I take; when He has tried me, I shall come forth as gold."

Job 23:10

Focus	Despair		Debate													Diagnosis	
	1 3		4												37	38 42	
D I V I S I O N S	Job's Affliction	Job's Lament	Eliphaz vs. Job (1)	Bildad vs. Job (1)	Zophar vs. Job (1)	Eliphaz vs. Job (2)	Bildad vs. Job (2)	Zophar vs. Job (2)	Eliphaz vs. Job (3)	Bildad vs. Job (3)	Job's Closing Monologue	Elihu's Four Speeches	The Lord's Two Speeches	Job's Acquittal		
	1 2	3	4 7	8 10	11 14	15 17	18 19	20 21	22 24	25 26	27 31	32 37	38/42:6	42:7-17		
	Conflict		Cycle 1			Cycle 2			Cycle 3				Con-clusion			
T O P I C S	God's Works		Men's Misunderstandings										God's Words			
	Pro-logue		Dialogue										Epi-lo-gue			
	Prose		Poetry										Prose			
Loca-tion	Land of Uz (Area of Edom/North Arabia)															
Time	Patriarchal Period (Perhaps c. 2000 B.C.)															

Talk Thru — The book of Job concerns the transforming crisis in the life of a great man who lived perhaps 4,000 years ago. Job lost everything he had—wealth, family, health—in a sudden series of catastrophes that forced him to wrestle with the question "Why?" The book begins with a heavenly debate between God and Satan, moves into an earthly debate between Job and his friends, and closes with a series of divine questions. Job's trust in God (1-2) changed to complaining and growing self-righteousness (3-31; see 32:1 and 40:8), but his repentance (42:1-6) led to his restoration (42:7-17). The trials brought about an important transformation: The man after the process was different from the man before the process. Job divides into three parts: Despair (1-3), Debate (4-37), and Diagnosis (38-42).

Despair (1-3): Job was not a logical candidate for disaster (see 1:1,8). His moral integrity and selfless service of God heighten the dilemma. Behind the scene, Satan ("accuser") charged that no one loves God from pure motives, but only for material blessings (1:10). To refute Satan's accusations, God allowed him to strike Job with two series of assaults. In his sorrow, Job lamented the day of his birth (3) but he did not deny God (1:21; 2:10).

Debate (4-37): Although Job's "comforters" came to wrong conclusions, they were his friends: of all who knew Job only they came; they mourned with him in seven days of silent sympathy; and they confronted Job without talking behind his back. But after Job broke the silence, a three-round debate followed with his friends ringing the changes on the same theme—Job must be suffering because of his sin. Job's responses to their simplistic assumptions made the debate cycles increase in emotional fervor. He first accused his friends of judging him and later appealed to the Lord as his judge and refuge:

	Bildad	Bildad	Bildad
The Three Cycles of Debate :	Eliphaz Zophar	Eliphaz Zophar	Eliphaz (Zophar silent)
	Job	Job	Job
Job's Response:	"You act as my judge"	"The Lord is my judge"	"The Lord is my refuge"

Job made three basic complaints: (1) God does not hear me (13:3,24; 19:7; 23:3-5; 30:20), (2) God is punishing me (6:4; 7:20; 9:17), (3) God allows the wicked to prosper (21:7). His defenses were much longer than his friends' accusations, and in the process of defending his innocence he became guilty of self-righteousness.

After Job's five-chapter closing monologue (27-31), Elihu freshened the air with a more perceptive and accurate view than those offered by Eliphaz, Bildad, or Zophar (32-37). He told Job that he needed to humble himself before God and submit to God's process of purifying his life through trials.

	Eliphaz	Bildad	Zophar	Elihu
Characteristic:	Theologian	Historian, legalist	Moralist, dogmatist	Young theologian, intellectual
Relies on:	Observation, Experience	Tradition	Assumption	Education
Personality:	Considerate	Argumentative	Rude, blunt	Perceptive, some conceit
Voice of:	Philosophy	History	Orthodoxy	Logic
Argument:	"If you sin, you suffer"	"You *must* be sinning"	"You *are* sinning"	"God purifies and teaches"
Advice to Job:	Only the wicked suffer	The wicked always suffer	The wicked are short-lived	Humble yourself and submit to God
Key verse:	4:8; 5:17	8:8	20:5	37:23
Concept of God:	Righteous; punishes wicked, blesses good	Judge; immovable lawgiver	Unbending, merciless	Disciplinarian, teacher
Name:	"God is Gold" or "God Dispenses (Judgment)"	"Son of Contention"	"Rough" or "Chirper"	"He is My God"

Diagnosis (38-42): After Elihu's preparatory discourse, God Himself ended the debate by speaking to Job out of the whirlwind. In His first speech, God revealed His power and wisdom as Creator and Preserver of the physical and animal world. Job responded by acknowledging his ignorance and insignificance; he could offer no rebuttal (40:3-5). In His second speech, God revealed His sovereign authority and challenged Job with two illustrations of his power to control the uncontrollable. This time Job responded by acknowledging his error with a repentant heart (42:1-6). Job could not understand God's ways in the realm of nature—how then could he understand God's ways in the spiritual realm? God made no reference to Job's personal sufferings and hardly touched on the real issue of the debate. But Job got a glimpse of the divine perspective, and when he acknowledged God's sovereignty over his life, his worldy goods were restored two-fold. Job prayed for his three friends who had cut him so deeply, but Elihu's speech was never rebuked. Thus, Satan's challenge became God's opportunity to build in Job's life. "Behold, we count those blessed who endured. You have heard of the endurance of Job and have seen the outcome of the Lord's dealings, that the Lord is full of compassion and is merciful" (Jas. 5:11; see Jas. 1:12).

Title — *'Iyyob* is the Hebrew title for this book, and the name has two possible meanings. If it was derived from the Hebrew word for persecution it means "persecuted one." It is more likely that it comes from the Arabic word "to come back" or "repent." If so, it means "repentant one." Both meanings apply to the book. The Greek title is *'Iob,* and the Latin title is *Iob.*

Author — The author of Job is unknown and there are no textual hints as to his identity. Commentators, however, have been generous with suggestions: Job, Elihu, Moses, Solomon, Isaiah, Hezekiah, Jeremiah, Baruch, and Ezra have all been nominated. The non-Hebraic cultural background of this book may point to Gentile authorship. There are no consistent rabbinic traditions, but one Talmudic tradition suggests that Moses wrote the book. The land of Uz (1:1) is adjacent to Midian where Moses lived for 40 years, and it is conceivable that Moses obtained a record of the dialogue left by Job or Elihu. This could explain how the Israelites possessed this non-Israelite story and gave it canonical status.

Job is considered by many to be the most sublime dramatic poem ever written, but there is no solid evidence regarding its authorship. But this is not a weighty issue because the text makes no specific claims.

Date and Setting — Lamentations 4:21 locates Uz in the area of Edom, southeast of the Dead Sea. This is also in the region of northern Arabia, and Job's friends came from nearby countries.

It is important to distinguish the date of the events in Job from the date of writing. It is difficult to be sure of the date of the events because there are no references to contemporary historical occurrences. But a number of facts indicate a patriarchal date for Job, perhaps between Genesis 11 and 12 or not long after the time of Abraham: (1) Job lived 140 years *after* the events in the book (42:16); his lifespan must have been close to 200 years. This fits the patriarchal period (Abraham lived 175 years; Gen. 25:7). (2) Job's wealth was measured in terms of livestock (1:3; 42:12) rather than gold and silver. (3) Like Abraham, Isaac, and Jacob, Job was the priest of his family and offered sacrifices. (4) There are no references to Israel, the exodus, the Mosaic law, or the tabernacle. (5) Fitting Abraham's time, the social unit in Job is the patriarchal family-clan. (6) The Chaldeans who murdered Job's servants (1:17) were nomads and had not yet become city-dwellers. (7) Job uses the characteristic patriarchal name for God, *Shaddai* "the Almighty" 31 times. This early term is found only 17 times in the rest of the Old Testament. The rare use of Yahweh "the LORD" also suggests a pre-Mosaic date. Ezekiel 14:14,20 and James 5:11 show that Job was a historical person.

Several theories have been set forth for the date of authorship: (1) It was written shortly after the events occurred, perhaps by Job or Elihu. (2) It was written by Moses in Midian (1485-1445 B.C.). (3) It was written in the time of Solomon (c. 950 B.C.). There are similarities in Job to other wisdom literature at this time; compare the praises of wisdom in Job 28 and Proverbs 8. The problem here is the great time lag of about 1,000 years. (4) It was written during or after the Babylonian captivity.

Theme and Purpose — The basic question of the book is "Why do the righteous suffer if God is loving and all-powerful?" Suffering itself is not the central theme; it is what Job *learned* from his suffering—the sovereignty of God over all creation. The debate in chapters 3-37 was whether God would allow this suffering to happen to a person who is innocent. The oversimplified solutions offered by Job's three friends were simply inadequate. Elihu's claim that God can use suffering to purify the righteous was closer to the mark. The conclusion at the whirlwind is that God is in fact sovereign and worthy of worship in *whatever* He chooses to do. Job had to learn to trust in the goodness and power of God in spite of outward circumstances by enlarging his concept of God. Even this "blameless" man (1:1) needed to repent when he became proud and self-righteous. He had to come to the end of his own resources, humble himself, and acknowledge the greatness and majesty of the Lord. Job teaches that God is Lord "in heaven, and on earth, and under the earth" (Phil. 2:10). He is omniscient, omnipotent, and good. As such, His ways are sometimes incomprehensible to men, but He can always be trusted. Without the divine perspective in 1-2 and 38-42, chapters 3-37 are a real mystery. Job did not have access to chapters 1-2, but he was responsible to trust God against appearances. Suffering is not always associated with sin; God can sovereignly use it to test and teach.

Contribution to the Bible — Job is a book of dramatic poetry that is unsurpassed in beauty, depth, and intensity. It makes rich use of synonymous, antithetic, and synthetic parallelism. In its setting Job offers a glimpse of non-Hebrew culture in patriarchal times. Its universal flavor is appropriate to the universal theme it develops.

Job reveals five ways in which God uses hardships that are reflected in Deuteronomy 8: (1) to humble us (22:29; Deut. 8:2), (2) to test us (2:3; Deut. 8:2), (3) to rearrange our priorities (42:5-6; Deut. 8:3), (4) to discipline us (5:17; Deut. 8:5), and (5) to prepare us for future blessings (42:10; Deut. 8:7).

Chapters 38-42 give the most intensive survey of creation in the Bible. Among other things, Job teaches that the earth is suspended in empty space (26:7) and implies that the earth is a sphere (22:14).

Christ in Job — Job acknowledges a Redeemer (see 19:25-27) and cries out for a Mediator (9:33; 33:23). The book raises problems and questions which were answered perfectly in Christ who identified with our sufferings (Heb. 4:15). Christ is the believer's Life, Redeemer, Mediator, and Advocate.

Psalms

"Let the words of my mouth and the meditation of my heart be acceptable in Thy sight, O LORD, my rock and my Redeemer."
Psalm 19:14

"My mouth will speak the praise of the LORD; and all flesh will bless His holy name forever and ever."
Psalm 145:21

Book	Book 1 (1-41)	Book 2 (42-72)	Book 3 (73-89)	Book 4 (90-106)	Book 5 (107-150)
Chief Author	David	David/ Korah	Asaph	Anony- mous	David/ Anony- mous
Number of Psalms	41	31	17	17	44
Basic Content	Songs of Worship	Hymns of National Interest		Anthems of Praise	
Topical Likeness to Pentateuch	Genesis: Man and Creation	Exodus: Deliver- ance and Redemp- tion	Leviticus: Worship and Sanctuary	Numbers: Wilder- ness and Wandering	Deutero- nomy: Scripture and Praise
Closing Doxology	41:13	72:18,19	89:52	106:48	150:1-6
Possible Compiler	David	Hezekiah/Josiah		Ezra/Nehemiah	
Possible Dates of Compilation	c. 1020- 970 B.C.	c. 970-610 B.C.		Until c. 430 B.C.	
Span of Authorship	About 1,000 Years (c. 1410-430 B.C.)				

Talk Thru — The book of Psalms is the largest and perhaps most widely used book in the Bible. It explores the full range of human experiences in a very personal and practical way. Its 150 "songs" run from the creation through the patriarchal, theocratic, monarchical, exilic, and post-exilic periods. The tremendous breadth of subject matter in the Psalms includes diverse topics like jubilation, war, peace, worship, judgment, Messianic prophecy, praise, and lament. The Psalms were set to the accompaniment of stringed instruments and served as the temple hymnbook and devotional guide for the Jewish people.

The Psalter is really five books in one, and each book ends with a doxology (see the chart). The last psalm is the closing doxology for Book 5 and for the Psalter as a whole. After the psalms were written, editorial superscriptions or instructions were added to 116 of them. These superscriptions are historically accurate and are even numbered as the first verses in the Hebrew text. They designate 57 psalms as *mizmor*, "psalm"—a song accompanied by a stringed instrument. Another 29 are called *shir*, "song" and 13 are called *maskil*, "contemplative poem." Six are called *miktam*, perhaps meaning "epigram" or "inscription poem." Five are termed *tepillah*, "prayer" (see Hab. 3), and only one is called *tehillah*, "praise" (Ps. 145). In addition to these technical terms, the psalms can be classified according to certain themes: creation psalms (8,19), exodus psalms (78), penitence psalms (6), pilgrimage psalms (120-134), and Messianic psalms (see Christ in Psalms). There are even nine acrostic psalms in which the first verse or line begins with the first verse of the Hebrew alphabet, the next begins with the second, and so on (9,10,25,34,37,111,112,119,145).

First Chronicles 16:4 supports another approach to classification: ". . . to invoke, to thank, and to praise the LORD, the God of Israel" (RSV). This leads to three basic types—lament, thanksgiving, and praise psalms. The following classification further divides the psalms into 10 types: (1) *Individual lament psalms*. Directly addressed to God, these psalms petition Him to rescue and defend an individual. They have these elements: (a) an introduction (usually a cry to God), (b) the lament, (c) a confession of trust in God, (d) the petition, (e) a declaration or vow of praise. This is the most abundant type (e.g., 3-7,12-13,22,25-28,35,38-40,42-43,51,54-57,59,61,63-64,69-71,86,88, 102,109,120,130,140-143). (2) *Communal lament psalms*. The only difference is that the nation rather than an individual makes the lament. These include 44,60,74,79-80,83,85,90,123. (3) *Individual thanksgiving psalms*. The psalmist publicly acknowledges God's activity on his behalf. These psalms thank God for something He has already done or express confidence in what He will yet do. They have these elements: (a) a proclamation to praise God, (b) a summary statement, (c) a report of deliverance, (d) a renewed vow of praise. These include 18,30,32,34,40-41,66,106,116,138. (4) *Communal thanksgiving psalms*. In these psalms the acknowledgment is made by the nation rather than an individual. See 124,129. (5) *General praise psalms*. These psalms revolve around the word "praise" and are more general than the thanksgiving psalms. The psalmist attempts to magnify the name of God and boast about His greatness (see 8,19,29,103-104,139,148,150). The joyous exclamation "hallelujah" ("praise the LORD!") is found in several of these psalms. (6) *Descriptive praise psalms*. These psalms praise God for His attributes and acts (e.g., 33,36,105,111,113,117,135-136,146-147). (7) *Enthronement psalms*. These psalms describe Yahweh's sovereign reign over all (see 47,93,96-99). Some anticipate the kingdom rule of Christ. (8) *Pilgrimage songs*. These psalms, also known as Songs of Zion, were sung by pilgrims traveling up to Jerusalem for the three annual religious feasts of Passover, Pentecost, and Tabernacles (see 43,46,48,76,84,87,120-134). (9) *Royal psalms*. The reign of the earthly as well as the heavenly King is portrayed in most of these psalms. These include 2,18,20-21,45,72,89,101,110,132,144. (10) *Wisdom and didactic psalms*. The reader is exhorted and instructed in the way of righteousness (see 1,37,119).

There is a problem with the so-called imprecatory ("to call down a curse") psalms. These psalms invoke divine judgment on one's enemies (see 7,35,40,55,58-59,69,79,109,137,139,144). Although some of them seem unreasonably harsh, a few things should be kept in mind: (1) they call for divine justice rather than human vengeance, (2) they ask for God to punish the wicked and thus vindicate His righteousness, (3) they condemn sin (there was not a sharp distinction between a sinner and his sin in the Hebrew mind), and (4) even Jesus called down a curse on several cities and told His disciples to curse cities that did not receive the gospel (Matt. 10:14-15).

A number of special musical terms (some obscure) are used

in the superscriptions of the psalms. "For the choir director" appears in 55 psalms indicating that there was a collection of psalms that was used by the conductor of music in the temple, perhaps for special occasions. "Selah" is used 71 times in the psalms and three times in Habakkuk 3. This may mark a pause, a musical interlude, or a crescendo.

Title — The book of Psalms was gradually collected and originally unnamed, perhaps due to the great variety of material. It came to be known as *sepher tehillim*, — the "Book of Praises" — because almost every psalm contained some note of praise to God. The Septuagint used the Greek word *Psalmoi* as its title for this book, meaning poems sung to the accompaniment of musical instruments. It also called it the *Psalterium* (a collection of songs), and this word is the basis for the term Psalter. The Latin title is *Liber Psalmorum*, the "Book of Psalms."

Author — Although critics have challenged the historical accuracy of the superscriptions regarding authorship, the evidence is strongly in their favor. Almost half (73) of the psalms are designated as Davidic: 3-9,11-32,34-41,51-65,68-70,86,101,103,108-110,122,124,131,133,138-145. David's wide experience as a shepherd, musician, warrior, and king (1011-971 B.C.) is reflected in these psalms. The New Testament reveals that the anonymous psalms 2 and 95 were also written by this king whose name means "Beloved of Yahweh" (Acts 4:25; Heb. 4:7). In addition to the 73 by David, 12 were by Asaph, "Collector," a priest who headed the service of music (50,73-83; Ezra 2:41); 10 were by the sons of Korah, "Bald," a guild of singers and composers (42,44-49,84-85,87; Num. 26:9-11); two were by Solomon, "Peaceful," Israel's most powerful king (72,127); one was by Moses, "Son of the Water," a prince, herdsman, and deliverer (90); one was by Heman, "Faithful," a wise man (88; 1 Kings 4:31; 1 Chron. 15:19); and one was by Ethan, "Enduring," a wise man (89; 1 Kings 4:31; 1 Chron. 15:19). The remaining 50 psalms are anonymous: 1-2, 10,33,43,66-67,71,91-100,102,104-107,111-121,123,125-126,128-130,132,135-137,146-150. Some of the anonymous psalms were traditionally attributed to Ezra.

Date and Setting — The psalms cover a huge time span

from Moses (c. 1410 B.C.) to the post-exilic community under Ezra and Nehemiah (c. 430 B.C.). Because of their broad chronological and thematic range, the psalms were written to different audiences under many conditions. They therefore reflect a multitude of moods and as such are relevant to every reader.

The five books were compiled over several centuries. As individual psalms were written, some were used in Israel's worship. A number of small collections were independently made like the pilgrimage songs and groups of Davidic psalms (1-41,51-70,138-145). These smaller anthologies were gradually collected into the five books. The last stage was the uniting and editing of the five books themselves. It is interesting that Book 1 uses the name Yahweh 272 times and Elohim only 15 times, while Book 2 uses Elohim 164 times and Yahweh only 30 times. David (1 Chron. 15:16), Hezekiah (2 Chron. 29:30; Prov. 25:1), and Ezra (Neh. 8) were involved in various stages of collecting the psalms. David was the originator of the temple liturgy of which his psalms were a part. The superscriptions of 13 psalms specify key events in his life: 1 Samuel 19:11 (Ps. 59); 21:11 (Ps. 56); 21:13 (Ps. 34); 22:1 (Ps. 142); 22:9 (Ps. 52); 23:19 (Ps. 54); 24:3 (Ps. 57); 2 Samuel 8:13 (Ps. 60); 12:13 (Ps. 51); 15:16 (Ps. 3); 15:23 (Ps. 63); 16:5 (Ps. 7); 22:2-51 (Ps. 18).

Here are four things to remember when interpreting the psalms: (1) When the superscription gives the historical event, the psalm should be interpreted in that light. When it is not given, there is little hope in reconstructing the historical occasion. Assuming occasions will probably hurt more than help the interpretive process. (2) Some of the psalms were associated with definite aspects of Israel's worship (e.g. 5:7; 66:13; 68:24-25), and this can help in understanding those psalms. (3) Many of the psalms use definite structure and motifs. (4) Many psalms anticipate Israel's Messiah and are fulfilled in Christ. But care must be taken not to allegorize them and forget the grammatical-historical method of interpretation.

Theme and Purpose

— There are several kinds of psalms, and they express different feelings and circumstances. But the common theme is worship—God is worthy of all praise because of who He is, what He has done, and what He will do. His goodness extends through all time and eternity. The psalms present a very personal response to the person and work of God as they reflect on His program for His people. There is a keen desire to see His program fulfilled and His name extolled. Many of the psalms survey the Word of God and the attributes of God, especially during difficult times. This kind of faith produces confidence in His power in spite of circumstances.

The psalms were used in the two temples and some were part of the liturgical service. They also served as an individual and communal devotional guide.

Contribution to the Bible — The book of Psalms is quoted more times in the New Testament than any other book. Our Lord frequently used the Psalms during the course of His earthly life (e.g., the Sermon on the Mount, teaching the multitudes, answering the Jewish leaders, cleansing the temple, during the last supper, and on the cross). The singing of psalms was a regular part of worship in the early church (cf. 1 Cor. 14:26; Eph. 5:19; Col. 3:16).

In addition to the book of Psalms, there are at least 11 other psalms in the Old Testament: (1) the song of the sea (Exod. 15:1-18), (2) the song of Moses (Deut. 32:1-43), (3) the song of Deborah (Judg. 5), (4) the song of Hannah (1 Sam. 2:1-10), (5) a psalm of David (2 Sam. 22:2-51; Ps. 18), (6) Job's lament psalms (Job 3,7,10), (7) a doxology in Isaiah (Isa. 12:4-6), (8) the song of Hezekiah (Isa. 38:9-20), (9) Jeremiah's lament psalms (Lam. 3:19-38; 5), (10) the prayer of Jonah (Jonah 2:1-9), (11) the prayer of Habakkuk (Hab. 3:2-19).

Christ in Psalms — Many of the psalms specifically anticipated the life and ministry of Jesus Christ, the One who came centuries later as Israel's promised Messiah ("anointed one"). The Psalms, like the four Gospels, give several perspectives on the person and work of Christ:

- *Jesus Christ, the King* (portrayed in Matthew)
  - 2: Christ rejected as King by the nations
  - 18: Christ is Protector and Deliverer
  - 20: Christ provides salvation
  - 24: Christ is King of Glory
  - 47: Christ rules in His kingdom
  - 110: Christ is King-Priest

21: Christ is given glory by God

132: Christ is enthroned

● *Jesus Christ, the Servant* (portrayed in Mark)

17: Christ is Intercessor

41: Christ is betrayed by a close friend

22: Christ is the dying Savior

69: Christ is hated without a cause

23: Christ is Shepherd

109: Christ loves those who reject Him

40: Christ is obedient unto death

● *Jesus Christ, the Son of Man* (portrayed in Luke)

8: Christ is made a little lower than angels

40: Christ's resurrection is realized

16: Christ's resurrection is promised

● *Jesus Christ, the Son of God* (portrayed in John)

19: Christ is Creator

118: Christ is the Chief Cornerstone

102: Christ is eternal

There are five different kinds of Messianic psalms: (1). *Typical Messianic.* The subject of the psalm is in some feature a type of Christ (see 34:20; 69:4,9). (2) *Typical Prophetic.* The psalmist uses language to describe his present experience which points beyond his own life and becomes historically true only in Christ (see 22). (3) *Indirectly Messianic.* At the time of composition the psalm referred to a king or the house of David in general, but awaits final fulfillment in Christ (see 2,45,72). (4) *Purely Prophetic.* Refers solely to Christ without reference to any other son of David (see 110). (5) *Enthronement.* Anticipates the coming of Yahweh and the consummation of His kingdom—will be fulfilled in the person of Christ (see 96-99).

Here are some of the specific Messianic prophecies in the book of Psalms:

Psalm	Prophecy	Fulfillment
2:7	God will declare Him to be His Son	Matthew 3:17
8:6	All things will be put under His feet	Hebrews 2:8
16:10	He will be resurrected from the dead	Mark 16:6-7
22:1	God will forsake Him in His hour of need	Matthew 27:46
22:7-8	He will be scorned and mocked	Luke 23:35

22:16	His hands and feet will be pierced	John 20:25,27
22:18	Others will gamble for His clothes	Matthew 27:35-36
34:20	Not one of His bones will be broken	John 19:32-33,36
35:11	He will be accused by false witnesses	Mark 14:57
35:19	He will be hated without a cause	John 15:25
40:7-8	He will come to do God's will	Hebrews 10:7
41:9	He will be betrayed by a friend	Luke 22:47
45:6	His throne will be forever	Hebrews 1:8
68:18	He will ascend to God's right hand	Mark 16:19
69:9	Zeal for God's house will consume Him	John 2:17
69:21	He will be given vinegar and gall to drink	Matthew 27:34
109:4	He will pray for His enemies	Luke 23:34
109:8	His betrayer's office will be fulfilled by another	Acts 1:20
110:1	His enemies will be made subject to Him	Matthew 22:44
110:4	He will be a priest like Melchizedek	Hebrews 5:6
118:22	He will be the chief cornerstone	Matthew 21:42
118:26	He will come in the name of the LORD	Matthew 21:9

Proverbs

"The fear of the LORD is the beginning of knowledge; fools despise wisdom and instruction."

Proverbs 1:7

"For the commandment is a lamp, and the teaching is light; and reproofs for discipline are the way of life."

Proverbs 6:23

(Also see 9:10; 15:33.)

Focus	Preparation For Wisdom		Proverbs on Wisdom				Precepts of Wisdom		
	1 9		10 29				30 31		
DIVISIONS	Purpose and Theme	A Father's Exhortations on Wisdom	Proverbs of Solomon (First Collection)	Words of Wise Men	Proverbs of Solomon (Second Collection)		Words of Agur	Words of King Lemuel	Alphabet of a Virtuous Wife
	1:1-7	1:8 9	10 22:16	22:17 24	25 29		30	31:1-9	31:10-31
TOPICS	Prologue		Maxims				Epilogue		
	Personification of Wisdom		Principles of Wisdom				Practice of Wisdom		
	Commendation of Wisdom		Counsel of Wisdom				Comparisons of Wisdom		
	Solomon			Wise Men	Solomon		Agur and Lemuel		
Location	Judah						Unknown		
Time	c. 950-700 B.C.								

Talk Thru— Proverbs is the most intensely practical book in the Old Testament because it teaches skillful living in the multiple aspects of everyday life. Its specific precepts include instruction on wisdom and folly, the righteous and the wicked, the tongue, pride and humility, justice and vengeance, the family, laziness and work, poverty and wealth, friends and neighbors, love and lust, anger and strife, masters and servants, life and death. Proverbs touches upon every facet of human relationships, and its principles transcend the bounds of time and culture. The Hebrew word for proverb *(mashal)* means "comparison, similar, parallel." A proverb uses a comparison or figure of speech to make a pithy but potent observation. Proverbs have been defined as simple illustrations that expose fundamental realities about life. These maxims are not theoretical but practical; they are easily memorized, based on real-life experience, and designed for use in the mainstream of life. The proverbs are general statements and illustrations of timeless truth which allow for, but do not condone, exceptions to the rule. The key word is *hokhmah*, "wisdom"—it literally means "skill" (in living). Wisdom is more than shrewdness or intelligence. Instead, it relates to practical righteousness and moral acumen. The book of Proverbs may be divided into three segments: Preparation for Wisdom (1-9), Proverbs on Wisdom (10-29), and Precepts of Wisdom (30-31).

Preparation for Wisdom (1-9): After a brief prologue that spells out the purpose and theme of the book (1:1-7), there is a series of 10 exhortations, each beginning with "My son" (1:8-9:18). These messages introduce the concept of wisdom in the format of a father's efforts to persuade his son to pursue the path of wisdom in order to achieve godly success in life. Wisdom rejects the invitation of crime and foolishness, rewards its seekers on every level, and its discipline provides freedom and safety (1-4). Wisdom protects one from illicit sensuality and its consequences, from foolish practices and laziness, and from adultery and the lure of the harlot (5-7). Wisdom is to be preferred to folly because of its divine origin and rich benefits (8-9). There are four kinds of fools ranging from those who are naive and uncommitted to scoffers who arrogantly despise the way of God. The fool is not mentally deficient; he is self-sufficient, ordering his life as if there were no God.

Proverbs on Wisdom (10-29): This section contains two

distinct Solomonic collections plus a number of precepts from wise men. There is a minimal amount of topical arrangement in these chapters. There are some thematic clusters (e.g., 26:1-12, 13-16, 20-22), but the usual units are one-verse maxims. It is helpful to assemble and synthesize these proverbs according to specific themes like money and speech. The first Solomonic collection (10:1-22:16) consists of 375 proverbs of Solomon. Chapters 10-15 contrast right and wrong in practice and all but 19 proverbs use antithetic parallelism. Chapters 16-22:16 offer a series of moral axioms and all but 18 proverbs use synonymous parallelism. The words of wise men (22:17-24:34) are given in two groups. The first group has 30 distinct sayings (22:17-24:22), and six more are found in the second group (24:23-34). The second Solomonic collection was copied and arranged by "the men of Hezekiah" (25:1). These proverbs in chapters 25-29 further develop the themes in the first Solomonic collection.

Precepts of Wisdom (30-31): The last two chapters of Proverbs act as an appendix of sayings by two otherwise unknown sages, Agur and Lemuel. Most of Agur's material (chapter 30) is given in clusters of numerical proverbs. The last chapter includes a 22-verse acrostic portrait (the first letters of the verses trace the 22-letter Hebrew alphabet) of a virtuous wife (31:10-31). This chapter is unique in ancient literature, and it reveals a high view of women. The person in these verses is (1) a good woman (13,15-16,19,25), (2) a good wife (11-12,23-24), (3) a good mother (14-15,18,21,27), and (4) a good neighbor (20,26). Her conduct, concern, speech, and future stand in sharp contrast to the harlot in chapter 7.

Title — Because Solomon, the pinnacle of Israel's wise men, was the principal contributor, the Hebrew title of this book is *mishle shelomoh*, the "Proverbs of Solomon" (1:1). The Greek title is *Paroimiai Salomontos*, the "Proverbs of Solomon." The Latin title *Liber Proverbiorum*, the "Book of Proverbs," combines the words *pro* "for" and *verba* "words" to describe the way the proverbs concentrate many words into a few. The Rabbinical writings called Proverbs *sepher hokhmah*, the "Book of Wisdom."

Author — Solomon's name appears at the beginning of the three sections he authored: 1:1 for chapters 1-9, 10:1 for chapters 10-22:16, and 25:1 for chapters 25-29. According to 1 Kings 4:32, he spoke 3,000 proverbs and 1,005 songs. Only about 800 of his 3,000 proverbs are included in the two Solomonic collections in this book. No man was better qualified than Solomon to be the principal contributor—he asked for wisdom (1 Kings 3:5-9) and God granted it to him (1 Kings 4:29-31) to such a degree that people from foreign lands came to hear him speak (1 Kings 4:34; 10: 1-13,24). His breadth of knowledge, aptitude, skill, and perception were extraordinary. In every area Solomon brought prosperity and glory to Israel until his latter years (cf. 1 Kings 11:4).

It is likely that Solomon collected and edited proverbs other than his own. According to Ecclesiastes 12:9, "he pondered, searched out and arranged many proverbs." The second collection of Solomonic proverbs in 25-29 was assembled by King Hezekiah's scribes because of his interest in spiritually benefiting his subjects with the Word of God. The prophets Isaiah and Micah ministered during Hezekiah's time, and it has been suggested that they also might have been involved in this collection.

Proverbs 22:17-24:34 consists of "the words of the wise" (22:17; 24:23). Some of these sayings are quite similar to those found in *The Wisdom of Amenemope,* a document of teachings on civil service by an Egyptian who probably lived between 1000 B.C. and 600 B.C. Wise men of this period went to hear one another, and it is probable that Amenemope borrowed certain aphorisms from Hebrew literature. If the *hakhamim* ("wise men") lived before Solomon's time, he may have been the collector and editor of this series of wise sayings.

There is no biblical information about Agur (chapter 30) or Lemuel (chapter 31). Agur ben Jakeh (30:1) is simply called an oracle, and Lemuel is called a king and an oracle (31:1). Both have been identified with Solomon, but there is no basis for this suggestion. The 22-verse acrostic on the virtuous wife (31:10-31) may or may not have been composed by Lemuel.

Date and Setting — Proverbs is a collection of topical maxims, not a historical book. It is a product of the wisdom school in Israel. According to Jeremiah 18:18 and Ezekiel 7:26, there were three groups who communicated to the people on behalf of God: the priests imparted the law, the prophets communicated the divine word and visions, and the sages or

elders gave counsel to the people. The sages provided the practical application of godly wisdom to specific problems and decisions. The "Preacher" of Ecclesiastes is a good example of the wisdom school (Eccles. 1:1,12; 7:27; 12:8-10). *Qoheleth* or "Preacher" meant one who addresses an assembly—he presided over a "school" of wise men and "taught the people knowledge" (Eccles. 12:9). "My son" in Proverbs and Ecclesiastes evidently refers to the pupil. This was parallel to Samuel's role of heading Israel's school of prophets.

Wisdom literature is also found in other countries of the ancient Near East. In Egypt, written examples can be found as early as 2700 B.C. (the writings of Ipuwer). Although the style was similar to Israel's wisdom literature, the proverbs and sayings of these countries differed from those of Israel in content because they lacked the orientation to the righteous standards of Yahweh.

Solomon's proverbs were written by 931 B.C. and his proverbs in chapters 25-29 were collected by Hezekiah about 230 years later (Hezekiah reigned from 715-686 B.C.). Under Solomon Israel was at its spiritual, political, and economic summit. Solomon probably wrote his proverbs in his middle years before his life began to crumble in carnality, materialism, and idolatry.

Theme and Purpose — Proverbs is one of the few biblical books that clearly spells out its purpose. The purpose statement in 1:2-6 is twofold: (1) to impart moral discernment and discretion (1:2a,3-5), and (2) to develop mental clarity and perception (1:2b,6). The words "wisdom and instruction" in 1:2a complement each other because wisdom *(hokhmah)* means skill, and instruction *(musar)* means discipline. No skill is perfected without discipline, and when a person has skill he has freedom to create something beautiful. Proverbs deals with the most fundamental skill of all: practical righteousness before God in every area of life. This requires knowledge, experience, and a willingness to put God first (see 3:5-7). Chapters 1-9 are designed to create a felt need for wisdom and Proverbs as a whole is designed both to prevent and to remedy ungodly lifestyles. The book served as a manual to impart the legacy of wisdom, prudence, understanding, discretion, knowledge, guidance, competence, correction, counsel, and truth from generation to generation.

The theme of Proverbs is found in 1:7a: "The fear of the LORD is the beginning of knowledge." To fear God is to stand in awe of His righteousness, majesty, and power and to trust Him by humbly depending upon Him. There is a reciprocal relationship here, because "the fear of the LORD is the beginning [foundation] of wisdom" (9:10), but wisdom leads to the knowledge and fear of God (see 2:1-5).

Contribution to the Bible — Proverbs along with Job and Ecclesiastes is the wisdom literature of the Old Testament. It is built upon the fear of Yahweh as the basis for practical holiness and skill in life. There is a universal and comprehensive tone in this book because it talks to everyone. The proverbs are generalized statements that are true to life even though individual cases may differ. Psalms emphasizes a walk before God and the devotional life, but Proverbs concentrates on a walk before men and the daily life. The proverbs are practical, moral, and concise—they should be read very slowly in small sections. Some are humorous as well (see 11:22; 19:24; 23:13,35; 24:33;25:24;26:13-16; 27:15-16; 30:15,21-23). There are at least 14 New Testament quotations or allusions to the Proverbs.

James has a number of similarities to the book of Proverbs. Compare Proverbs and James on the tongue: (a) P 12:18-19 and J 1:26, (b) P 15:1-2 and J 3:5, (c) P 18:21; 21:6 and J 3:6, (d) P 21:23 and J 1:19; 3:8, (e) P 25:15 and J 3:3, (f) P 25:23 and J 4:1. The comparison of earthly and divine wisdom in James also resembles Proverbs. Man's wisdom in James 3:15-16 is (1) earthly (P 14:2), (2) natural (P 7:18), (3) demonic (P 27:20), (4) jealous (P 6:34), (5) selfish (P 28:25), (6) disorderly (P 11:29), and (7) evil (P 8:13). God's wisdom in James 3:17 is (1) pure (P 15:26), (2) peaceable (P 3:1-2), (3) gentle (P 11:2), (4) reasonable (P 14:15), (5) full of mercy and good fruits (P 11:17; 3:18), (6) unwavering (P 21:6), and (7) without hypocrisy (P 28:13).

Christ in Proverbs — In Proverbs 8, wisdom is personified and seen in its perfection. It is divine (8:22-31), it is the source of biological and spiritual life (8:35-36; 3:18), it is righteous and moral (8:8-9), and it is available to all who will receive it (8:1-6,32-35). This wisdom became incarnate in Christ "in whom are hidden all the treasures of wisdom and knowledge" (Col. 2:3). "But by His doing you are in Christ Jesus, *who became to us wisdom from God,* and righteousness and sanctification, and redemption" (1 Cor. 1:30; cf. 1 Cor. 1:22-24).

Ecclesiastes

"And I saw every work of God, I concluded that man cannot discover the work which has been done under the sun. Even though man should seek laboriously, he will not discover; and though the wise man should say, 'I know,' he cannot discover."

Ecclesiastes 8:17

"The conclusion, when all has been heard, is: fear God and keep his commandments, because this applies to every person."

Ecclesiastes 12:13
(Also see 1:2,14; 3:14.)

Focus	Excla- mation 1:1-11	Exper- ience 1:12 2:26	Exploration 3 6	Exhortation and Explanation 7 12:7				Epilogue 12:8-14
D I V I S I O N S	Theme and Illustrations 1:1-11	Experiential Search for Meaning 1:12 2:26	Futility in Every Area of Life 3 6	Lessons on Practical Wisdom 7 9:12	Observations on Wisdom and Folly 9:13 11:6	Exhortations on Using Life Well 11:7 12:7		Conclusion: The Source of Real Meaning 12:8-14
T O P I C S	Dec- lara- tion	Demon- strations	Develop- ment	Deductions				Denoue- ment
	Sub- ject	Sermons						Summary
	"Vanity Under the Sun" vs. "Fear of the Lord"							
Loca- tion	Universal (Under the Sun)							
Time	Decades of Searching							

Talk Thru — Ecclesiastes is a profound and problematic book. It is the record of an intense search for meaning and satisfaction in life on this earth, especially in view of all the inequities and apparent absurdities that surround us. It takes the perspective of the greatest answers that wisdom under the sun can produce. If the "Preacher" is identified as Solomon, Ecclesiastes was written from a unique vantage point. He was qualified beyond all others to write this book with the greatest mental, material, and political resources ever combined in one man. This book is extremely difficult to synthesize, and several alternate approaches have been used. The one used here is: Exclamation (1:1-11), Experience (1:12-2:26), Exploration (3-6), Exhortation and Explanation (7-12:7), and Epilogue (12:8-14).

Exclamation (1:1-11): After a one-verse introduction, the Preacher states his theme: "Vanity of vanities! All is vanity" (1:2). Life under the sun appears to be futile and perplexing. Verses 3-11 illustrate this theme in the endless and apparently meaningless cycles found in nature and history.

Experience (1:12-2:26): The Preacher describes his multiple experiential quest for meaning and satisfaction as he explored his vast resources. He began with wisdom (1:12-18) but found that "increasing knowledge results in increasing pain." Due to his intense perception of reality he experienced just the reverse of "ignorance is bliss." The Preacher moved from wisdom to laughter, hedonism, and wine (2:1-3) and then turned to works, women, and wealth (2:4-11)—but all led to emptiness. He realized that wisdom is far greater than foolishness, but both seem to lead to futility in view of the brevity of life and universality of death (2:12-17). He concludes by acknowledging that contentment and joy are found only in God.

Exploration (3-6): At this point, Ecclesiastes turns from an experiential to a philosophical quest, but the conclusion remains the same. The Preacher considers the unchanging order of events and the fixed laws of God. Time is short, and there is no eternity on earth (3:1-15). The futility of death seems to cancel the difference between righteousness and wickedness (3:16-22). Chapters 4-5 explore the futility in social relationships (oppression, rivalry, covetousness, power) and in religious relationships (formalism, empty prayer, vows). In addition, the world's offerings produce disappointment, not satisfaction. Ultimate meaning can only be found in God.

Exhortation and Explanation (7-12:7): A series of lessons on practical wisdom are given in 7:1-9:12. Levity and pleasure-seeking are seen as superficial and foolish; it is better to have sober depth of thought. Wisdom and self-control provide perspective and strength in coping with life. One should enjoy prosperity and consider in adversity—God made both. Avoid the twin extremes of self-righteousness and immorality. Sin invades all men, and wisdom is cut short by evil and death. The human mind cannot grasp ultimate meaning. Submission to authority helps one avoid unnecessary hardship, but real justice is often lacking on earth. The uncertainties of life and certainty of the grave show that God's purposes and ways often cannot be grasped. One should therefore magnify opportunities while they last because fortune can suddenly change.

Observations on wisdom and folly are found in 9:13-11:6. Wisdom, the most powerful human resource, is contrasted with the meaningless talk and effort of fools. In view of the unpredictability of circumstances, wisdom is the best course to follow in order to minimize grief and misfortune. Wisdom involves discipline and diligence. In 11:7-12:7 the Preacher offers exhortations on using life well. Youth is too brief and precious to be squandered in foolishness or evil. A person should live well in the fullness of each day before God and acknowledge Him early in life. This section closes with an exquisite allegory of old age (12:1-7).

Epilogue (12:8-14): The Preacher concludes that the "good life" is only attained by revering God. Those who fail to seriously take God and His will into account are doomed to lives of foolishness and futility. Life will not wait upon the solution of all its problems, but real meaning can still be found by looking not "under the sun" but beyond the sun to the "one Shepherd" (12:11).

Title — The Hebrew title *qoheleth* is a rare term, found *only* in Ecclesiastes (1:1,2,12; 7:27; 12:8,9,10). It comes from the word *qahal*, "to convoke an assembly, to assemble." Thus, it means "one who addresses an assembly, a preacher." The Septuagint used the Greek word *'Ekklesiastes* as its title for this book. Derived from the word *'ecclesia*, "assembly, congregation, church" it simply means "preacher." The Latin *Ecclesiastes* means "speaker before an assembly."

Author

— The minority of scholars today hold Ecclesiastes to be Solomonic. Nevertheless, there are powerful arguments that Qoheleth and Solomon were one.

External Evidence: Jewish Talmudic tradition attributes the book to Solomon but suggests that Hezekiah's scribes may have edited the text (see Prov. 25:1). Solomonic authorship of Ecclesiastes was also the universal Christian position until the time of Luther. (Luther's position that it was written by a literary impersonator of Solomon after the exile has become the standard view even though it logically implies that the author was a moral deceiver.)

Internal Evidence: The author calls himself "the son of David, king in Jerusalem" in 1:1,12. Solomon was the best qualified Davidic descendant for the quest in this book. He was the wisest man who ever taught in Jerusalem (see 1:16 and 1 Kings 4:29-30). The descriptions of Qoheleth's exploration of pleasure (2:1-3), impressive accomplishments (2:4-6), and unparalleled wealth (2:7-10) were fulfilled only by King Solomon. The proverbs in this book are similar to those in the book of Proverbs (e.g., Eccles. 7 and 10). According to 12:9, Qoheleth collected and arranged many proverbs, perhaps referring to the two Solomonic collections in Proverbs. The unity of authorship of Ecclesiastes is supported by the seven references to Qoheleth.

Date and Setting

— Critics argue that the literary forms in Ecclesiastes are post-exilic, but they are in fact unique, and cannot be used in dating this book. The phrase "all who were over Jerusalem before me" in 1:16 has been used to suggest a date after Solomon's time, but there *were* many kings and wise men in Jerusalem before the time of Solomon. But Solomon was the only son of David who reigned over Israel from Jerusalem (1:12).

Ecclesiastes was probably written late in Solomon's life, around 935 B.C. If this is so, the great glory that Solomon ushered in early in his reign was already beginning to fade, and the disruption of Israel into two kingdoms would soon take place. Jewish tradition asserts that Solomon wrote Song of Solomon in his youthful years, Proverbs in his middle years, and Ecclesiastes in his last years. This book may be expressing his regret for his folly and wasted time due to carnality and idolatry (cf. 1 Kings 11).

There are no references to historical events other than personal aspects of Qoheleth's life. This allows for a universal quality. The location was Jerusalem (1:1,12,16), the seat of Israel's rule and authority.

Theme and Purpose — Ecclesiastes reports the results of a diligent quest for purpose, meaning, and satisfaction in human life. The Preacher poignantly sees the emptiness and futility of power, popularity, prestige, and pleasure apart from God. The word *vanity* appears 37 times to express the many things that cannot be understood about life. All earthly goals and ambitions when pursued as ends in themselves lead to dissatisfaction and frustration. Life "under the sun" (used 29 times) seems to be filled with inequities, uncertainties, changes in fortune, and violations of justice. But Ecclesiastes does not give an answer of atheism or skepticism; God is referred to throughout. In fact, it claims that the search for man's *summum bonum* must end in God. Satisfaction in life can only be found by looking beyond this world. Ecclesiastes gives an analysis of negative themes but it also develops the positive theme of overcoming the vanities of life by fearing a God who is good, just, and sovereign (12:13-14). Wisdom involves seeing life from a divine perspective and trusting God in the face of apparent futility and lack of purpose. Life is a daily gift from God and it should be enjoyed as much as possible (see 2:24-26; 3:12-13,22; 5:18-20; 8:15; 9:7-10; 11:8-9). Our comprehension is indeed limited, but there are many things we *can* understand. Qoheleth recognized that God will ultimately judge all people. Therefore he exhorted: "fear God and keep His commandments" (12:13).

Contribution to the Bible — Ecclesiastes is the most philosophical book in the Bible, and its perspective is that of human wisdom (1:13,16-17) more than the divine "Thus says the LORD." Because of its point of view, the book contains several statements that contradict the general teaching of Scripture when used out of context (see 1:15; 2:24; 3:19-20; 7:16-17; 8:15; 9:2,5; 10:19; 11:9). Thus, there was a running debate over officially recognizing it as part of the Old Testament canon until Jewish scholars finally settled it in the Council of Jamnia (c. A.D. 90). Different positions continue to be held concerning its inspiration. (1) Some believe it is uninspired because of its

fatalism (3:15), pessimism (4:2), hedonism (2:24; 8:15), and materialism (3:19-21). It is a naturalistic work with some references to God. (2) Others believe the book is partly inspired as the best that the human mind can produce apart from God. The concluding exhortation to fear God (12:13-14) is the key to the book. (3) Ecclesiastes has difficult passages because of its vantage point, but it is inspired. For example, 3:19-20 says that the deaths of men and animals are alike; both go to the grave. But this does not teach that there is no afterlife. It is a true statement—humans and animals die, decompose, and disappear. The apparent problems caused by Ecclesiastes are overcome when the purpose of the author and the fact of progressive revelation are taken into account.

The book is built more on general than on special revelation. Nevertheless, it develops clear truths about God and man: God's existence (3:14; 5:2), God's sovereignty and power (6:2; 7:13; 9:1), God's justice (5:8; 8:12-13), man's sinfulness (7:20; 9:3), man's finiteness (8:8,17), man's duty (9:7-10; 12:13), man's immortality (3:11; 12:7), and divine punishment and rewards (2:26; 3:17; 8:12; 11:9; 12:14). The exclusive use of *Elohim* ("God," 41 times) rather than *Yahweh* ("LORD") shows that the Creator/creature relationship rather than the Redeemer/redeemed relationship is being considered. Qoheleth's search shows that empiricism (1-2) and rationalism (3-12) are not enough without the third way of knowing—revelation.

This series of sermons by the Preacher illustrates that life under the sun is futile without a relationship with the One who made the sun.

Life Under the Sun	Life Under the Son
1:3 What advantage is work under the sun	He who began a good work in you will perfect it until the day of Christ Jesus (Phil. 1:6)
1:9 Nothing new under the sun	If any man is in Christ, he is a new creation . . . new things have come (2 Cor. 5:17)
1:14 All deeds are vanity under the sun	Be steadfast, immovable . . . knowing that your toil is not in vain in the Lord (1 Cor. 15:58)

2:18	The fruit of labor is hated under the sun	Bearing fruit in every good work and increasing in the knowledge of God (Col. 1:10)
6:12	Man is mortal under the sun	Whoever believes in Him should not perish but have everlasting life (John 3:16)
8:15	Pleasure is temporary under the sun	For it is God who is at work in you, both to will and to work for His good pleasure (Phil. 2:13)
8:17	Man cannot discover God's work under the sun	Now I know in part, but then I shall know fully (1 Cor. 13:12)
9:3	All men die under the sun	God has given us eternal life, and this life is in His Son (1 John 5:11)
9:11	Strength and speed under the sun	God has chosen the weak things of the world to shame the things which are strong (1 Cor. 1:27)
12:2	Life under the sun will cease	In order that you may know that you have eternal life (1 John 5:13)

Christ in Ecclesiastes—Ecclesiastes convincingly portrays the emptiness and perplexity of life without a relationship with the Lord. Each person has eternity in his heart (3:11), and only Christ can provide ultimate satisfaction, joy, and wisdom. Man's highest good is found in the "one Shepherd" (12:11) who offers abundant life (John 10:9-10).

Song of Solomon

"My beloved is mine, and I am his; he pastures his flock among the lilies."

Song of Solomon 2:16

"Many waters cannot quench love, nor will rivers overflow it; if a man were to give all the riches of his house for love, it would be utterly despised."

Song of Solomon 8:7

Focus	Beginning of Love		Broadening of Love	
	1 5:1		5:2 8	
DIVISIONS	Falling in Love	United in Love	Struggling in Love	Growing in Love
	1 3	4 5:1	5:2 6	7 8
TOPICS	Courtship	Wedding	Problem	Progress
	Fostering of Love	Fulfillment of Love	Frustration of Love	Faithfulness of Love
	Courtship and Marriage		Adjustments in Marriage	
Locations	The Country and the Palace			
Time	Perhaps a Year			

Talk Thru — Solomon wrote 1,005 songs (1 Kings 4:32), but this beautiful eulogy of love stood out among them as the "Song of Songs" (1:1). The great literary value of this song can be seen in its rich use of metaphors and oriental imagery as it extols the purity, beauty, and satisfaction of love. It is never crass but often intimate as it explores the dimensions of the relationship between two lovers: attraction, desire, companionship, pleasure, union, separation, faithfulness, and praise. Like Ecclesiastes, this little book is not easily outlined, and various schemes can be used. It abounds with sudden changes of speakers, and they are not identified. The beginning of love is seen in 1:1-5:1, and the broadening of love is found in 5:2-8:14.

Beginning of Love (1:1-5:1): King Solomon had a vineyard in the country of the Shulammite (6:13; 8:11). The Shulammite had to work in the vineyard with her brothers (1:6; 8:11-12), and when Solomon visited, he won her heart and eventually took her to the palace in Jerusalem as his bride. She was tanned from hours of work outside in the vineyard, but she was "most beautiful among women" (1:6,8).

This song is arranged like scenes in a one-act drama with three main speakers—the bride (the Shulammite), the king (Solomon), and a chorus (the daughters of Jerusalem). It is not always clear who is speaking, but this is a likely arrangement:

The bride: 1:2-4a,5-7,12-14,16-17; 2:1,3-6,8-17; 3:1-4; 4:16; 5:2-8,10-16; 6:2-3,11-12; 7:9b-13; 8:1-3,6-7,10-12,14.
The groom: 1:8-10,15; 2:2,7; 3:5; 4:1-15; 5:1; 6:4-10,13; 7:1-9a; 8:4,5b,13.
The chorus: 1:4b,11; 3:6-11; 5:9; 6:1,13; 8:5a,8-9.

Chapters 1-3 give a series of recollections of the courtship: (1) the bride's longing for affection at the palace before the wedding (1:2-8), (2) expressions of mutual love in the banquet hall (1:9-2:7), (3) a springtime visit of the king to the bride's home in the country (2:8-17), (4) the Shulammite's dream of separation from her beloved (3:1-5), (5) the ornate wedding procession from the bride's home to Jerusalem (3:6-11).

In 4:1-5:1, Solomon praises his bride from head to toe with a superb chain of similies and metaphors. Her virginity is compared to "a garden locked" (4:12), and the garden is entered when the marriage is consummated (4:16-5:1). The union is commended, possibly by God, in 5:1b.

Broadening of Love (5:2-8:14): Some time after the wedding, the Shulammite had a troubled dream (5:2) in the palace while Solomon was away. In her dream, Solomon came to her door but she answered too late—he was gone. She panicked and searched for him late at night in Jerusalem. Upon his return, Solomon assured her of his love and praised her beauty (6:4-7:10). The Shulammite begins to think of her country home and tries to persuade her beloved to return there with her (7:11-8:4). The journey takes place in 8:5-7 as their relationship continues to deepen. Their love will not be overthrown by jealousy or circumstances. At her homecoming (8:8-14), the Shulammite reflects on her brothers' care for her when she was young (8:8-9). She remained virtuous ("I was a wall," 8:10) and is now in a position to look out for her brothers' welfare (8:11-12). The song concludes with a dual invitation of lover and beloved (8:13-14).

Title — The Hebrew title *shir hashirim* comes from 1:1, "The Song of Songs." This is in the superlative and speaks of Solomon's most exquisite song. The Greek title *Asma Asmaton* and the Latin *Canticum Canticorum* also mean "song of songs" or "the best song." The name *Canticles* ("songs") is derived from the Latin title. Because Solomon is mentioned in 1:1, the book is also known as the Song of Solomon.

Author — Solomonic authorship is rejected by critics who claim it is a later collection of songs. Many take 1:1 to mean "which is about or concerning Solomon." But the internal evidence of the book is strongly in favor of the traditional position that Solomon is its author. Solomon is specifically mentioned seven times (1:1,5; 3:7,9,11; 8:11,12) and he is identified as the groom. There is evidence of royal luxury and rich imported goods (e.g., 3:6-11). The king by this time also had 60 queens and 80 concubines (6:8). Solomon's harem at its fullest extent reached 700 queens and 300 concubines (1 Kings 11:3). First Kings 4:32-33 says that Solomon composed 1,005 songs and had intimate knowledge of the plant and animal world. This greatest of his songs alludes to 21 species of plants and 15 species of animals. It cites geographical locations in the north and in the south, indicating that they were yet one kingdom. For example, 6:4 mentions both Tirzah and Jerusalem, the northern and southern capitals (after Solomon's time, Samaria became the northern capital). Because of the poetic imagery, the

Song of Solomon uses 49 words which occur nowhere else in Scripture.

Date and Setting — This song was written primarily from the point of view of the Shulammite, but Solomon was its author, probably early in his reign, c. 965 B.C. There is a problem of how a man with a harem of 140 women (6:8) could extol the love of the Shulammite as though she was his only bride. It may be that Solomon's relationship with the Shulammite was the only pure romance he ever experienced. The bulk of his marriages were political arrangements. It is significant that the Shulammite was a vineyard keeper of no great means. This book was also written before he plunged into gross immorality and idolatry. "For it came about when Solomon was old, his wives turned his heart away after other gods; and his heart was not wholly devoted to the LORD his God" (1 Kings 11:4).

The Shulammite addresses the king as "my beloved" and the king addresses his bride as "my love." The daughters of Jerusalem were probably attendants to the Shulammite. The term "Shulammite" appears only in 6:13, and it may be derived from the town of Shunem which was southwest of the Sea of Galilee in the tribal area of Issachar. The song refers to 15 geographic locations from Lebanon in the north to Egypt in the south: Kedar (1:5), Egypt (1:9), En-gedi (1:14), Sharon (2:1), Jerusalem (2:7), Lebanon (3:9), Mount Gilead (4:1), Amana (4:8), Senir (4:8), Hermon (4:8), Tirzah (6:4), Heshbon (7:4), Damascus (7:4), Carmel (7:5), and Baal-hamon (8:11).

Theme and Purpose — The purpose of this book depends on the viewpoint taken as to its primary thrust. Is it fictional, allegorical, or historical? (1) *Fictional:* Some hold that this song is a fictional drama that portrays Solomon's courtship and marriage of a poor but beautiful girl from the country. But the book gives every indication that the story really happened. (2) *Allegorical:* In this view, the primary purpose of the Song was to illustrate the truth of God's love for His people whether the events were fictional or not. Some commentators insist that the book is indeed historical but its primary purpose is typical, that is, to present Yahweh's love for His bride Israel and/or Christ's love for His Church. But this interpretation is subjective and lacking in evidence. There are other places in Scripture where the husband/wife relationship is used symbolically (cf. Ezek. 16; 23; Hos. 1-3), but these are always indicated as symbols. This may be an application of the book but it should not be the primary interpretation. (3) *Historical:* The Song of Songs is a poetic record of Solomon's actual romance with a Shulammite woman. The various scenes in the book exalt the joys of love in courtship and marriage and teach that physical beauty and sexuality in marriage should not be despised as base or unspiritual. It offers a proper perspective of human love and avoids the extremes of lust and asceticism. Only when sexuality was viewed in the wrong way as something akin to evil was an attempt made to allegorize the book. But this is part of God's creation with its related desires and pleasures, and it is reasonable that He would provide us with a guide to a pure sexual relationship between a husband and wife. In fact, the union of the two sexes was originally intended to illustrate the oneness of the Godhead (see Gen. 1:27; 2:24; 1 Cor. 6:16-20). Thus, the Song is a bold and positive endorsement by God of marital love in all its physical and emotional beauty. This interpretation does not mean that the book has no spiritual illustrations and applications. It certainly illustrates God's love for His covenant people Israel, and anticipates Christ's love for His bride, the Church.

Contribution to the Bible — The Song is a unit rather than a collection of songs. It is a dramatic poem built on a dialogue betwen the same two characters (and an occasional chorus) throughout. There is a continuity of style, imagery, and expression in this unique biblical book. Solomon emphasized the intellect in Ecclesiastes, but the emotions clearly dominate his Song.

This book was one of the *antilegomena* ("spoken against")—its inclusion in the canon of Scripture was delayed because of questions over its religious value, its use of God's name only once (8:6), its unusual subject matter, and the lack of quotations of the Song in the rest of Scripture. The Song has traditionally been read at the feast of the Passover.

Christ in Song of Solomon — In the Old Testament, Israel was regarded as the bride of Yahweh (see Isa. 54:5-6; Jer. 2:2; Ezek. 16:8-14; Hos. 2:16-20). In the New Testament, the Church is seen as the bride of Christ (see 2 Cor. 11:2; Eph. 5:23-25; Rev. 19:7-9; 21:9). The Song of Solomon illustrated the former and anticipated the latter.

Walk Thru the Poetical Books

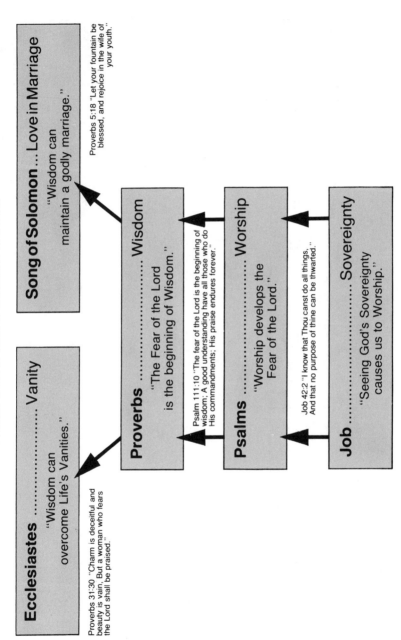

Ecclesiastes ...... Vanity

"Wisdom can overcome Life's Vanities."

Proverbs 31:30 "Charm is deceitful and beauty is vain, But a woman who fears the Lord shall be praised."

Song of Solomon ... Love in Marriage

"Wisdom can maintain a godly marriage."

Proverbs 5:18 "Let your fountain be blessed, and rejoice in the wife of your youth."

Proverbs ...... Wisdom

"The Fear of the Lord is the beginning of Wisdom."

Psalm 111:10 "The fear of the Lord is the beginning of wisdom; A good understanding have all those who do His commandments; His praise endures forever."

Psalms ...... Worship

"Worship develops the Fear of the Lord."

Job 42:2 "I know that Thou canst do all things, And that no purpose of thine can be thwarted."

Job ...... Sovereignty

"Seeing God's Sovereignty causes us to Worship."

Integration of the Old Testament

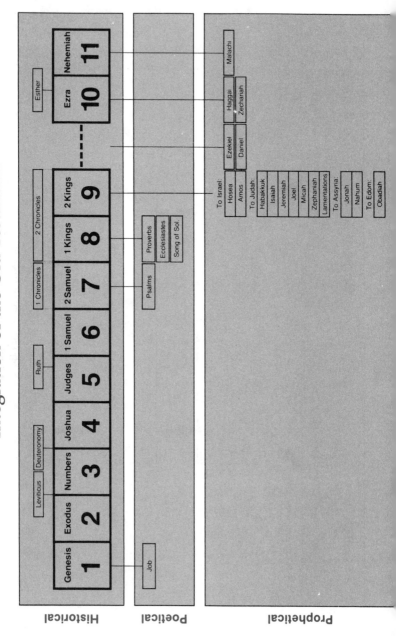

Historical

Genesis	Exodus	Numbers	Joshua	Judges	1 Samuel	2 Samuel	1 Kings	2 Kings		Ezra	Nehemiah
1	**2**	**3**	**4**	**5**	**6**	**7**	**8**	**9**		**10**	**11**

Leviticus Deuteronomy

Ruth

1 Chronicles 2 Chronicles

Esther

Poetical

Job

Psalms

Proverbs
Ecclesiastes
Song of Sol

Prophetical

To Israel:
Hosea
Amos

To Judah:
Habakkuk
Isaiah
Jeremiah
Joel
Micah
Zephaniah
Lamentations

To Assyria:
Jonah
Nahum

To Edom:
Obadiah

Ezekiel
Daniel

Haggai
Zechariah

Malachi

144

Introduction to the Major Prophets

The Prophets as a Whole — The 17 prophetical books comprise about one-fourth of Scripture and are crucial from a theological and historical point of view. Yet their message and meaning evade more people than any other section of the Bible, principally because of neglect.

Designation: The second division of the Hebrew Bible was known as the Prophets and consisted of the Former Prophets and Latter Prophets. The Former Prophets were actually the historical books of Joshua, Judges, Samuel, and Kings. These books chronicled God's dealings with the theocratic nation from the time of Joshua to the Babylonian captivity. Thus, they furnish the background to the writing prophets. The Latter Prophets are Isaiah, Jeremiah, Ezekiel, and the 12 minor prophets. The term "latter" speaks more of their place in the canon than of chronology. These prophets left written records of their ministry, but the oral prophets (e.g., Nathan, Ahijah, Iddo, Jehu, Elijah, Elisha, Oded, Shemaiah, Azariah, Hanani, Jahaziel, and Huldah) left no records that survived. The writing prophets were later divided into the major and minor prophets as we know them today. The major prophets were so designated because of their greater length (Lamentations excepted).

Characteristics: These men were called prophets, seers, watchmen, men of God, messengers, and servants of the Lord. The most frequently used title is *nabi*, "prophet" (over 300 times), referring to one who has been called or appointed to proclaim the message of God Himself. The word *roeh*, "seer" speaks of one who perceives things that are not in the realm of natural sight or hearing. The English word "prophet" is derived from two Greek words that literally mean "speak for." This emphasizes the role of these people as divinely chosen spokesmen who received and related God's messages, whether in oral, visual, or written form. God communicated to them through a variety of means including dreams, visions, angels, nature, miracles, and an audible voice.

Samuel was, in a sense, the first of the real prophets (Acts 3:24; 13:20; Heb. 11:32). He was the first to create a colony of prophets, and he presided over them at Ramah (1 Sam. 19:20). True prophets were divinely called and endowed with special abilities. Because of their moral and spiritual message which was grounded in the law, their lives had to be consistent with their words. Deuteronomy 18:18-20 prescribed that a true prophet would speak in Yahweh's name and that his short-term prophecies must be completely accurate.

Message: Although the prophets had a ministry of *foretelling* future events, their primary role was that of *forthtelling*. This demanded spiritual insight as well as foresight, because they proclaimed the consequences of specific attitudes and practices of their day. They dipped into the past for lessons and exhortations concerning the present. And they spoke of the need of present reforms to avert future judgment. The prophetic message had four major themes: (1) The prophets exposed the sinful practices of the people. It required considerable courage to tell the people what they needed to hear instead of succumbing to the temptation of telling them what they wanted to hear. God's messengers could not compromise their harsh treatment of sin as sin, knowing that the only hope for the people was a humble turning to the Lord and acknowledgment of their guilt. Like watchmen who alerted the people of coming danger, their messages were very practical. (2) The prophets called the people back to the moral, civil, and ceremonial law of God. They reminded the people about the character of God and urged them to trust Him with all their hearts. God has a rich purpose for them, but they must believe and obey Him. (3) They warned the people of coming judgment. God must condemn the nation if its princes, priests, and people continue to arrogantly reject God's moral and spiritual principles. They are responsible for their disobedience to their covenant commitment with God. Yahweh is the sovereign Lord of history, and the Gentile nations will also be judged if they rebel against His dominion. (4) The prophets anticipated the coming Messiah. History is linear, not cyclical. It has a definite goal, and God will sovereignly move all things to a consummation in the Messianic age. His name will be honored and His voice obeyed by all people of the earth. Biblical prophecy is unique because of its clarity and specific fulfillment. Over 300 Old Testament prophecies were precisely fulfilled by Messiah in His first advent, and over 400 more remain to be fulfilled when He comes again. "Of Him all the prophets bear witness" (Acts 10:43).

In short, the prophetic message is twofold: condemnation because of the sin of man, but consolation because of the grace of God.

Interpretation: The prophets spoke in the context and background of their times, and it is important to understand their historical and cultural circumstances. They emphasized four chronological points — their own day, the captivity and return, the first coming of Christ, and the Messianic kingdom. The chronology was not as important in their minds as the events themselves, and they sometimes blurred the distinctions between these four periods. Some events were literally fulfilled, some were partially fulfilled, and some are yet unfulfilled. Their messages use symbols and figures of speech, but they point to real events.

There is a great diversity and individuality among the prophets ranging from the sophistication of Isaiah to the simplicity of Amos. Their personalities, backgrounds, interests, and writing styles vary widely, but they shared a common conviction, courage, and commitment. They wrote from the ninth to the fifth centuries B.C. and spanned God's program from their day to the new heaven and new earth. Of the 17 prophetic books, 12 were pre-exilic, two were exilic, and three were post-exilic.

The Major Prophets — Isaiah: This pinnacle of the prophets has a two-fold message of condemnation (1-39) and consolation (40-66). Isaiah analyzes the sins of Judah and pronounces God's judgment on the nation. He broadens his scope to include judgment on the surrounding nations and

moves to universal judgment followed by blessing. After a historical parenthesis concerning King Hezekiah, Isaiah consoles the people with a message of future salvation and restoration. Yahweh is the sovereign Savior who will rescue His people.

Jeremiah: Judah had reached the depths of moral and spiritual decay, and Jeremiah was called to the heart-breaking and unpopular ministry of declaring the certain judgment of God against the nation. Jeremiah faithfully ministered in spite of rejection and persecution, and the dreaded day finally came. Judah's defiance of God's holiness led to her downfall, but God graciously promised to establish a new covenant with His people.

Lamentations: This beautifully structured series of five lament poems is Judah's funeral for the fallen city of Jerusalem. After his 40 years of warning, Jeremiah's awful words came true. His sorrow is obvious in his vivid descriptions of the defeat, destruction and desolation of Jerusalem.

Ezekiel: The prophet Ezekiel ministered to the Jewish captives in Babylon before and after the fall of Jerusalem. Like Jeremiah, he had to convince the people that the city was doomed and that the captivity would not be brief. Ezekiel also described the fate of Judah's foes and ended with a great apocalyptic vision of Judah's future.

Daniel: This crucial book abounds with detailed prophecies and visions of the future. It outlines God's sovereign plan for the Gentile nations (2-7) and moves on to a portrait of Israel during the time of Gentile domination (8-12). At a time when the Jews had little hope, Daniel provided encouragement by revealing God's power and plans for their future.

Isaiah

"Come now, and let us reason together," says the Lord, "though
your sins are as scarlet, they will be as white as snow; though
they are red like crimson, they will be like wool. If you consent
and obey, you will eat the best of the land; but if you refuse and
rebel, you will be devoured by the sword." Truly, the mouth of
the Lord has spoken."

Isaiah 1:18-20

"All of us like sheep have gone astray, each of us has turned to
his own way; but the Lord has caused the iniquity of us all to fall
on Him."

Isaiah 53:6

(Also see 6:3; 41:10; 57:15.)

Focus	Prophetic Condemnation			Historic Contribution	Prophetic Consolation		
	1 35			36 39	40 66		
DIVISIONS	Condemnation of Judah	Condemnation of Surrounding Nations	Universal Condemnation and Blessing	Historical Interlude	The Sovereignty of God	The Salvation of God	The Restoration of God
	1 12	13 23	24 35	36 39	40 48	49 57	58 66
TOPICS	Judgment			Transition	Hope		
	Groan: God's Nation				Glory: Nation's God		
	Corruption (1:4)				Comfort (40:1)		
	Need for Salvation: Judah, the Sinful Servant				Provision of Salvation: Messiah, the Suffering Servant		
Locations	Judah	Surrounding Nations	All Nations	Jerusalem	Israel and All Nations		
Time	About 41 Years of History (722-681 B.C.)				536 B.C. to the First and Second Advents of Christ		

Talk Thru — Isaiah, the "Mt. Everest of Hebrew prophecy," is like a miniature Bible. Its first 39 chapters stress the righteousness, holiness, and justice of God and correspond to the 39 books of the Old Testament. This portion of the book pronounces judgment on immoral and idolatrous people beginning with Judah, then the nations surrounding Judah, and finally the whole world. Judgment is coming, and sin ultimately leads to punishment. The last 27 chapters of Isaiah portray Yahweh's glory, compassion, and grace and correspond to the 27 books of the New Testament. Messiah will come as a Savior to bear a cross and as a Sovereign to wear a crown. He Himself will bear God's judgment for sin and provide hope for Jew and Gentile. It is interesting that the names of Isaiah's two sons summarize the two divisions of this great book: Maher-shalal-hash-baz means "swift is the booty, speedy is the prey" (chapters 1-39) and Shear-jashub means "a remnant shall return" (chapters 40-66).

Isaiah, the "Shakespeare of the prophets," has often been called the "evangelical prophet" because of his incredibly clear and detailed Messianic prophecies. The "Gospel according to Isaiah" has three major sections: Prophetic Condemnation (1-35), Historic Contribution (36-39), and Prophetic Consolation (40-66).

Prophetic Condemnation (1-35): Isaiah's first message of condemnation is aimed at his own countrymen in Judah (1-12). Chapter 1 is a capsulized message of the entire book. Judah is riddled with moral and spiritual disease; the people are neglecting God as they bow to ritualism and selfishness. But Yahweh graciously invites them to repent and return to Him because this is their only hope of avoiding judgment. Isaiah's call to proclaim God's message is found in chapter 6, and this is followed by the Book of Immanuel (7-12). These chapters repeatedly refer to Messiah (see 7:14; 8:14; 9:2,6-7; 11:1-2) and anticipate the blessing of His future reign.

The prophet moves from local to regional judgment as he proclaims a series of oracles against the surrounding nations (13-23). The 11 nations are Babylonia, Assyria, Philistia, Moab, Damascus (Syria), Ethiopia, Egypt, Babylonia (again), Edom, Arabia, Jerusalem (Judah), and Tyre. Isaiah's little apocalypse (24-27) depicts universal tribulation followed by the blessings of the kingdom. Chapters 28-33 pronounce six woes on Israel and Judah for specific sins. Isaiah's prophetic condemnation closes with a general picture of international devastation that will precede universal blessing (34-35).

Historic Contribution (36-39): This historical parenthesis looks back to the Assyrian invasion of Judah in 701 B.C. and anticipates the coming Babylonian invasion of Judah. Judah escaped captivity by Assyria (36-37; 2 Kings 18-19), but they will not escape from the hands of Babylonia (38-39; 2 Kings 20). God answered King Hezekiah's prayers and delivered Judah from Assyrian destruction by Sennacherib. Hezekiah also turned to the Lord in his illness and was granted a 15-year extension of his life. But he foolishly showed all his treasures to the Babylonian messengers, and Isaiah told him that the Babylonians would one day carry his treasure and descendants to their land.

Prophetic Consolation (40-66): Having pronounced Judah's divine condemnation, Isaiah comforts them with God's promises of hope and restoration. The basis for this hope is the sovereignty and majesty of God (40-48). Of the 216 verses in these nine chapters, 115 speak of God's greatness and power. The Creator is contrasted with idols, the creation of men. His sovereign character is Judah's assurance of future restoration. Babylonia will indeed carry them off but it will be judged and destroyed, and God's people will be released from captivity. Chapters 49-57 concentrate on the coming Messiah who will be their Savior and suffering Servant. This Rejected but exalted One will pay for their iniquities and usher in a kingdom of peace and righteousness upon the whole earth. All who acknowledge their sins and trust in Him will be delivered (58-66). In that day Jerusalem will be remade, Israel's borders will be enlarged, and Messiah will reign in Zion. God's people will confess their sins and His enemies will be judged. Peace, prosperity, and justice will prevail, and God will make all things new.

Title — *Yesha'yahu* and its shortened form *yeshaiah* mean "Yahweh is salvation." This name is an excellent summary of the contents of the book. The Greek form in the Septuagint is *Hesaias*, and the Latin form is *Esaias* or *Isaias*.

Author — Isaiah, the "St. Paul of the Old Testament," was evidently from a distinguished Jewish family. His education is evident in his impressive vocabulary and style. His work is comprehensive in scope and beautifully communicated. Isaiah maintained close contact with the royal court, but his exhortations against alliances with foreign powers were not always well received. This great poet and prophet was uncompromising, sincere, and compassionate. His wife was a prophetess and he fathered at least two sons (7:3, 8:3). He spent most of his time in Jerusalem, and Talmudic tradition says he was sawed in two during the reign of Manasseh (cf. Heb. 11:37).

The unity of this book has been challenged by critics who hold that a "Deutero-Isaiah" wrote chapters 40-66 after the Babylonian captivity. They argue that 1-39 has an Assyrian background while 40-66 is set against a Babylonian background. But Babylon is mentioned more than twice as often in 1-39 as in 40-66. The only shift is one of perspective from the present into the future. Critics also argue that there are radical differences in the language, style, and theology of the two sections. Actually, the resemblances between 1-39 and 40-66 are greater than the differences. These include similarities in thoughts, images, rhetorical ornaments, characteristic expressions, and local coloring. It is true that the first section is more terse and rational while the second section is more flowing and emotional, but much of this is caused by the subject matter difference of condemnation versus consolation. Critics often forget that content, time, and circumstances typically affect any author's style. In addition, there is no theological contradiction between the emphasis on Messiah as King in 1-39 and as suffering Servant in 40-66. While the thrust is different, Messiah is seen in both sections as Servant and King. Another critical argument is that Isaiah could not have predicted the Babylonian captivity and the return under Cyrus (mentioned by name in 44-45) 150 years in advance. This is simply an anti-supernatural assumption that ignores the predictive claims of the book (see 42:9). This view cannot explain the amazing Messianic prophecies of Isaiah that were literally fulfilled in the life of Christ (see Christ in Isaiah).

The unity of Isaiah is supported by the book of Ecclesiasticus, the Septuagint, and the Talmud. The New Testament also claims that Isaiah wrote both sections. John 12:37-41 quotes from Isaiah 6:9-10 and 53:1 and attributes it all to Isaiah. In Romans 9:27 and 10:16-21, Paul quotes from Isaiah 10, 53, and 65 and gives the credit to Isaiah. The same is true of Matthew 3:3; 12:17-21; Luke 3:4-6; and Acts 8:28.

If 40-66 was written by another prophet after the events

took place, it is a misleading and deceptive work. Furthermore, it would lead to the strange conclusion that Israel's greatest prophet is the only writing prophet of the Old Testament to go unnamed.

Date and Setting — Isaiah's long ministry ranged from about 740 to 680 B.C. (1:1). He began his ministry near the end of Uzziah's reign (790-739) and continued through the reigns of Jotham (739-731), Ahaz (731-715), and Hezekiah (715-686). Assyria was growing in power under Tiglath-pileser who turned toward the west after his conquests in the east. He plucked up the small nations that dotted the Mediterranean coast including Israel and much of Judah. Isaiah lived during this time of military threat to Judah and warned its kings against trusting in alliances with other countries rather than the power of Yahweh. As a contemporary of Hosea and Micah, he prophesied during the last years of the northern kingdom but ministered to the southern kingdom of Judah who was following the sins of her sister Israel. After Israel's demise in 722 B.C., he warned Judah of judgment not by Assyria but by Babylonia, even though Babylonia had not yet risen to power.

Isaiah ministered from the time of Tiglath-pileser (745-727) to the time of Sennacherib (705-681) of Assyria. He outdated Hezekiah by a few years because 37:38 records the death of Sennacherib in 681 B.C. Hezekiah was succeeded by his wicked son Manasseh who overthrew the worship of Yahweh and no doubt opposed the work of Isaiah.

Theme and Purpose — The basic theme of this book is found in Isaiah's name: *salvation* is of the Lord. The word salvation appears 26 times in Isaiah but only seven times in all the other prophets combined. Chapters 1-39 portray man's great need for salvation, and chapters 40-66 reveal God's great provision of salvation. Salvation is of God, not man, and He is seen as the supreme Ruler, the sovereign Lord of history, and the only Savior. Isaiah solemnly warned Judah of approaching judgment because of moral depravity, political corruption, social injustice, and especially spiritual idolatry. Because the nation would not turn away from its sinful practice, Isaiah announced the ultimate overthrow of Judah. Nevertheless, God would remain faithful to His covenant by preserving a godly remnant and promising salvation and deliverance through the coming Messiah. The Savior will come out of Judah and accomplish the twin work of redemption and restoration. The Gentiles will come to His light and universal blessing will finally come.

Contribution to the Bible — Isaiah is quoted in the New Testament far more than any other prophet. He is mentioned 21 times by name, and chapter 53 alone is quoted or alluded to at least 85 times in the New Testament. Isaiah is characterized by systematic presentation, brilliant imagery, broad scope, clarity, beauty, and power.

Some of his prophecies have been fulfilled but many await fulfillment. Our Lord, for example, quoted Isaiah 61:1-2 in Luke 4:18-20 but stopped mid-sentence: " . . . to proclaim the favorable year of the Lord." The next phrase in Isaiah reads "and the day of vengeance of our God." The first part was indeed fulfilled by Christ, but the second awaits fulfillment when He comes again, not as the suffering Servant, but as the ruling King.

Christ in Isaiah — When he speaks about Christ, Isaiah sounds more like a New Testament writer than an Old Testament prophet. His Messianic prophecies are clearer and more explicit than those of any other Old Testament book. They describe many aspects of the person and work of Christ in His first and second advents, and often blend the two together. Here are a few of the Christological prophecies with their New Testament fulfillments: 7:14 (Matt. 1:22-23); 9:1-2 (Matt. 4:12-16); 9:6 (Luke 2:11; Eph. 2:14-18); 11:1 (Luke 3:23,32; Acts 13:22-23); 11:2 (Luke 3:22); 28:16 (1 Pet. 2:4-6); 40:3-5 (Matt. 3:1-3); 42:1-4 (Matt. 12:15-21); 42:6 (Luke 2:29-32); 50:6 (Matt. 26:67; 27:26,30); 52:14 (Phil. 2:7-11); 53:3 (Luke 23:18; John 1:11; 7:5); 53:4-5 (Rom. 5:6,8); 53:7 (Matt. 27:12-14; John 1:29; 1 Pet. 1:18-19); 53:9 (Matt. 27:57-60); 53:12 (Mark 15:28); 61:1-2a (Luke 4:17-19,21). The Old Testament has over 300 prophecies about the first advent of Christ, and Isaiah contributes a number of them. The odds that even 10 of them could be fulfilled by one person is a statistical marvel. Isaiah's Messianic prophecies that await fulfillment in the Lord's second advent include: 4:2; 11:2-6,10; 32:1-8; 49:7;

52:13,15; 59:20-21; 60:1-3; 61:2b-3.

Isaiah 52:13-53:12 is the central chapter of the consolation section (40-66). Its five stanzas present five different aspects of the saving work of Christ: (1) 52:13-15 — His whole-hearted sacrifice (burnt offering); (2) 53:1-3 — His perfect character (meal offering); (3) 53:4-6 — He brought atonement that issues in peace with God (peace offering); (4) 53:7-9 — He paid for the transgression of the people (sin offering); (5) 53:10-12 — He died for the effects of sin (trespass offering).

Jeremiah

"So now then, speak to the men of Judah and against the inhabitants of Jerusalem saying, 'Thus says the Lord, "Behold, I am fashioning calamity against you and devising a plan against you. Oh turn back, each of you from his evil way, and reform your ways and your deeds.' " "But they will say, 'It's hopeless! For we are going to follow our own plans, and each of us will act according to the stubbornness of his evil heart.' "

Jeremiah 18:11-12
(Also see 1:10; 3:14; 9:23-24; 17:5-10.)

Focus	Call of Jeremiah	Concerning Judah					Concerning the Nations	Consummation of Judgment
	1	2				45	46 51	52
D I V I S I O N S	Call of the Prophet	Condemnations of the Prophet	Conflicts of the Prophet	Consolations of the Prophet	Circumstances of the Prophet		Condemnation of Nine Countries	Concluding Supplement
	1	2 25	26 29	30 33	34 45		46 51	52
T O P I C S	Ministry	Message to Judah	Misery in Judah				Message to the Nations	Message Vindicated
	Designation of the Prophet	Declarations Against Judah					Declarations Against the Nations	Descriptions of Jerusalem's Fall
	Prologue	Prophetic Declarations (Sermons & Signs)						Postlude
Locations	Judah						Surrounding Nations	Babylonia
Time	About 47 Years (627 to c. 580 B.C.)							

156

Talk Thru — Jeremiah is an autobiography of the life and ministry of one of Judah's greatest prophets during its darkest days. He was called as a prophet during the reign of Josiah, the last of Judah's good kings. But even Josiah's well-intentioned reforms could not stem the tide of apostasy. The downhill slide of the nation continued virtually unabated through a succession of four godless kings during Jeremiah's ministry. The people wallowed in apostasy and idolatry and grew even more treacherous than Israel was before its captivity (3:11). They perverted the worship of the true God and gave themselves over to spiritual and moral decay. Because they refused to repent or even listen to God's prophet, the divine cure required radical surgery. Jeremiah proclaimed an approaching avalanche of judgment. Babylonia would be God's instrument of judgment, and this book refers to that nation 164 times, more than the rest of the Bible together. Jeremiah faithfully proclaimed the divine condemnation of rebellious Judah for 40 years and was rewarded with opposition, beatings, isolation, and imprisonment. His sympathy and sensitivity caused him to grieve over the rebelliousness and imminent doom of his nation. He often wanted to resign from his prophetic office because of the harshness of his message and his reception, but he persevered to Judah's bitter end. He was the weeping prophet (9:1; 13:17) — lonely, rejected, and persecuted.

Although Jeremiah is not easy to arrange chronologically or thematically, its basic message is clear: surrender to God's will is the only way to escape calamity. Judgment cannot be halted, but promises of restoration are sprinkled through the book. Its divisions are: Call of Jeremiah (1), Concerning Judah (2-45), Concerning the Nations (46-51), and Consummation of Judgment (52).

Call of Jeremiah (1): Jeremiah was called and sanctified before birth to be God's prophet. This introductory chapter surveys the identification, inauguration, and instructions of the prophet.

Concerning Judah (2-45): Jeremiah's message was communicated through a variety of parables, sermons, and object lessons. The prophet's life became a daily illustration to Judah, and most of the book's object lessons are found in this section (13:1-11,12-14; 14:1-9; 16:1-9; 18:1-8; 19:1-13; 24:1-10; 27:1-11; 32:6-15; 43:8-13). In a series of 12 graphic messages, Jeremiah lists the causes of Judah's coming judgment. The Gentile nations were more faithful to their false gods than Judah was to Yahweh. They became a false vine by following idols and were without excuse. The people are condemned for their empty profession, disobedience to God's covenant, and spiritual harlotry. God had bound Judah to Himself, but like a rotten waistband, they had become corrupt and useless. Jeremiah offered a confession for the people but their sin was too great; the prophet could only lament for them. As a sign of imminent judgment he was forbidden to marry and participate in the feasts. Because the nation would not trust God or keep the sabbath, the land would receive a sabbath rest when they were in captivity. Jerusalem will be invaded and the rulers and people will be deported to Babylon. Restoration will only come under the new shepherd, Messiah, the nation's future king. Jeremiah announced the duration of the captivity as 70 years in contrast to the messages of the false prophets who claimed it would not happen.

Because of his message (2-25), Jeremiah suffered misery and opposition (26-45). He was rejected by the prophets and priests who called for his death, but he was spared by the elders and officials. In his sign of the yoke he proclaimed the unpopular message that Judah must submit to divine discipline. But he assures the nation of restoration and hope under a new covenant (30-33). A remnant will be delivered and there will be a coming time of blessing. Jeremiah's personal experiences and sufferings are the focal point of 34-45 as opposition against the prophet mounts. Since he was no longer allowed in the temple he sent his assistant Baruch to read his prophetic warnings. His scroll was burnt by Jehoiakim and Jeremiah was imprisoned. After the destruction of the city Jeremiah was taken to Egypt by fleeing Jews, but he prophesied that Nebuchadnezzar would invade Egypt as well.

Concerning the Nations (46-51): These chapters are a series of prophetic oracles against nine nations: Egypt, Philistia, Moab, Ammon, Edom, Damascus (Syria), Arabia, Elam, and Babylonia. Only Egypt, Moab, Ammon, and Elam are given a promise of restoration.

Consummation of Judgment (52): Jeremiah's 40-year declaration of doom was finally vindicated in an event so significant that it is recorded in detail four times in Scripture (2 Kings 25; 2

Chron. 36; Jer. 39; 52). In this historical supplement, Jerusalem is captured, destroyed, and plundered. The leaders are killed and the captives taken to Babylon.

Title

Title — *Yirmeyahu* or *yirmeyah* literally means "Yahweh throws," perhaps in the sense of laying a foundation. It may effectively mean "Yahweh establishes, appoints, or sends." The Greek form of the Hebrew name in the Septuagint is *Hieremias*, and the Latin form is *Jeremias*.

Author

Author — Jeremiah was the son of Hilkiah the priest and lived just over two miles north of Jerusalem in Anathoth. As an object lesson to Judah he was not allowed to marry (16:2). Because of his radical message of God's judgment through the coming Babylonian invasion, he led a life of conflict. He was threatened in his hometown of Anathoth, tried for his life by the priests and prophets of Jerusalem, put in stocks, forced to flee from king Jehoiakim, publicly humiliated by the false prophet Hananiah, and thrown in a cistern.

The critical view of this book assumes that it contains several traditions of Jeremiah's words coupled with deuteronomistic preaching. This assumption has no foundation in fact, history, or tradition. It is a subjective rejection of the positive internal and external testimony to Jeremiah as the author. The book clearly states that Jeremiah is its author (1:1). Jeremiah dictated all his prophecies to his secretary Baruch from the beginning of his ministry until the fourth year of Jehoiakim. After this scroll was destroyed by the king, Jeremiah dictated a more complete edition to Baruch (see 36-38) and later sections were also composed. Only chapter 52 was evidently not written by Jeremiah. This supplement is almost identical to 2 Kings 24:18-25:30 and it may have been added by Baruch. There was more than one edition, because the Hebrew text is somewhat longer and arranged differently than the Septuagint text. Perhaps Baruch made a more comprehensive collection of his master's sermons and rearranged the material.

Daniel alluded to Jeremiah's prophecy of the 70-year captivity (25:11-14; 29:10; Dan. 9:2), and Jeremiah's authorship is also confirmed by Ecclesiasticus, Josephus, and the Talmud. The New Testament makes explicit and implicit references to Jeremiah's prophecy: Matthew 2:17-18 (31:15); Matthew 21:13;

Mark 11:17; Luke 19:4b (7:11); Romans 11:27 (31:33); Hebrews 8:8-13 (31:31-34).

Date and Setting

Date and Setting — Jeremiah was a contemporary of Zephaniah, Habakkuk, Daniel, and Ezekiel. His ministry stretched from 627 to about 580 B.C. Josiah, Judah's last good king (640-609), instituted spiritual reforms when the Book of the Law was discovered in 622 B.C. Jeremiah was on good terms with Josiah and lamented when he was killed in 609 B.C. by Pharaoh Necho of Egypt. By this time, Babylonia had already overthrown Nineveh, the capital city of Assyria (612 B.C.). Jehoahaz replaced Josiah as king of Judah but reigned only three months before he was deposed and taken to Egypt by Necho. Jehoiakim (609-597) was Judah's next king, but he reigned as an Egyptian vassal until 605 B.C. when Egypt was defeated by Babylonia at Carchemish. Nebuchadnezzar took Palestine and deported key people like Daniel to Babylon. Judah's king Jehoiakim was now a Babylonian vassal, but he rejected Jeremiah's warnings in 601 B.C. and rebelled against Babylonia. Jehoiachin became Judah's next king in 597 B.C. but was replaced by Zedekiah three months later when Nebuchadnezzar captured Jerusalem and deported Jehoiachin to Babylon. Zedekiah was the last king of Judah because his attempted alliance with Egypt led to Nebuchadnezzar's occupation and overthrow of Jerusalem in 586 B.C.

Thus, there were three stages in Jeremiah's ministry: (1) From 627 to 605 B.C. he prophesied while Judah was threatened by Assyria and Egypt. (2) From 605 to 586 B.C. he proclaimed God's judgment while Judah was threatened and besieged by Babylonia. (3) From 586 to about 580 B.C. he ministered in Jerusalem and Egypt after Judah's downfall.

Theme and Purpose

Theme and Purpose — In Jeremiah, God is seen as patient and holy—He has delayed judgment and appealed to his people to repent before it is too late. As the object lesson at the potter's house demonstrated, a ruined vessel could be repaired while still wet (18:1-4), but once dried, a marred vessel was fit only for the garbage heap (19:10-11). God's warning was clear: Judah's time for repentance would soon pass. Because they defied God's words and refused to repent, the Babylonian captivity was inevitable. Jeremiah listed the moral and spiritual causes for their coming catastrophe, but he also proclaimed God's gracious promise of hope and restoration. There will always be a remnant, and God will establish a new covenant.

Contribution to the Bible — While Isaiah is generally chronological, Jeremiah is not. Following the order of Judah's last kings, this is a possible arrangement of his oracles: Josiah (1-6); Jehoahaz (22:10-12); Jehoiakim (7-20; 25-26; 35-36; 45-46:12; 47-49); Jehoiachin (22-23); Zedekiah (21; 24; 27-34; 37-39); Gedaliah (Nebuchadnezzar's puppet governor of Judah, 40-44).

Jeremiah presents Yahweh as the sovereign Creator and Lord of all people and nations. His love is holy and His compassion is righteous. As the only true God, He hates idolatry and the immorality it produces. Loss of reverence for Yahweh leads to moral degradation and dissolution. During the course of Jeremiah's life, these are the changes that took place:

Beginning	End
Reformation	Retrogression
Assyria in power	Babylonia in power
Jews in the land	Jews deported to Babylon
Jeremiah in Jerusalem	Jeremiah in Egypt
Jeremiah addressing the masses	Jeremiah addressing a remnant
Davidic throne occupied	Davidic throne empty

Christ in Jeremiah — Messiah is clearly seen in 23:1-8 as the coming Shepherd and righteous Branch who will "reign as king and act wisely and do justice and righteousness in the land. In His days Judah will be saved, and Israel will dwell securely; and this is His name by which He will be called, the LORD our righteousness" (23:5b-6). He will bring in the new covenant (31:31-34) which will fulfill God's covenants with Abraham (Gen. 12:1-3; 17:1-8), Moses and the people (Deut. 28-30), and David (2 Sam. 7:1-17).

The curse on Jehoiachin (Jeconiah, Coniah) in 22:28-30

meant that no physical descendant would succeed him to the throne. Matthew 1:1-17 traces the genealogy of Christ through Solomon and Jeconiah to His legal (but not His physical) father Joseph. But no son of Joseph could sit upon the throne of David, for he would be under the curse of Jehoiachin. Luke 3:23-38 traces Christ's lineage backward from Mary (His physical parent) through David's other son Nathan (3:31), thereby avoiding the curse. The righteous Branch will indeed reign on the throne of David.

Lamentations

"How lonely sits the city that was full of people! She has become like a widow who was once great among the nations!"

Lamentations 1:1a

"Is it nothing to all you who pass this way? Look and see if there is any pain like my pain which was severely dealt out to me, which the Lord inflicted on the day of His fierce anger."

Lamentations 1:12
(Also see 2:17; 3:22-23; 5:21.)

Focus	Jerusalem Deserted 1	Jerusalem Destroyed 2	Jeremiah's Distress 3	Jerusalem Defeated 4	Jeremiah's Desire 5
DIVISIONS	Desolation and Sorrow of Jerusalem 1	Indignation of Jehovah upon Jerusalem 2	Lamentation and Prayer of Jeremiah 3	Description of the Siege of Jerusalem 4	Supplication for the Restoration of Jerusalem 5
TOPICS	Lament 1	Lament 2	Lament 3	Lament 4	Lament 5
	God's Chastening and Control				God's Character
	Acrostic Laments				Non-Acrostic Prayer
Location	The Remains of Jerusalem				
Time	Soon After the Fall of Jerusalem (586 or 585 B.C.)				

Talk Thru — For 40 years Jeremiah suffered rejection and abuse for his warnings of coming judgment. When Nebuchadnezzar finally came and destroyed Jerusalem in 586 B.C., a lesser man might have taunted "I told you so!" But Jeremiah compassionately identified with the tragic overthrow of Jerusalem and composed five beautiful and emotional lament poems as a funeral for the once proud city. These dirges reflect the tender heart of the man who was divinely commissioned to communicate a harsh message to a sinful and stiff-necked people. The city, the temple, the palace, and the walls have been reduced to rubble and its inhabitants have been deported to distant Babylonia. Jeremiah's five mournful poems can be entitled: Jerusalem Deserted (1), Jerusalem Destroyed (2), Jeremiah's Distress (3), Jerusalem Defeated (4), and Jeremiah's Desire (5).

Jerusalem Deserted (1): This poem consists of a lamentation by Jeremiah (1-11) and a lamentation by the personified Jerusalem (12-22). The city has been left desolate because of its grievous sins and her enemies "mocked at her ruin" (1:7). Jerusalem pleads with God to regard her misery and recompense her adversaries.

Jerusalem Destroyed (2): In his second elegy, Jeremiah moves from Jerusalem's desolation to a description of her destruction. Babylonia destroyed the city, but only as the Lord's instrument of judgment. Jeremiah presents an eyewitness account of the thoroughness and severity of Jerusalem's devastation (1-10). Through the Babylonians, God terminated all religious observances, removed the priests, prophets, and kings, and razed the temple and palaces. Jeremiah grieves over the suffering the people brought on themselves through rebellion against God (11-19), and Jerusalem's supplications complete the lament (20-22).

Jeremiah's Distress (3): In the first 18 verses, Jeremiah enters into the miseries and despair of his people and makes them his own. But there is an abrupt turn in verses 19-39 as the prophet reflects on the faithfulness and loyal love of the compassionate God of Israel. These truths enable him to find comfort and hope in spite of his dismal circumstances. Jeremiah expresses his deep sorrow (40-54) and petitions God for deliverance and requital (55-66).

Jerusalem Defeated (4): The prophet rehearses the siege of

Jerusalem and remembers the suffering and starvation of the rich and the poor (1-12). He also reviews the causes of the siege, especially the sins of the prophets and priests and their foolish trust in human aid (13-20). This poem closes with a warning to Edom of future punishment and a glimmer of hope for Jerusalem (21-22).

Jerusalem's Desire (5): Jeremiah's last elegy is a melancholy description of his people's lamentable state. Their punishment is complete (1-18), and Jeremiah prayerfully desires the restoration of his nation (19:22).

Title—The Hebrew title of this book comes from the first word of chapters 1, 2, and 4: *'ekah,* "Ah, how!" Another Hebrew word *qinoth,* "elegies, lamentations," has also been used as the title because it better represents the contents of the book. The Greek title *Threnoi* means "dirges, laments," and the Latin title *Threni* ("tears, lamentations") was derived from this word. The subtitle in Jerome's Vulgate reads: "Id est lamentationes Jeremiae prophetae," and this became the basis for the English title "The Lamentations of Jeremiah."

Author — The author of Lamentations is unnamed in the book, but internal and external evidence is consistently in favor of Jeremiah.

External Evidence: The universal consensus of early Jewish and Christian tradition attributes this book to Jeremiah. The superscription to Lamentations in the Septuagint says: "And it came to pass, after Israel had been carried away captive, and Jerusalem had become desolate, that Jeremiah sat weeping, and lamented with this lamentation over Jerusalem saying . . ." This is also the position of the Talmud, the Aramaic Targum of Jonathan, and early Christian writers like Origen and Jerome. In addition, 2 Chronicles 35:25 says that "Jeremiah chanted a lament for Josiah." This was an earlier occasion, but Jeremiah was familiar with the lament form.

Internal Evidence: The scenes in this graphic book were clearly portrayed by an eyewitness of Jerusalem's siege and fall soon after the destruction took place (cf. 1:13-15; 2:6,9; 4:1-12). Jeremiah witnessed the fall of Jerusalem and remained behind after the captives were deported (see Jer. 39). Although some critics claim that the style of Lamentations is different from

Jeremiah, the similarities are in fact striking and numerous, especially in the poetic sections of Jeremiah. Compare these passages from Lamentations and Jeremiah: 1:2 (Jer. 30:14); 1:15 (Jer. 8:21); 1:16 and 2:11 (Jer. 9:1,18); 2:22 (Jer. 6:25); 4:21 (Jer. 49:12). The same compassion, sympathy, and grief over Judah's downfall are evident in both books.

Date and Setting — The historical background of Lamentations can be found in Jeremiah, Date and Setting. The book was written soon after Jerusalem's destruction (Jer. 39; 52) at the beginning of the exile. Nebuchadnezzar laid siege on Jerusalem from January, 588 B.C. to July, 586 B.C. It fell on July 19 and the city and temple were burned on August 15. Jeremiah probably wrote these five elegies before he was taken by his disobedient countrymen into Egypt not long after the destruction (Jer. 43:1-7).

Theme and Purpose — There are three themes that run through the five laments of Jeremiah. The most prominent is the theme of mourning over Jerusalem's holocaust. The holy city has been laid waste and desolate—God's promised judgment for sin has come. In his sorrow, Jeremiah speaks for himself, for the captives, and sometimes for the personified city. The second theme is a confession of sin and acknowledgment of God's righteous and holy judgment upon Judah. The third theme is least prominent but very important: it is a note of hope in God's future restoration of His people. Yahweh has poured out His wrath, but in His mercy He will be faithful to His covenant promises. "The LORD's lovingkindnesses indeed never cease, for His compassions never fail. They are new every morning; great is Thy faithfulness" (3:22-23).

Contribution to the Bible — In the Hebrew text, the first four chapters of Lamentations are alphabetic acrostics. The first word in each of the 22 verses of chapters 1, 2, and 4 begins with the 22 successive letters of the Hebrew alphabet. Chapter 3 has 66 verses because three verses are allotted to each Hebrew letter. Chapter 5 has 22 verses but it is not an acrostic poem. In addition, chapters 1 and 2 have three lines per verse, chapter 4 has two lines per verse, and chapters 3 and 5 have only one line per verse. This elaborate structure stands in balanced contrast to

the passionate and dramatic outpouring of grief in these five lament poems. The acrostic form may have been used to express the full range (from A to Z) of their sufferings, and it may also have been an aid to memory and liturgical use. Jeremiah also chose to use "limping meter" in his poetic lines because this melancholy rhythm was used in funeral dirges. This technique adds to the plaintive mood of lamentation. The Jews publicly read this vivid and tragic book each year to commemorate Jerusalem's destruction in 586 B.C. and again in A.D. 70. In the Hebrew Bible it was placed in the *Megilloth* (the "five rolls") along with the Song of Solomon, Ruth, Esther, and Ecclesiastes. But it follows Jeremiah in the Septuagint as it does in English versions.

While the book of Jeremiah primarily anticipates the fall of Jerusalem, Lamentations reflects back upon it:

Jeremiah's Two Glimpses of Jerusalem's Fall

Christ in Lamentations — The weeping prophet Jeremiah is a type of Christ, the Prophet who wept over the same city six centuries later. "O Jerusalem, Jerusalem, who kills the prophets and stones those who are sent to her! How often I wanted to gather your children together, the way a hen gathers her chicks under her wings, and you were unwilling. Behold, your house is being left to you desolate!" (Matt. 23:37-38). Like Christ, Jeremiah identified himself personally with the plight of Jerusalem and with human suffering caused by sin.

Lamentations also has elements which typify Christ's life and ministry as the man of sorrows who was acquainted with grief. He was afflicted (1:12; 3:19), despised, and derided by His enemies (2:15-16; 3:14,30).

Ezekiel

"Now the end is upon you, and I shall send My anger against you; I shall judge you according to your ways, and I shall bring all your abominations upon you."

Ezekiel 7:3

"And say to them, 'Thus says the Lord God, "Behold, I will take the sons of Israel from among the nations where they have gone, and I will gather them from every side and bring them into their own land.' "

Ezekiel 37:21

Focus	Judah's Fall				Judah's Foes		Judah's Future	
	1			24	25	32	33	48
D I V I S I O N S	Ezekiel's Preparation and Commission	Ezekiel's Signs and Sermons	Vision of the Departing Glory	Signs, Sermons, and Parables of Judgment	Judgment on Surrounding Nations	Judgment on Egypt	Restoration of Judah and Israel	New Temple, Worship and Land
	1 3	4 7	8 11	12 24	25 28	29 32	33 39	40 48
T O P I C S	Condemnation of Judah				Condemnation of Nations		Consolation for Judah	
	Judah's End				Judah's Enemies		Judah's Expectations	
	Before the Siege (592-587)				During the Siege (586)		After the Siege (585-570)	
	Judgment						Restoration	
Location	Ezekiel in Babylon							
Time	22 Years (592-570 B.C.)							

168

Talk Thru— Ezekiel prophesied among the Jewish exiles in Babylon during the last days of Judah's decline and downfall. His message of judgment was similar to that of his older contemporary Jeremiah who had remained in Jerusalem. Judah will be judged because of her unfaithfulness, but God promises her future restoration and blessing. Like Isaiah and Jeremiah, Ezekiel proclaimed a message of horror and hope, of condemnation and consolation. But Ezekiel places special emphasis on the glory of Israel's soverign God who says "They shall know that I am the LORD." Ezekiel spoke of Judah's fall (1-24), Judah's foes (25-32), and Judah's future (33-48).

Judah's Fall (1-24): Ezekiel 1-3 records the prophet's preparation for his great ministry. God gave Ezekiel an overwhelming vision of His divine glory and commissioned him to be His prophet (compare the experiences of Moses in Exodus 3:1-10, Isaiah in 6:1-10, Daniel in 10:5-14, and John in Revelation 1:12-19). Ezekiel was given instruction, enablement, and responsibility. In chapters 4-24 Ezekiel directed his prophecies against the nation God had chosen for Himself. The prophet's signs and sermons (4-7) point to the certainty of Judah's judgment. In 8-11, Judah's past sins and coming doom are seen in a series of visions of the abominations in the temple, the slaying of the wicked, and the departing glory of God. The priests and princes are condemned as the glory leaves the temple, moves to the Mount of Olives, and disappears in the east. Chapters 12-24 speak of the causes and extent of Judah's coming judgment through dramatic signs, powerful sermons, and parables. Judah's prophets are counterfeits and her elders are idolatrous. They have become a fruitless vine and an adulterous wife. Babylon will swoop down like an eagle and pluck them up, and they will not be aided by Egypt. The people are responsible for their own sins, and they are not being unjustly judged for the sins of their ancestors. Judah has been unfaithful, but God promises that her judgment will ultimately be followed by restoration.

Judah's Foes (25-32): Judah's nearest neighbors may gloat over her destruction, but they will be next in line. They too will suffer the fate of siege and destruction by Babylonia. Ezekiel shows the full circle of judgment on the nations that surround Judah by following them in a clockwise circuit: Ammon, Moab, Edom, Philistia, Tyre, and Sidon (25-28). He spends a disproportionate amount of time on Tyre, and many scholars believe that the "king of Tyre" in 28:11-19 may be Satan, the real power behind the nation. Chapters 29-32 contain a series of oracles against Egypt. Unlike the nations in 25-28 that were destroyed by Nebuchadnezzar, Egypt will continue to exist, but as "the lowest of the kingdoms." Since that time it never recovered its former glory or influence.

Judah's Future (33-48): The prophecies in these chapters were given after the overthrow of Jerusalem. Now that the promised judgment has come, Ezekiel's message no longer centers on coming judgment but on the positive theme of comfort and consolation. Just as surely as judgment came, blessing will also come; God's people will be regathered and restored. The mouth of God's watchman Ezekiel opened when he was told that Jerusalem was taken. Judah had false shepherds (rulers), but the true Shepherd will lead them in the future. The vision of the valley of dry bones pictures the reanimation of the nation by the Spirit of God. Israel and Judah will be purified and reunited. There will be an invasion by the northern armies of Gog, but Israel will be saved because the LORD will destroy the invading forces.

In 572 B.C., 14 years after the destruction of Jerusalem, Ezekiel returned in a vision to the fallen city and was given detailed specifications of the reconstruction of the temple, the city, and the land (40-48). After an intricate description of the new outer court, inner court, and temple (40-42), Ezekiel views the return of the glory of the Lord to the temple from the east. Regulations concerning worship in the coming temple (43-46) are followed by revelations concerning the new land and city (47-48).

Title — The Hebrew name *yehezqe'l* means "God strengthens" or "strengthened by God." Ezekiel was indeed strengthened by God for the prophetic ministry to which he was called (3:8-9). This name occurs twice in this book and nowhere else in the Old Testament. The Greek form in the Septuagint is *Iezekiel* and the Latin form in the Vulgate is *Ezechiel*.

Author — Ezekiel the son of Buzi (1:3) had a wife who died as a sign to Judah when Nebuchadnezzar began his final siege on Jerusalem (24:16-24). Like Jeremiah, he was a priest who was called to be a prophet of the Lord. His prophetic ministry shows a priestly emphasis in his concern with the temple, priesthood, sacrifices, and Shekinah (the glory of God). Ezekiel was privileged to receive a number of visions of the power and plan of God, and he was careful and artistic in his written presentation.

Some objections have been raised, but there is no good reason to overthrow the strong evidence in favor of Ezekiel's authorship. This autobiographical book uses the first person singular throughout as the work of a single personality. This person is identified as Ezekiel in 1:3 and 24:24, and internal evidence supports the unity and integrity of Ezekiel's prophetic record. The style, language, and thematic development are consistent through the book, and there are several distinctive phrases that are repeated throughout, like "They shall know that I am the LORD," "son of man," "the word of the LORD came unto me," and the "glory of the LORD."

Date and Setting — Nebuchadnezzar destroyed Jerusalem in three stages. First, in 605 B.C., he overcame Jehoiakim and carried off key hostages including Daniel and his friends. Second, in 597 B.C., the rebelliousness of Jehoiakim and Jehoiachin brought further punishment, and Nebuchadnezzar made Jerusalem submit a second time. He carried off 10,000 hostages including Jehoiachin and Ezekiel. Third, in 586 B.C., Nebuchadnezzar destroyed the city after a long siege and disrupted all of Judah. If "thirtieth year" in 1:1 means Ezekiel's age, he was 25 years old when he was taken to Babylon and 30 years old when he received his prophetic commission (1:2-3). This means he was about 17 when Daniel was deported in 605 B.C., so that Ezekiel and Daniel were about the same age. Both men were about 20 years younger than Jeremiah who was ministering in Jerusalem. According to this chronology, Ezekiel was born in 622 B.C., deported to Babylon in 597, prophesied from 592 to at least 570, and died c. 560. Thus, he overlapped the end of Jeremiah's ministry and the beginning of Daniel's ministry. By the time he arrived in Babylon, Daniel was already well-known, and he is mentioned three times in Ezekiel's prophecy (14:14,20; 28:3). Ezekiel's Babylonian home was at Tel-Abib, the principal colony of Jewish exiles along the river Chebar, Nebuchadnezzar's "Grand Canal" (1:1; 3:15, 24).

From 592 to 586 B.C., Ezekiel found it necessary to convince the disbelieving Jewish exiles that there was no hope of immediate deliverance. But it was not until they heard that Jerusalem was destroyed that their false hopes of returning were dashed.

Ezekiel no doubt wrote this book shortly after the incidents recorded in it occurred. His active ministry lasted for at least 22 years (1:2; 29:17), and his book was probably completed by about 565 B.C.

Theme and Purpose — Like most of the other prophets, Ezekiel's two-fold theme was condemnation (1-32) and consolation (33-48). His ministry to the early Jewish exiles in Babylon was similar to Jeremiah's ministry in Jerusalem. He surveyed the sins which were bringing God's judgment upon the people of Judah and exposed the foolishness of their false hopes of an early return to their homeland. God's judgment on Jerusalem and its temple would surely strike and the Babylonian exile would not be brief. When the city fell, Ezekiel comforted the people by assuring them of God's covenant promise of future blessing and complete restoration. Ezekiel's section on divine consolation is more detailed and extensive than that of his contemporary Jeremiah.

Ezekiel places a strong emphasis on the sovereignty, glory, and faithfulness of God. He concentrates on the temple with its perversion, destruction, and restoration. Another temple-related theme is Ezekiel's fascinating portrayal of God's heavenly glory (1:28; 3:12,23), God's departing glory (9:3; 10:4,18-19; 11:22-23), and God's earthly glory (43:1-5; 44:4). The sovereign purpose of God through judgment and blessing alike is that His people come to know that He is the Lord.

Contribution to the Bible — Ezekiel is a book of methodical style, careful dating, and diligent organization. But this exacting framework houses an unsurpassed depth of mystery and richness of vibrant imagery, symbolism, parables, allegories, and apocalyptic visions. God told him "I have set you as a sign to the house of Israel" (12:6). Nine signs are found in chapters 4-24 and a tenth is in chapter 37: 4:1-3,4-8,9-17; 5:1-17;12:1-7,17-20; 21:1-17,18-23; 22:17-31; 24:15-27; 37:15-17. Ezekiel records six visions (1:4-28; 2:9-3:13; 3:22-23; 8-11; 37:1-10; 40-48) and six parables (15:1-8; 16; 17:1-21,22-24; 23; 24:1-14). Apocalyptic passages are scattered throughout the book (6:1-14;

7:5-12; 20:33-44; 28:25-26; 34:25-31; 36:8-15,33-36; 38-39; 47:1-12).
Some of his images and visions are difficult to interpret, and this
is especially true of chapters 40-48. Students of the Bible are
divided over a spiritual and literal interpretation of these chapters. Those who hold the spiritual view argue that the sacrificial
system has been fulfilled and abolished in Christ, that there is
no temple in the new Jerusalem (Rev. 21:22), and that these
descriptions are being spiritually fulfilled in the church. Those
who hold the literal view argue that the detailed measurements
and lengthy descriptions would be meaningless unless understood literally, that the sacrifices are memorial in nature, that
this will be in effect only in the millennial kingdom before the
new Jerusalem of Revelation 21 appears, and that Israel's
covenant promises are not fulfilled in the church.

Christ in Ezekiel — Ezekiel 17:22-24 depicts Messiah as a
tender twig that becomes a stately cedar on a lofty mountain. He
is called the Branch in Isaiah (11:1), Jeremiah (23:5; 33:15), and
Zechariah (3:8, 6:12). Messiah is the King who has the right to
rule (21:26-27), and He is the true Shepherd who will deliver and
feed His flock (34:11-31).

Daniel

"Daniel answered and said, 'Let the name of God be blessed forever and ever, for wisdom and power belong to Him. And it is He who changes the times and the epochs; He removes kings and establishes kings; He gives wisdom to wise men, and knowledge to men of understanding. It is He who reveals the profound and hidden things; He knows what is in the darkness, and the light dwells with Him.'"

Daniel 2:20-22

(Also see 2:44; 4:17,25,32.)

Focus	The Prophet	The Prophetic Plan for the Gentiles						The Prophetic Plan for Israel		
	1	2					7	8		12
DIVISIONS	Daniel's Training and Testing	Nebuchadnezzar's Dream and God's Plan	Nebuchadnezzar's Image and the Fiery Furnace	Nebuchadnezzar's Tree Vision and Humbling	Belshazzar's Feast and God's Judgment	Darius' Decree and Daniel's Deliverance	Daniel's Dream of the Four Beasts	Daniel's Vision of the Ram and Goat	Daniel's Prophecy of the Seventy Weeks	Daniel's Vision of Israel's Future
	1	2	3	4	5	6	7	8	9 10	12
TOPICS	Daniel's Background	Daniel the Interpreter						Daniel the Dreamer		
	Hebrew	Aramaic						Hebrew		
	Convincing Gentiles of God's Power					Convincing Jews of God's Purposes				
	Historical Narratives					Apocalyptic Visions				
Rulers	Babylonia					Persia	Babylonia	Persia		
	Nebuchadnezzar				Belshazzar	Darius	Belshazzar	Darius	Cyrus	
	1			4	5	6	7 8	9	10	12
Time	70 Years (605-536 B.C.)									

Talk Thru — Daniel, the "Apocalypse of the Old Testament," presents a surprisingly detailed and comprehensive sweep of prophetic history. After an introductory chapter in Hebrew, Daniel switches to Aramaic in chapters 2-7 to describe the future course of the Gentile world powers. Then in 8-12, Daniel reverts back to his native language to survey the future of the Jewish nation under Gentile dominion. The theme of God's sovereign control in the affairs of world history clearly emerges and provides comfort to the Jews whose nation was destroyed by the Babylonians. The Babylonians, Persians, Greeks, and Romans will come and go, but God will establish His kingdom through His people forever. Daniel's three divisions are: The Prophet (1), The Prophetic Plan for the Gentiles (2-7), and The Prophetic Plan for Israel (8-12).

The Prophet (1): This chapter introduces the book by giving the background and preparation of the prophet. Daniel was deported along with other promising youths and placed in an intensive training program in Nebuchadnezzar's court. Their names and diets were changed so that they would lose their Jewish identification, but Daniel's resolve to remain faithful to the Lord was rewarded. He and his friends were granted wisdom and knowledge.

The Prophetic Plan for the Gentiles (2-7): Only Daniel could relate and interpret Nebuchadnezzar's disturbing dream of the great statue (2). God empowered Daniel to foretell the way in which He would sovereignly raise and depose four Gentile empires. Messiah's kingdom will end the times of the Gentiles. Because of his position revealed in the dream, Nebuchadnezzar erected a golden image and demanded that all bow to it (3). The persecution and preservation of Daniel's friends in the fiery furnace again illustrated the power of God. After Nebuchadnezzar refused to respond to the warning of his vision of the tree (4), he was humbled by God until he acknowledged the supremacy of God and the foolishness of his pride. The feast of Belshazzar marked the end of the Babylonian kingdom (5). Belshazzar was judged because of his arrogant defiance of God. In the reign of Darius, a plot against Daniel backfired when he was divinely delivered in the den of lions (6). Daniel's courageous faith was rewarded, and Darius learned a lesson about the might of the God of Israel. The vision of the four beasts (7) supplements the four-part statue vision of

175

chapter 2 in its depiction of the Babylonian, Persian, Greek, and Roman empires. But once again, "the saints of the Highest One will receive the kingdom and possess the kingdom for ever" (7:18).

The Prophetic Plan for Israel (8-12): The focus in chapter 8 narrows to a vision of the ram and goat which shows Israel under the Medo-Persian and Grecian empires. Alexander the Great is the big horn of 8:21 and Antiochus Epiphanes is the little horn of 8:23. After Daniel's prayer of confession for his people, he was privileged to receive the revelation of the 70 weeks (9). This gives the chronology of God's perfect plan for the redemption and deliverance of the people of Israel. The book climaxes in one huge vision which gives amazing details of Israel's future history (10-12). Chapter 11 chronicles the coming kings of Persia and Greece, the wars between the Ptolemies of Egypt and the Seleucids of Syria, and the persecution led by Antiochus. God's people will be saved out of tribulation and resurrected (12).

Title — The name *daniye'l* or *dani'el* means "God is (my) judge," and the book is of course named after the author and principal character. The Greek form *Daniel* in the Septuagint is the basis for the Latin and English titles.

Author — Daniel and his three friends were evidently born into noble Judean families and were "youths in whom there was no defect, who were good-looking, showing intelligence in every branch of wisdom, endowed with understanding, and discerning knowledge" (1:4). He was given three years of training in the best of Babylon's schools (1:5). As part of the reidentification process, he was given a new name that honored one of the Babylonian deities—Belteshazzar meant "Bel protect his life" (see 1:7; 4:8; Jer. 51:44). Daniel's wisdom and divinely-given interpretive abilities brought him into a position of prominence, especially in the courts of Nebuchadnezzar and Darius. He is one of the few well-known Bible characters about whom nothing negative is ever written. His life was characterized by faith, prayer, courage, consistency, and lack of compromise. This "highly esteemed" man (9:23; 10:11,19) was mentioned three times by his sixth century B.C. contemporary Ezekiel as an example of righteousness.

Daniel claimed to write this book (12:4) and he uses the autobiographical first person from 7:2 onward. The Jewish Talmud agrees with this testimony, and Christ attributed a quote from 9:27 to "Daniel the prophet" (Matt. 24:15).

Date and Setting — Babylonia rebelled against the Assyrian Empire in 626 B.C. and overthrew the Assyrian capital of Nineveh in 612 B.C. Babylonia became the master of the Middle East when it defeated the Egyptian armies in 605 B.C. Daniel was among those taken captive to Babylon that year when Nebuchadnezzar subdued Jerusalem. He ministered for the full duration of the Babylonian captivity as a prophet and a governmental official and continued on after Babylon was overcome by the Medes and Persians in 539 B.C. His prophetic ministry was directed to the Gentile courts of Babylonia (Nebuchadnezzar and Belshazzar) and Persia (Darius and Cyrus) as well as his Jewish countrymen. Zerubbabel led a return of the Jews to Jerusalem in the first year of Cyrus, and Daniel lived and ministered at least until the third year of Cyrus (536 B.C.; 10:1). Daniel's final edition of his book was no doubt written by his ninetieth year (c. 530 B.C.). As he predicted, the Persian Empire continued until Alexander the Great (11:2-3) who stretched the Greek Empire as far east as India. The Romans later displaced the Greeks as rulers of the Middle East.

For various reasons, many critics have argued that Daniel is a fraudulent book that was written in the time of the Maccabees in the second century B.C., not the sixth century B.C. as it claims. But their arguments are not compelling: (1) The prophetic argument holds that Daniel could not have made such accurate predictions; it must be a "prophecy after the events." Daniel 11 alone contains over 100 specific prophecies of historical events that literally came true. The author must have lived at the time of Antiochus Epiphanes (175-163 B.C.) and probably wrote this to strengthen the faith of the Jews. But this argument was developed out of a theological bias that assumes true prophecy cannot take place. It also implies that the work was intentionally deceptive. (2) The linguistic argument claims that the book uses a late Aramaic in 2-7 and that the Persian and Greek words also point to a late date. But recent discoveries show that Daniel's Aramaic is actually a form of the early Imperial Aramaic. Daniel's use of some Persian words is no argument for a late date since he lived into the Persian period under Cyrus. The only Greek words are names of instruments in chapter 3, and this comes as no surprise since there were Greek mercenaries in the Assyrian and Babylonian armies. Far more Greek words would be expected if the book were written in the second century B.C. (3) The historical argument asserts that Daniel's historical blunders argue for a late date. But recent evidence has demonstrated the historical accuracy of Daniel. Inscriptions found at Haran show that Belshazzar reigned in Babylon while his father Nabonidus was fighting the invading Persians. And Darius the Mede (5:31,6:1) has been identified as Gubaru, a governor appointed by Cyrus.

Theme and Purpose — Daniel was written to encourage the exiled Jews by revealing God's sovereign program for Israel during and after the period of Gentile domination. The times of the Gentiles began with the Babylonian captivity, and Israel would suffer under Gentile powers for many years. But this period is not permanent, and a time will come when God will establish the Messianic kingdom which will last forever. Daniel repeatedly emphasizes the sovereignty and power of God over human affairs. "The Most High is ruler over the realm of mankind, and bestows it on whomever He wishes" (4:25b). The God who directs the forces of history has not deserted His people. They must continue to trust in Him, because His promises of preservation and ultimate restoration are as sure as the coming of the Messiah.

Contribution to the Bible — While Ezekiel empha-sizes the nation's religious restoration, Daniel concentrates on its political restoration. Daniel was clearly a prophet, but he did not occupy the prophetic office by making public proclamations to the people as God's representative like Jeremiah and Ezekiel. Therefore, this book was placed in the "Writings," the third division of the Hebrew Bible, rather than the Prophets. Because it is apocalyptic literature, Daniel has many similarities to Revelation, particularly in its imagery and symbolism. Some believe that it was fulfilled before or during the first century A.D., but others believe that portions await fulfillment. The second view argues that since the events of the 69 weeks were literally fulfilled in the four kingdoms, the events of the seventi-

eth week will be literally fulfilled in the future.

Christ in Daniel — Christ is the great stone who will crush the kingdoms of this world (2:34-35,44), the Son of Man who is given dominion by the Ancient of Days (7:13-14), and the coming Messiah who will be cut off (9:25-26). It is likely that Daniel's vision in 10:5-9 was an appearance of Christ (cf. Rev. 1:12-16).

The vision of the 69 weeks in 9:25-26 pinpoints the coming of Messiah. The decree of 9:25 took place on March 4, 444 B.C. (Neh. 2:1-8). The 69 weeks of seven years each equals 483 years, or 173,880 days (using 360-day prophetic years). This leads to March 29, 33 A.D., the date of the triumphal entry. This is checked by noting that B.C. 444 to A.D. 33 is 476 years, and 476 times 365.24219 days per year equals 173,855 days. Adding 25 days for the difference between March 4 and March 29 gives 173,880 days.

Prophets of Israel and Judah

Name	Date	Audience	World Power	Biblical Context	Old Testament References to the Prophet	Theme
Isaiah	c 740-680	Pre-exile: Judah	Assyria	2 Kgs. 15:1-20:21 2 Chr. 26:16-32:33	2 Kgs. 19-20 (passim); 2 Chr. 26:22; 32:20, 32; Isa. (passim).	Salvation is of the Lord
Jeremiah	c 627-580	Pre-exile: Judah	Assyria & Babylonia	2 Kgs. 22:3-25:30 2 Chr. 34:1-36:21	2 Chr. 35:25; 36:12, 21f; Ezra 1:1; Dan. 9:2; Jer. (passim).	Warning of Coming Judgment
Ezekiel	c 593-571	Exile: Exiles in Babylonia	Babylonia	2 Kgs. 24:8-25:30 2 Chr. 36:9-21	Ezek. 1:3; 24:24	Glory of the Lord
Daniel	c 605-535	Exile: Exiles in Babylonia	Babylonia & Medo-Persia	2 Kgs. 23:34-25:30 2 Chr. 36:4-23	Ezek. 14:14, 20; 28:3; Dan. (passim)	Sovereignty of God over men and nations
Hosea	c 755-715	Pre-exile: Israel	Assyria	2 Kgs. 14:23-18:12	Hos. 1:1, 2.	Loyal love of God
Joel	c 835	Pre-exile: Judah	Assyria	2 Chr. 12:1-21 2 Chr. 24:1-27	Joel 1:1.	Day of the Lord
Amos	c 760-753	Pre-exile: Israel	Assyria	2 Kgs. 14:23-15:7	Amos 1:1; 7:8-14; 8:2.	Judgment on Israel
Obadiah	c 848-841	Pre-exile: Edom	Assyria	2 Kgs. 8:16-24 2 Chr. 21:1-20	Obad. 1	Doom on Edom
Jonah	c 782-753	Pre-exile: Assyria	Assyria	2 Kgs. 13:10-25; 14:23-29	2 Kgs. 14:25; Jonah (passim).	Salvation to the Gentiles
Micah	c 735-700	Pre-exile: Judah	Assyria	2 Kgs. 15:32-19:37 2 Chr. 27:1-32:23	Micah 1:1; Jer. 26:18.	Injustice of Judah and Justice of God
Nahum	c 664-654	Pre-exile: Assyria	Assyria	2 Kgs. 21:1-18 2 Chr. 33:1-20	Nah. 1:1.	The Destruction of Nineveh
Habakkuk	c 609-605	Pre-exile: Judah	Babylonia	2 Kgs. 23:31-24:7 2 Chr. 36:1-8	Hab. 1:1; 3:1.	The Just shall Live by Faith
Zephaniah	c 632-628	Pre-exile: Judah	Assyria	2 Kgs. 22:1-2 2 Chr. 34:1-7	Zeph. 1:1.	Judgment and Blessing in the Day of the Lord
Haggai	c 520	Post-exile: Jews who returned to Jerusalem from Babylonia	Medo-Persia	Ezra 5:1-6:15	Ezra 5:1; 6:14; Hag. (passim).	Rebuilding the Temple
Zechariah	c 520-480	Post-exile: Jews who returned to Jerusalem from Babylonia	Medo-Persia	Ezra 5:1-6:15	Ezra 5:1; 6:14; Neh. 12:16; Zech. 1:1, 7; 7:1, 8.	Future Blessing for Israel
Malachi	c 432-424	Post-exile: Jews who returned to Jerusalem from Babylonia	Medo-Persia	Neh. 13:1-31	Mal. 1:1.	Appeal to Backsliders

Introduction to the Minor Prophets

While the 17 prophetic books of the Old Testament are the "dark continent of Scripture," people are even more unfamiliar with the 12 minor prophets as a whole than they are with the five major prophets. These 12 books became known as the "minor prophets" late in the 4th century A.D. not because they were considered less important or less inspired, but because they are generally shorter than the five major prophets, especially books like Isaiah and Jeremiah. Their messages are more succinct than those of the major prophets, but they are just as powerful.

Before the time of Christ these 12 books were joined together to make one scroll known collectively as *The Twelve*. Their combined length (67 chapters) is about equal to that of Isaiah. The only chronological significance of the order of the minor prophets in the English Bible is that the first six were written before the last six:

Canonical Order	Chronological Order	Approximate Dates
1. Hosea	1. Obadiah	840
2. Joel	2. Joel	835
3. Amos	3. Jonah	760
4. Obadiah	4. Amos	755
5. Jonah	5. Hosea	740
6. Micah	6. Micah	730

7. Nahum	7. Nahum	660
8. Habakkuk	8. Zephaniah	625
9. Zephaniah	9. Habakkuk	607
10. Haggai	10. Haggai	520
11. Zechariah	11. Zechariah	515
12. Malachi	12. Malachi	430

The minor prophets from Obadiah to Malachi cover a 400-year span of history moving through the Assyrian, Babylonian, and Persian Empires. Three were prophets to the northern kingdom (Jonah, Amos, Hosea), six were prophets to the southern kingdom (Obadiah, Joel, Micah, Nahum, Zephaniah, Habakkuk), and three were post-exilic prophets (Haggai, Zechariah, Malachi). Although all the minor prophets are named, very little is known about most of them. Their backgrounds and personalities are quite diverse, but the four basic prophetic themes are found in all of them (see Introduction to the Major Prophets).

Hosea: The unhappy story of Hosea and his faithless wife Gomer illustrates the loyal love of God and the spiritual adultery of Israel. Hosea exposes the sins of Israel and contrasts them to God's holiness. The nation must be judged for its sins but it will be restored in the future because of the love and faithfulness of God.

Joel: This book looks back to a recent locust plague that decimated the land of Judah to illustrate the far more terrifying Day of the Lord. The land will be invaded by a fearsome army that will make the locusts seem mild in comparison. Nevertheless, God appeals to the people to repent in order to divert the coming disaster. Because the people will not change, judgment will come, but it will be followed by great blessing.

Amos: The northern kingdom was in its heyday when Amos warned the people of their coming doom. In eight pronouncements of judgment, Amos spirals around the surrounding countries before landing on Israel. He then delivers three sermons to list the sins of the house of Israel and call for repentance. The people reject Amos' warnings and their coming judgment is portrayed in a series of five visions. But Amos closes his book with a brief word of future hope.

Obadiah: This obscure prophet of the southern kingdom directs his brief oracle to the nation of Edom that bordered

Judah on the southeast. Edom (descended from Esau) refused to act as his brother's keeper toward Judah (descended from Jacob). Because they gloated when Jerusalem was invaded, their judgment would be nothing less than total destruction.

Jonah: With a prophetic message of only one line, Jonah is the most biographical of all the prophets. The repentant response of the people of Nineveh to Jonah's terse oracle causes the God of mercy to spare the city. But the central teaching of the book is the lesson on compassion God has to teach His reluctant prophet. Jonah learns to look beyond his nation and trust the Creator of all people.

Micah: The prophecy of Micah begins with a word of divine retribution against Israel and Judah because of the radical corruption on every level of society: rulers, prophets, priests, judges, businessmen, and landlords. But God's covenant promises will be fulfilled in the future kingdom of Messiah. Judgment will ultimately be followed by forgiveness and restoration, and the book ends on a strong note of promise.

Nahum: About 125 years after Nineveh repented under the preaching of Jonah, Micah predicted the imminent destruction of the same city. The people in the Assyrian capital have reverted back to idolatry and brutality, and Assyria has overthrown the northern kingdom of Israel. Because of God's holiness and power, Nineveh will surely be destroyed in spite of its apparent invincibility.

Habakkuk: Very close to the end of the kingdom of Judah, Habakkuk asks God why He is not dealing with the wickedness of his nation. When God tells him He is about to use the Babylonians as His rod of judgment, Habakkuk asks a second question: How can He judge Judah with a nation that is even more wicked? After the Lord's second response, the prophet magnifies the name of God for His power and purposes.

Zephaniah: In no uncertain terms, Zephaniah develops the theme of the coming day of the Lord as a day of awesome judgment followed by great blessing. Zephaniah begins with the coming judgment of Judah and broadens his scope to include the Gentiles as well. Because Judah refuses to seek the Lord, it stands condemned. But a remnant will exult when God restores the fortunes of His people.

Haggai: After the Babylonian exile, the Jews began to rebuild the temple but allowed the work to stop while they rebuilt their own houses instead. Because of their failure to put God first, they were not enjoying His blessing in the land. Haggai urges the people to finish the temple because of God's promise that it would be filled with glory. After chastening the people for their contamination, Haggai closes with a promise of future blessing.

Zechariah: A contemporary of Haggai, Zechariah also exhorts the Jews to complete the construction of the temple. Zechariah's method of motivating them is one of encouragement — the temple is central to Israel's spiritual heritage, and it is related to the coming of Messiah. Zechariah's series of visions, messages, and burdens offer some of the clearest Messianic prophecies in Scripture. God reveals that His program for his people is far from completed.

Malachi: By the time of the last Old Testament prophet, the spiritual and moral climate of the people has grown cold. Their worship is meaningless and indifferent, and as they grow more distant from God, they become characterized by religious and social compromise. A terrible day of judgment is coming when "all the arrogant and every evildoer will be chaff" to be burned, "But for you who fear My name the sun of righteousness will rise with healing in its wings."

Hosea

"As they had their pasture, they became satisfied, and being satisfied, their heart became proud; therefore, they forgot Me."

Hosea 13:6

"Return, O Israel, to the LORD your God, for you have stumbled because of your iniquity."

Hosea 14:1

(Also see 6:4-6; 14:4.)

Focus	Illustration of God and Israel			Israel's Sin and God's Holiness	Israel's Suffering and God's Justice	Israel's Salvation and God's Love
	1		3	4 7	8 10	11 14
D I V I S I O N S	Marriage of Hosea and Gomer	Unfaithfulness of Gomer	Reunion of Hosea and Gomer	Reprobation of Israel	Retribution of Israel	Restoration of Israel
	1	2	3	4 7	8 10	11 14
T O P I C	Sin	Judg- ment	Restor- ation	Sin	Judgment	Restoration
	Sins Illustrated			Sin Exposed	Sin Judged	Sinners Forgiven
	Faithless Wife and Forgiving Husband			Faithless Nation and Forgiving Lord		
	The Marriage of Hosea (Narrative)			The Message of Hosea (Sermons)		
Loca- tion	Northern Kingdom of Israel					
Time	About 755 B.C. to 710 B.C.					

Talk Thru — Hosea was called by God to prophesy during Israel's last hours just as Jeremiah would prophesy years later to the crumbling kingdom of Judah. As one commentator noted, "What we see in the prophesy of Hosea are the last few swirls as the kingdom of Israel goes down the drain." This book represents God's last gracious effort to plug the drain. Hosea's personal tragedy was an intense illustration of Israel's national tragedy. It is a story of one-sided love and faithfulness which represents the relationship between Israel and Yahweh. Just as Gomer was married to Hosea, Israel was betrothed to God. Both relationships gradually disintegrated — Gomer ran after other men, and Israel ran after other gods. Israel's spiritual adultery is illustrated in Gomer's physical adultery. The development of the book can be traced in this way: Illustration of God and Israel (1-3), Israel's Sin and God's Holiness (4-7), Israel's Suffering and God's Justice (8-10), Israel's Salvation and God's Love (11-14).

Illustration of God and Israel (1-3): Hosea married a woman named Gomer who bore him three children appropriately named by God as signs to Israel. Jezreel, Lo-ruhamah, and Lo-ammi mean "God scatters," "not pitied," and "not my people." Similarly, God will judge and scatter Israel because of her sin.

Gomer sought other lovers and deserted Hosea. In spite of the depth to which her sin carried her, Hosea redeemed her from the slave market and restored her.

Israel's Sin and God's Holiness (4-7): Because of his own painful experience, Hosea could feel some of the sorrow of God over the sinfulness His people. His loyal love for Gomer was a reflection of God's concern for Israel. But Israel had fallen into the dregs of sin and was hardened to God's gracious last appeal to return. The people had flagrantly violated all of God's commandments, and they are indicted by the holy God for their crimes. Even now God would heal and redeem them (7:1,13), but in their arrogance and idolatry they rebelled.

Israel's Suffering and God's Justice (8-10): These chapters give the verdict of the case God has just presented. Israel's disobedience will lead to her dispersion. "For they sow the wind" (4-7), "and they reap the whirlwind" (8-10). Israel spurned repentance, and the judgment of God could no longer be delayed.

Israel's Salvation and God's Love (11-14): God is holy (4-7) and just (8-10), but He is also loving and gracious (11-14). God must discipline, but because of His endless love, He will ultimately save and restore His wayward people. "How can I give you up, O Ephraim? . . . I will heal their apostasy, I will love them freely, for My anger has turned away from them" (11:8; 14:4).

Title

Title — The names Hosea, Joshua, and Jesus are all derived from the same Hebrew root word. The word *hoshea* means "salvation," but Joshua and Jesus have an additional idea: "Yahweh is salvation" (see Joshua, Title). As God's messenger, Hosea offered the possibility of salvation if only the nation would turn from idolatry back to God. Israel's last king, Hoshea, had the same name as the prophet even though the English Bible spells them differently. Hosea in the Greek and Latin is *Osee*.

Author

Author — There is little critical refutation of the claim in 1:1 that Hosea is the author of this book. His home town is not given, but his familiarity and obvious concern with the northern kingdom indicate that he lived in Israel, not Judah. This is also seen when he calls the king of Samaria "our King" (7:5). Hosea was the son of Beeri (1:1), husband of Gomer (1:3), and father of two sons and a daughter (1:4,6,9). Nothing more is known of him since he is not mentioned elsewhere in the Bible.

Hosea had a real compassion for his people, and his personal suffering because of Gomer gave him some understanding of God's grief over their sin. Thus his words of coming judgment were passionately delivered but tempered with a heart of tenderness. He upbraids his people for their lying, murder, insincerity, ingratitude, idolatry, and covetousness with cutting metaphors and images, but his messages are punctuated with consolation and future hope.

Date and Setting

Date and Setting — Hosea addressed the northern kingdom of Israel (5:1), often called Ephraim after the largest tribe (5:3, 5, 11, 13). According to 1:1, he ministered during the reigns of Uzziah (767-739), Jotham (739-731), Ahaz (731-715), and Hezekiah (715-686), kings of Judah. When Hosea began his ministry, Jeroboam II (782-753) was still reigning in Israel. This makes Hosea a younger contemporary of Amos, another prophet to the northern kingdom. Hosea was also a contemporary of Isaiah and Micah who ministered to the southern kingdom. Hosea's long career continued after the time of Jeroboam II and spanned the reigns of the last six kings of Israel from Zechariah (753-752) to Hoshea (732-722). Hosea evidently compiled this book in the early years of Hezekiah, and his ministry stretched from c. 755 B.C. to c. 710 B.C. The book of Hosea represents about 40 years of sermons.

When Hosea began his ministry, Israel was enjoying a temporary period of political and economic prosperity under Jeroboam II. But this was short-lived, and Israel began to crumble after Tiglath-pileser III (745-727) strengthened Assyria. The reigns of Israel's last six kings were relatively brief since four were murdered and a fifth was carried captive to Assyria. Confusion and decline characterized the last years of the northern kingdom, and they refused to heed Hosea's warning of imminent judgment. The people were in a spiritual stupor, riddled with sin and idolatry.

Theme and Purpose — The themes of chapters 1-3 echo throughout the rest of the book. The adultery of Gomer (1) illustrates the sin of Israel (4-7); the degradation of Gomer (2) represents the judgment of Israel (8-10); and Hosea's redemption of Gomer (3) pictures the restoration of Israel (11-14). More than any other Old Testament prophet, Hosea's personal experiences illustrated his prophetic message. In his relationship to Gomer, Hosea portrayed God's faithfulness, justice, love, and forgiveness toward His people. The theme of God's holiness is developed in contrast to Israel's corruption and apostasy. Hosea utters about 150 statements concerning the sins of Israel, and more than half deal specifically with idolatry. The theme of God's justice is contrasted with Israel's lack of justice. There was never a good king in Israel, and judgment is long overdue. The theme of God's love is seen in contrast to Israel's hardness and empty ritual. God's loyal love is unconditional and ceaseless; in spite of Israel's manifold sins, God tries every means to bring His people back to Himself. He pleads with the people to return to Him, but they will not. "Return, O Israel, to the LORD your God, for you have stumbled because of your iniquity" (14:1).

Contribution to the Bible — Hosea is the first of the 12

minor prophets, perhaps because of its size. The New Testament quotes or alludes to its vivid statements several times: 1:10 (Rom. 9:25-27; 2 Cor. 6:18), 2:23 (Rom. 9:25-26; 1 Pet. 2:10), 6:6 (Matt. 9:13; 12:7); 10:8 (Luke 23:30; Rev. 6:16), 11:1 (Matt. 2:14-15), 13:14 (1 Cor. 15:55), and 14:2 (Heb. 13:15).

There are different views concerning Hosea's marriage to Gomer. Some see it as a fictional allegory of God and Israel, but there is little basis for this position. Chapters 1-3 are presented as a straightforward narrative, and there are no indications that it is fictitious. Although Hosea was told to take a "wife of harlotry" (1:2), this does not necessarily mean that Gomer was a harlot before her marriage to Hosea. This passage may be looking ahead to what she would become.

Christ in Hosea — Matthew 2:15 applied Hosea 11:1 to Christ in Egypt: "When Israel was a youth I loved him, and out of Egypt I called My son." Matthew quotes the second half of this verse to show that the exodus of Israel from Egypt as a new nation was a prophetic type of Israel's Messiah who was also called out of Egypt in His childhood. Both Israel and Christ left Palestine to take refuge in Egypt.

Christ's identification with our plight and His loving work of redemption can be seen in Hosea's redemption of Gomer from the slavemarket.

Joel

"Alas for the day! For the day of the LORD is near, and it will come as destruction from the Almighty."

Joel 1:15

"Then you will know that I am the LORD your God, dwelling in Zion My holy mountain. So Jerusalem will be holy, and strangers will pass through it no more."

Joel 3:17

Focus	The Day of the Locust		The Day of the Lord		The Day of Deliverance			
	1:1 1:20		2:1 2:17		2:18 3:21			
D I V I S I O N S	The Devastation of the Land	The Desolation of the Land	The Invasion of the Land	The Invitation to Repent	The Recovery of the People	The Reception of the Spirit	The Retribution upon the Nations	The Restoration of the People
	1:1 1:14	1:15 1:20	2:1 2:11	2:12 2:17	2:18 2:27	2:28 2:32	3:1 3:17	3:18 3:21
T O P I C S	Historic Invasion		Prophetic Invasion		Promised Blessing		Final Triumph	
	Destruction				Restoration			
	God's Dealings in Nature		God's Dealings with Israel and the Nations					
	History		Prophecy					
Loca-tion	Southern Kingdom of Judah							
Time	About 835 B.C.							

Talk Thru — The brief book of Joel develops the crucial theme of the coming day of the Lord (1:15; 2:1,2,11,31; 3:14,18). It is a time of awesome judgment upon people and nations that have rebelled against God. But it is also a time of future blessing upon those who have trusted in Him. The theme of disaster runs through the book (locust plagues, famine, raging fires, invading armies, celestial phenomena), but promises of hope are interspersed in the pronouncements of coming judgment. The outline of Joel is: The Day of the Locust (1:1-20), The Day of the Lord (2:1-17), and The Day of Deliverance (2:18-3:21).

The Day of the Locust (1:1-20): Joel begins with an account of a recent locust plague that devastated the land. The black cloud of insects stripped the grapevines and fruit trees and ruined the grain harvest. The economy was brought to a standstill, and the people were in a desperate situation (1:13-14).

The Day of the Lord (2:1-17): Joel made effective use of this natural catastrophe as an illustration of a far greater judgment to come. Compared to the terrible day of the Lord, the destruction by the locusts would seem insignificant. The land will be invaded by a swarming army — like locusts they will be speedy and voracious. The desolation caused by this army will be dreadful: "The day of the LORD is indeed great and very awesome, and who can endure it?" (2:11b).

Even so, it is not too late for the people to avert disaster. The prophetic warning is designed to bring them to the point of repentance (2:12-17). " 'Yet even now,' declared the LORD, 'return to Me with all your heart, and with fasting, weeping, and mourning' " (2:12). But God's gracious offer fell on deaf ears.

The Day of Deliverance (2:18-3:21): The swarming, creeping, stripping and gnawing locusts (1:4; 2:25) will come again in a fiercer form. But God promises that judgment will be followed by great blessing in a material (2:18-27) and spiritual (2:28-32) sense.

These rich promises are followed by a solemn description of the judgment of all nations in the valley of decision (3:14) in the end times. The nations will give an account of themselves to the God of Israel who will judge those who rebelled against Him. Yahweh alone controls the course of history. "Then you will know that I am the LORD your God, dwelling in Zion My holy mountain" (3:17). Joel ends with the kingdom blessings upon the remnant of faithful Judah. "But Judah will be inhabited forever, and Jerusalem for all generations" (3:20).

Title— The Hebrew name *yo'el* means "Yahweh is God." This name is appropriate to the theme of the book which emphasizes God's sovereign acts in history. The courses of nature and nations are in His hand. The Greek equivalent is *'Ioel,* and the Latin is *Joel.*

Author— Although there are several other Joels in the Bible, the prophet Joel is known only from this book. In the introductory verse, Joel identifies himself as the son of Pethuel ("persuaded of God," 1:1). His frequent references to Zion and the house of the Lord (1:9,13-14; 2:15-17,23,32; 3:1,5-6,16-17,20-21) suggest that he probably lived not far from Jerusalem. Because of his statements about the priesthood in 1:13-14; 2:17, some think Joel was a priest as well as a prophet. In any case, Joel was a clear, concise, and uncompromising preacher of repentance.

Date and Setting — Since there are no explicit time references in this book, it cannot be dated with certainty. Some commentators assign a late date (usually post-exilic) to Joel for these reasons: (1) It does not mention the northern kingdom; this indicates it was written after the 722 B.C. demise of Israel. (2) The references to priests but not kings fits the post-exilic period. (3) Joel does not refer to Assyria, Syria, or Babylonia, evidently because these countries have already been overthrown. (4) If Joel 3:2 refers to the Babylonian captivity this also supports the post-exilic date. (5) The mention of the Greeks in 3:6 argues for a late date. Commentators who believe Joel was written in the 9th century B.C. answer the above arguments in this way: (1) Joel's failure to mention the northern kingdom is an argument from silence. His prophecy was directed to Judah, not Israel. (2) Other early prophets omit references to a king (Obadiah, Jonah, Nahum, Habakkuk). This also fits the political situation in 841-835 B.C.; Athaliah usurped the throne upon the death of her husband Ahaziah. Joash, the legitimate heir to the throne, was a minor and protected by the high priest Jehoiada. When Athaliah was removed from power in 835, Joash came to the throne but ruled under the regency of Jehoiada. Thus, the prominence of the priests and lack of reference to a king in Joel fit this historical context. (3) It is true that Joel does not mention Assyria or Babylonia, but the countries Joel *mentions* are more crucial. These are Phoenicia, Philistia, Egypt, and Edom, and these countries were prominent in the 9th century but not later. Assyria and Babylonia are not mentioned because they had not yet reached a position of power. Also, if Joel was post-exilic, a reference to Persia would be expected. (4) Joel 3:2 does not refer to the Babylonian captivity but to an event that has not yet occurred. (5) Greeks are mentioned in Assyrian records back into the 8th century B.C. It is just an assumption to state that the Hebrews had no knowledge of the Greeks at an early time.

There is also evidence of borrowing between Joel and Amos (cf. Joel 3:16 and Amos 1:2; Joel 3:18 and Amos 9:13). The context of the books suggests that Amos, an 8th-century prophet, borrowed from Joel. Also, Joel's style is more like Hosea and Amos than that of post-exilic writers. The evidence seems to favor a date of about 835 B.C. for Joel, during the reigns of Athaliah or Joash. Since Joel does not mention idolatry, it may have been written after the purge of Baal worship and most other forms of idolatry in the early reign of Joash under Jehoiada the priest. As an early prophet of Judah, Joel would have been a contemporary of Elisha in Israel.

Theme and Purpose—The key theme of Joel is the day of the Lord in retrospect and prospect. The terrible locust plague that recently occurred in Judah was used by Joel to illustrate the coming day of judgment when God directly intervenes in human history to vindicate His righteousness. This will be a time of unparalleled retribution upon Israel (2:1-11) and the nation: (3:1-17), but it will culminate in great blessing and salvation for all who trust in the Lord (2:18-32; 3:18-21). "And it will come about that whoever calls on the name of the LORD will be delivered" (2:32a).

Joel was written as a warning to the people of Judah of their need to humbly turn to the Lord with repentant hearts (2:12-17) so that God could bless rather than buffet them. If they continue to spurn God's gracious call for repentance, judgment will be inevitable. Joel stresses the sovereign power of Yahweh over nature and nations, and shares how God uses nature to get the attention of men.

Contribution to the Bible — Joel is characterized by graphic style and vivid descriptions. He makes striking use of a historical event as an illustrative foundation for the overall message of the book. Although Obadiah was the first prophet to mention the day of the Lord (Obad. 15), Joel was the first to develop this important biblical theme. Other references to the day of the Lord include: Isaiah 2:12,17-20; 3:7-18; 4:1-2; 13:6-9; Jeremiah 46:10; Ezekiel 13:5; 30:3; Amos 5:18; Zephaniah 1:7,14; Malachi 4:5; 1 Corinthians 5:5; 1 Thessalonians 5:2. It is clear from 2 Thessalonians 2:2 and 2 Peter 3:10 that the day of the Lord is a future event from the New Testament perspective. Peter quoted Joel 2:28-32 in his sermon on the day of Pentecost in Acts 2:16-21, but stopped in the middle of verse 32. In His Olivet Discourse (Matt. 24:29), Jesus associated the events mentioned in Joel 2:10,31; 3:15 with the signs of His second coming. The apostle Paul applied Joel 2:32 to the salvation available to Jews and Gentiles who trust in Christ (Rom. 10:12-13).

Christ in Joel — Christ promised to send the Holy Spirit after His ascension to the Father (John 16:7-15; Acts 1:8). When this was fulfilled on the day of Pentecost, Peter said, "This is what was spoken of through the prophet Joel" (Joel 2:28-32; Acts 2:16-21). Joel also portrays Christ as the One who will judge the nations in the valley of Jehoshaphat ("Yahweh judges") in 3:2,12.

Amos

"You only have I chosen among all the families of the earth;
Therefore, I will punish you for all your iniquities."

Amos 3:2

"Therefore, I will make you go into exile beyond Damacus," says
the LORD, whose name is the God of hosts."

Amos 5:27

(Also see 1:2; 4:12; 5:4,24.)

Focus	Pronounce-ment of Judgment	Provocations For Judgment	Pictures of Judgment	Promises after Judgment
	1　　　　2	3　　　　6	7　　　　9:10	9:11　　　　9:15
D I V I S I O N S	Amos' Funnel of Fire (Judgment upon the Nation)	The Sins and Judgment of Israel	Portraits of Israel's Judgment	Restoration of Israel
T O P I C S	Eight Oracles	Three Sermons	Five Visions	Three Promises
	Vengeance	Vindication	Visions	Victory
	Sentences	Sermons	Scenes	Securities
	"Thus says the Lord"	"Hear this word"	"Thus God showed Me"	" 'I will,' declares the Lord"
Loca-tions	Surrounding Nations	Northern Kingdom of Israel		
Time	About 760-753 B.C.			

Talk Thru — Amos' message of the coming doom of the northern kingdom of Israel seemed preposterous to the people. External circumstances never looked better in the north — it was a time of booming business, bulging boundaries, and soaring optimism. But the internal conditions never looked worse — injustice, greed, hypocrisy, oppression, and arrogance. It is no surprise that Amos' earnest and forceful message against Israel's sins and abuses was poorly received. The "prophet of Israel's Indian summer" presented a painfully clear message: "prepare to meet your God, O Israel" (4:12). The four divisions of Amos are: Pronouncements of Judgment (1-2), Provocations for Judgment (3-6), Pictures of Judgment (7-9:10) and Promises After Judgment (9:11-15).

Pronouncements of Judgment (1-2): Amos was called by God to the unenviable task of leaving his homeland in Judah to preach a harsh message of judgment to Israel. Each of his eight oracles in chapters 1-2 begins with the statement "For three transgressions of _____ and for four." The fourth transgression is equivalent to the last straw; the iniquity of each of the eight countries is full. Amos begins with the nations that surround Israel as his catalog of catastrophe gradually spirals in on Israel itself. Seven times God declares, "I will send fire" (1:4,7,10,12,14; 2:2,5), a symbol of judgment.

Provocations for Judgment (3-6): In these chapters, Amos delivers three sermons, each beginning with the phrase "Hear this word" (3:1; 4:1; 5:1). The first sermon (3) is a general pronouncement of judgment because of Israel's iniquities. The second sermon (4) exposes the crimes of the people and describes the ways God chastened them in order to draw them back to Himself. Five times He said, "Yet you have not returned to Me" (4:6,8,9,10,11). The third sermon (5-6) lists the sins of the house of Israel and calls them to repent. But they hate integrity, justice, and compassion, and their refusal to turn to Yahweh will lead to their exile. Although they arrogantly wallow in luxury, their time of prosperity will suddenly come to an end.

Pictures of Judgment (7-9:10): Amos' three sermons are followed by five visions of coming judgment upon the northern kingdom. The first two judgments of locusts and fire did not come to pass because of Amos' intercession. The third vision of the plumbline is followed by the only narrative section in the book (7:10-17). Amaziah the priest of Bethel wanted Amos to go back to Judah. The fourth vision pictures Israel as a basket of rotten fruit overripe for judgment. The fifth vision is a relentless depiction of Israel's unavoidable judgment.

Promises After Judgment (9:11-15): Amos has hammered upon the theme of divine retribution with oracles, sermons, and visions. Nevertheless, he ends his book on a note of consolation, not condemnation. God promises to reinstate the Davidic line (9:11-12), to renew the land (9:13), and to restore the people (9:14-15).

Title — The name *'amos* is derived from the Hebrew root *'amas*, "to lift a burden, to carry." Thus, his name means "burden" or "burden bearer." Amos lived up to the meaning of his name by bearing up under his divinely given burden of declaring judgment to rebellious Israel. The Greek and Latin titles are *'Amos* and *Amos.*

Author — The only Old Testament appearance of the name Amos is in this book (he should not be confused with Amoz, the father of Isaiah). Concerning his background, Amos said, "I am not a prophet, nor am I the son of a prophet; for I am a herdsman and a grower of sycamore figs" (7:14). But he was gripped by God and divinely commissioned to bring his prophetic burden to Israel (3:8b; 7:15). He came from the rural area of Tekoa in Judah, 12 miles south of Jerusalem, where he tended a special breed of small sheep that produced wool of the best quality. As a grower of sycamore figs, he had to puncture the fruit before it ripened to allow the insects inside to escape. Amos lived a disciplined life, and his knowledge of the wilderness often surfaces in his messages (cf. 3:4-5, 12; 5:8,19; 9:9). Amos was from the country, but he was well-educated in the Scriptures. His keen sense of morality and justice is obvious, and his objective appraisal of Israel's spiritual condition was not well received, especially since he was from Judah. He delivered his message in Bethel because it was the residence of the king of Israel and a center of idolatry. His frontal attack on the greed, injustice, and self-righteousness of the people of the northern kingdom made his words unpopular.

Date and Setting — Amos prophesied "in the days of Uzziah king of Judah, and in the days of Jeroboam son of Joash,

king of Israel, two years before the earthquake" (1:1). Uzziah reigned in 767-739 B.C., and Jeroboam II reigned in 782-753 B.C., leaving an overlap from 767 B.C. to 753 B.C. Over 200 years later, Zechariah referred to this earthquake in Uzziah's reign (Zech. 14:5). Amos 7:11 anticipates the 722 B.C. Assyrian captivity of Israel and indicates that at the time of writing, Jeroboam II was not yet dead. Thus, Amos prophesied in Bethel around 755 B.C. Astronomical calculations indicate that a solar eclipse took place in Israel on June 15, 763 B.C. This event was probably fresh in the minds of Amos' hearers (see 8:9).

Amos ministered after the time of Obadiah, Joel, and Jonah and just before Hosea, Micah, and Isaiah. At this time, Uzziah reigned over a prosperous and militarily successful Judah. He fortified Jerusalem and subdued the Philistines, Ammonites, and Edomites. In the north, Israel was ruled by the capable king Jeroboam II. Economic and military circumstances were almost ideal, but prosperity only increased the materialism, immorality, and injustice of the people (2:6-8; 3:10; 4:1; 5:10-12; 8:4-6). During these years, Assyria, Babylonia, Syria, and Egypt were relatively weak. Thus, the people of Israel found it hard to imagine the coming disaster predicted by Amos. But it was only three decades until the downfall of Israel.

Theme and Purpose — The basic theme of Amos is the coming judgment of Israel because of the holiness of Yahweh and the sinfulness of His covenant people. Amos unflinchingly and relentlessly visualizes the causes and course of Israel's quickly approaching doom. God is gracious and patient, but His justice and righteousness will not allow sin to go unpunished indefinitely. The sins of Israel are heaped as high as heaven: empty ritualism, oppression of the poor, idolatry, deceit, self-righteousness, arrogance, greed, materialism, callousness. The people have repeatedly broken every aspect of their covenant relationship with God. Nevertheless, God's mercy and love are evident in His offer of deliverance if the people will only turn back to Him. God graciously sent Amos as a reformer to warn the people of Israel of their fate if they refused to repent. But they rejected his plea, and the course of judgment could not be altered.

Contribution to the Bible — The proportion of

judgment compared to hope and blessing is higher in Amos than in the other prophets. Only the last five verses offer a word of consolation and promise. Amos stands as one of the Bible's most direct and incisive prophets. Consider, for example, his description of the greedy women of Samaria: "Hear this word, you cows of Bashan who are on the mountain of Samaria" (4:1). Amos was the first of the two writing prophets to the northern kingdom (3:1,12; 7:10,14-15). Unlike Hosea, he was a resident of Judah, not Israel. Here are some *generalized* comparisons between their two books:

Hosea	Amos
1. Preaches against idolatry	1. Preaches against injustice
2. Commands the people to know God	2. Commands the people to seek God
3. Rebukes religious inequities	3. Rebukes social inequities
4. Aims at their worship of God	4. Aims at their walk with God
5. Stresses their need for the knowledge of God	5. Stresses their need for justice
6. "I don't delight in your sacrifices"	6. "I hate your offerings"
7. Majors on image worship	7. Little on image worship
8. Describes Israel as a privileged people	8. Describes Israel as a privileged people
9. Much about the loyal love of God	9. Little about the loyal love of God
10. Called for repentance	10. Aroused the conscience
11. Addresses Israel as family	11. Addresses Israel as a state
12. Deals with his homeland	12. Deals with foreigners
13. A national message	13. A universal message
14. Refers much to the past	14. Refers little to the past
15. Grace of God	15. Righteousness of God
16. Lovingkindness	16. Wrath
17. Complex character	17. Simple character
18. A poet	18. A philosopher
19. A mystic	19. A moralist
20. Sympathetic	20. Stern

Amos displays a detailed understanding of the Pentateuch. Compare these examples: 2:7 (Deut. 23:17-18); 2:8 (Exod. 22:26); 2:12 (Num. 6:1-21); 4:4 (Deut. 14:28; 26:12); 4:5 (Lev. 2:11; 7:13). Amos is quoted in Matthew, Acts, and Romans: 4:11 (Rom. 9:29); 5:25-27) (Acts 7:42-43); 8:9 (Matt. 24:29); 9:11-12 (Acts 15:16-18).

Christ in Amos — The clearest anticipation of Christ in Amos is found at the end of the book. He has all authority to judge (1:1-9:10), but He will also restore His people (9:11-15).

Obadiah

"Because of violence to your brother Jacob, you will be covered with shame, and you will be cut off forever."

Obadiah 10

"For the day of theLORD draws near on all the nations. As you have done, it will be done to you. Your dealings will return on your own head."

Obadiah 15

Focus	Condemnation		Cause		Consummation		
	1	9	10	14	15		21
D I V I S I O N S	Revelation of Edom's Judgment		Reasons for Edom's Judgment		Removal of Edom		Restoration of Judah
	1	9	10	14	15	16	17 21
T O P I C S	Arrogance of Edom		Antagonism of Edom		Annihilation of Edom		
	Arraignment		Indictment		Sentence		
	Destruction of Edom				Day of the Lord		Deliverance of Judah
	Security on the Mountain of Esau (v. 3)				Sentence on the Mountain of Esau (v. 21)		
Loca-tion	Edom				The Nations		Israel and Judah
Time	Probably c. 840 B.C.						

Talk Thru — The struggle between Esau and Jacob contin-ued in the form of an ongoing struggle between their descen-dants in the nations of Edom and Israel. Edom (Esau) refused to act as a brother to Judah (Jacob), and maintained a fierce enmity with the offspring of Jacob for over 1,000 years. This national rivalry became especially heinous when the Edomites reveled over the defeat and looting of Jerusalem by a foreign power. Instead of being his brother's keeper, Edom participated in the crime.

Obadiah is the shortest book in the Old Testament (only 21 verses), but it embodies one of its strongest messages of judgment. For Edom, there are no pleas to return, no words of consolation or hope. Edom's fate is sealed, and there are no conditions for possible deliverance. God will bring total destruc-tion upon Edom, and there will be no remnant. Obadiah is Edom's day in court, complete with Edom's arraignment, indict-ment, and sentence. This "prophet of poetic justice" describes how the Judge of the earth will overthrow the pride of Edom and restore the house of Jacob. The three sections of Obadiah are Condemnation (1-9), Cause (10-14), and Consummation (15-21).

Condemnation (1-9): The first section of Obadiah makes it clear that the coming overthrow of Edom is a certainty, not a condition. Edom was arrogant (3) because of its secure position in Mt. Seir, a mountainous region south of the Dead Sea. Its capital city of Sela (Petra) was protected by a narrow canyon that prevented invasion by an army. But God said this will make no difference. Even a thief would not take everything, but when God destroys Edom it will be totally ransacked. Nothing will avert God's complete judgment.

Cause (10-14): These verses describe Edom's major crime of gloating over the invasion of Jerusalem. Edom rejoiced when foreigners plundered Jerusalem, and became as one of them. On the day when they should have been allies with Judah, they instead became aggressors against Judah.

Consummation (15-21): Obadiah looks beyond the destruc-tion of Edom to the coming day of the Lord when all nations will be judged (15-16). This is followed by a prophetic consolation directed to Judah ("the house of Jacob") and Israel ("the house of Joseph"). In these closing verses of hope for God's people (17-21), God promises that they will possess not only their own land, but also that of Edom and Philistia.

Title — The Hebrew name *'obadyah* means "worshiper of Yahweh" or "servant of Yahweh." The Greek title in the Septuagint is *'Obdiou*, and the Latin title in the Vulgate is *Abdias.*

Author — Obadiah was an obscure prophet who probably lived in the southern kingdom of Judah. Nothing is known of his hometown or family, but it is not likely that he came out of the kingly or priestly line because his father is not mentioned (1:1). There are 13 Obadiahs in the Old Testament, and there have been some attempts to identify the author of this book with one of the other 12. Four of the better prospects are: (1) the officer in Ahab's palace who hid God's prophets in a cave (1 Kings 18:3); (2) one of the officials sent out by Jehoshaphat to teach the law in the cities of Judah (2 Chron. 17:7); (3) one of the overseers who took part in repairing the temple under Josiah (2 Chron. 34:12); or (4) a priest in the time of Nehemiah (Neh. 10:5).

Date and Setting — Obadiah mentions no kings, so verses 10-14 provide the only historical reference point. But scholars disagree over which invasion of Jerusalem Obadiah had in mind. There are four possibilities: (1) In 926 B.C., Shishak of Egypt plundered the temple and palace of Jerusalem in the reign of Rehoboam (1 Kings 14:25-26). But at this time, Edom was still subject to Judah. This does not fit Obadiah 10-14 which indicates that Edom was independent of Judah. (2) During the reign of Jehoram (848-841 B.C.), the Philistines and Arabians invaded Judah and looted the palace (2 Chron. 21:16-17). Edom revolted in the reign of Jehoram and became a bitter antagonist (2 Kings 8:20-22; 2 Chron. 21:8-20). This fits the description of Obadiah. (3) In 790 B.C., King Jehoash of Israel invaded Judah (2 Kings 14; 2 Chron. 25). But Obadiah calls the invaders "strangers" (vs. 11). This would be an inappropriate term for describing the army of the northern kingdom. (4) In 586 B.C., Nebuchadnezzar of Babylonia defeated and destroyed Jerusalem (2 Kings 24-25).

The two best candidates are (2) and (4). Obadiah 10-14 seems to fit (2) better then (4) because it does not indicate the total destruction of the city which took place when Nebuchadnezzar burned the palace and temple and razed the walls. And Nebuchadnezzar certainly would not "cast lots of Jerusalem" (11) with anyone. Also, all of the other prophets who speak of the destruction of 586 identify Nebuchadnezzar and the Babylonians as the agents, but Obadiah leaves the enemy unidentified. For these and other reasons, it appears likely that the plundering of Jerusalem in Obadiah was by the Philistines between 848 and 841 B.C. This would make Obadiah a contemporary of Elisha and the earliest of the writing prophets, predating Joel by a few years.

The history of Edom began with Esau who was given the name Edom ("red") because of the red stew for which he traded his birthright. Esau moved to the mountainous area of Seir and absorbed the Horites, the original inhabitants. Edom refused to allow Israel to pass through their land on the way to Canaan. The Edomites opposed Saul and were subdued under David and Solomon. They fought against Jehoshaphat and successfully rebelled against Jehoram. They were again conquered by Judah under Amaziah, but they regained their freedom during the reign of Ahaz. Edom was later controlled by Assyria and Babylonia, and·in the 5th century B.C. the Edomites were forced by Nabataeans to leave their territory. They moved to the area of southern Palestine and became known as Idumaeans. Herod the Great, an Idumaean, became King of Judea under Rome in 37 B.C. In a sense, the enmity between Esau and Jacob was continued in Herod's attempt to murder Jesus. The Idumaeans participated in the rebellion of Jerusalem against Rome and were defeated along with the Jews by Titus in A.D. 70. Ironically, the Edomites applauded the destruction of Jerusalem in 586 B.C. (see Ps. 137:7) but died trying to defend it in A.D. 70. After that time, they were never heard of again. As Obadiah predicted, they would be 'cut off forever' (vs. 10); "there will be no survivor of the house of Esau" (vs. 18).

Theme and Purpose — The major theme of Obadiah is a declaration of Edom's coming doom because of its arrogance and cruelty to Judah: "I will make you small among the nations" (2); "the arrogance of your heart has deceived you" (3); "O how you will be ruined!" (5); "O how Esau will be ransacked" (6); "then your mighty men will be dismayed" (9); "you will be covered with shame" (10); "you will be cut off forever" (10); "as

you have done, it will be done to you" (15). Even the last few verses which primarily deal with Israel, speak of Edom's downfall (17-21). The secondary theme of Obadiah is the future restoration of Israel and faithfulness of Yahweh to His covenant promises. God's justice will ultimately prevail.

Contribution to the Bible — Obadiah is the hardest prophetical book to date, but the best candidates are c. 840 B.C. and c. 586 B.C. If the former, Obadiah is the earliest of the writing prophets. His book is extremely short but complete with the two basic prophetic themes of condemnation (1-16) and consolation (17-21). Obadiah concentrates on the judgment of Edom, but other prophets are not silent about Edom's doom: see Isaiah 21; 34; Jeremiah 9; 25; 27; 49; Ezekiel 25; 35-36; Joel 3; Amos 1; Malachi 1. Evidence indicates that the prophets Joel, Amos, and Jeremiah made use of Obadiah: 1 (Jer. 49:14); 2 (Jer. 49:15); 3-4 (Jer. 49:16); 5 (Jer. 49:9); 6 (Jer. 49:10); 8 (Jer. 49:7); 9 (Jer. 49:22); 10 (Joel 3:19); 11 (Joel 3:3); 15 (Joel 1:15); 16 (Jer. 49:12); 17 (Joel 3:17); 18 (Amos 1:12); 19 (Amos 9:12). Obadiah offers one of the clearest biblical examples of pride going before a fall (1 Cor. 10:12).

Christ in Obadiah — Christ is seen in Obadiah as the Judge of the nations (15-16), the Savior of Israel (17-20), and the Possessor of the kingdom (21; "and the kingdom will be the Lord's").

Jonah

"And he prayed to the Lord and said, "Please Lord, was not this what I said while I was still in my own country? Therefore, in order to forestall this I fled to Tarshish, for I knew that Thou art a gracious and compassionate God, slow to anger and abundant in loving kindness, and one who relents concerning calamity."

Jonah 4:2

(Also see 2:9; 4:10-11).

Focus	Disobedience of Jonah 1	Distress of Jonah 2	Declaration of Jonah 3	Displeasure of Jonah 4
D I V I S I O N S	Jonah and the Storm 1	Jonah and the Fish 2	Jonah and the City 3	Jonah and the Gourd 4
T O P I C S	Fleeing	Fearing	Following	Fuming
	Going from God	Going Back to God	Going With God	Going Ahead of God
	"I won't go"	"I will go"	"I'm here"	"I shouldn't have come"
Loca-tion	Mediterranean Sea		Nineveh	
Time	About 760 B.C.			

Talk Thru — Jonah is an unusual book because of its message and messenger. Unlike other Old Testament books, it revolves exclusively around a Gentile nation. God is concerned for the Gentiles as well as His covenant people Israel. But God's messenger was a reluctant prophet who did not want to proclaim his message for fear that the Assyrians would respond and be spared by the compassionate God of Israel. Everything in the book obeyed God except the prophet himself — the storm, the lots, the sailors, the fish, the Ninevites, the plant, the worm, and the east wind. All these were used to teach Jonah a lesson on compassion and obedience. The four chapters depict the disobedience (1), distress (2), declaration (3), and displeasure (4) of Jonah.

Disobedience of Jonah (1): This chapter records the commission of Jonah (1:1-2), the disobedience of Jonah (1:3), and the consequences for Jonah (1:4-17). Jonah did not want to see God spare the notoriously cruel Assyrians. To preach a message of repentance to them would be like abetting Israel's enemy. In his patriotic zeal, Jonah put his country before his God and refused to represent Him in Nineveh. Instead of going 500 miles northeast to Nineveh, Jonah attempted to go 2,000 miles west to Tarshish (Spain). But the Lord used a creative series of countermeasures to accomplish His desired result. Jonah's efforts to thwart God's plan were futile. God prepared "a great fish" to preserve Jonah and deliver him on dry land.

Distress of Jonah (2): The fish and its divinely appointed rendezvous with the sinking prophet became a powerful reminder to Jonah of the sovereignty of God in every circumstance. While inside the fish, Jonah uttered a declarative praise psalm which alluded to several psalms that were racing through his mind (Pss. 3:8, 31:22, 42:7; 69:1). In his unique "prayer closet," Jonah offered thanksgiving for his deliverance from drowning. When he acknowledged that "salvation is from the LORD" (2:9), he was finally willing to obey and be used by God. After he was vomited onto land, Jonah had a long time to reflect upon his experiences during his 500-mile eastward trek to Nineveh.

Declaration of Jonah (3): Jonah obeyed his second commission to go to Nineveh (3:1-3) where he "became a sign to the Ninevites" (Luke 11:30). The prophet was a walking audiovisual from God, his skin no doubt bleached from his stay in the fish. As he proceeded through the city, his one-sentence sermon brought incredible results — it was the most responsive evangelistic effort in history. Jonah's words of coming judgment were followed by a proclamation by the king of the city to fast and repent. Because of His great mercy, God "relented concerning the calamity which He had declared He would bring upon them" (3:10).

Displeasure of Jonah (4): In these verses, Yahweh's love and grace are contrasted with Jonah's anger and lack of compassion. He was unhappy with the good results of his message because He knew Yahweh would now spare Nineveh. God used a plant, a worm, and a wind to teach Jonah a lesson in compassion. Jonah's emotions shifted to the extremes of fierce anger (4:1), despondency (4:3), great joy (4:6), and despair (4:8). In a humorous but meaningful account, Jonah was forced to see that he had more concern for a plant than for hundreds of thousands of people (if 120,000 children are in mind in 4:11, the population of the area was about 600,000). Jonah's lack of a divine perspective made his repentance a greater problem than the repentance of Nineveh. But he evidently learned his lesson, because he was willing to share his story in this book.

Title — *Yonah* is the Hebrew word for "dove." The Septuagint Hellenized this word into *'Ionas*, and the Latin Vulgate used the title *Jonas*.

Author — The first verse introduces Jonah as "the son of Amittai." Nothing more would be known about him if it were not for another reference to him in 2 Kings 14:25 as a prophet in the reign of Jeroboam II of Israel. Under Jeroboam, the borders of Israel were expanded "according to the word of the LORD, the God of Israel, which He spoke through His servant Jonah the son of Amittai, the prophet, who was of Gath-hepher." Gath-hepher was three miles north of Nazareth in lower Galilee, making Jonah a prophet of the northern kingdom. The Pharisees were wrong when they said, "Search, and see that no prophet arises out of Galilee" (John 7:52), because Jonah was a Galilean. One Jewish tradition says that Jonah was the son of the widow of Zarephath whom Elijah raised from the dead (1 Kings 17:8-24).

Some critics claim that Jonah was written during the 5th to

3rd centuries B.C. as a historical fiction to oppose the "narrow nationalism" of Ezra and Nehemiah by introducing universalistic ideas. An anonymous writer created this work to counteract the Jewish practice of excluding the Samaritans from worship and divorcing foreign wives. To support this view, it is noted that the book is written in the third person with no claim that Jonah authored it. The use of Aramaic words and the statement that "Nineveh *was* an exceedingly great city" (3:3) indicate a late date after Nineveh's fall in 612 B.C.

Conservative scholars refute this claim with these arguments: (1) The idea of God's inclusion of the Gentiles in His program is found elsewhere in the Scripture (cf. Gen. 9:27; 12:3; Lev. 19:33-34; 1 Sam. 2:10; Isa. 2:2; Joel 2:28-32). (2) Aramaic words occur in early as well as late Old Testament books. Aramaic is found in Near Eastern texts as early as 1500 B.C. (3) The fact that the book does not explicitly say that it was written by Jonah is an argument from silence. (4) The third-person style was a common practice among biblical writers. (5) The text in 3:3 literally means "had become." At the time of the story, Nineveh had already become a very large city. (6) Jonah was a historical prophet (2 Kings 14:25), and there are no hints that the book is fictional or allegorical. (7) Christ supported the historicity of the book (Matt. 12:39-41).

Date and Setting — Jonah was a contemporary of Jeroboam II of Israel (782-753 B.C.) who ministered after the time of Elisha and just before the time of Amos and Hosea. Israel under Jeroboam II was enjoying a period of resurgence and prosperity (see Amos, Date and Setting). Conditions were looking promising after many bleak years, and nationalistic fervor was probably high. During these years Assyria was in a period of mild decline. Weak rulers had ascended the throne. but Assyria still remained a threat. By the time of Jonah, Assyrian cruelty had become legendary. Graphic accounts of their cruel treatment of captives have been found in ancient Assyrian records, especially in the 9th and 7th centuries B.C. The repentance of Nineveh probably occurred in the reign of Ashurdan III (773-755 B.C.) Two plagues (765 and 759) and a solar eclipse (763) may have prepared the people for Jonah's message of judgment.

Theme and Purpose — Jonah reveals the power of God in nature (1-2;4) and the mercy of God in human affairs (3-4). The prophet learned that "salvation is from the Lord " (2:9), and God's gracious offer extends to all who repent and turn to Him. Jewish nationalism blinded God's covenant people to an understanding of His concern for the Gentiles. Jonah wanted God to show no mercy to the Ninevites, but he later learned how selfish and unmerciful his position was.

Contribution to the Bible — Unlike the other prophetical books, Jonah places more emphasis on the messenger than the message. In the Hebrew, the prophetic message consists of only five words (3:4). The 48 verses of this biographical book provide a clear character development and a powerful portrait of human emotions. Jonah was the only prophet sent directly to the Gentiles and the only prophet who tried to conceal his message. Jonah learned a number of principles: (1) It is impossible to succeed in running away from God. (2) There is no limit to what God can use to get one's attention. (3) Failure does not disqualify a person from God's service. (4) Disobedience to God creates turmoil in the life of a believer. (5) Patriotism should never stand between a believer and the plan of God.

More than any other Old Testament book, Jonah reveals the universal concern of Yahweh for all men. It is interesting that Nineveh responded better to the preaching of Jonah than Israel and Judah ever responded to any of their prophets.

Jonah has often been challenged because of its miraculous elements, especially the great fish. But this is a preconceived view that does not allow the God of creation to directly use His creation for special purposes. In addition, there are published accounts of men who have survived being swallowed by whales — certain whales have the capacity to engorge a man in one swallow. But the Hebrew word does not specify what kind of "fish" was involved in Jonah's case.

Christ in Jonah — Jonah is the only prophet whom Jesus likened to Himself. "But He answered and said to them, 'An evil and adulterous generation craves for a sign; and yet no sign shall be given to it but the sign of Jonah the prophet; for just as Jonah was three days and three nights in the belly of the sea monster, so shall the Son of Man be three days and three nights in the heart of the earth. The men of Nineveh shall stand up with this generation at the judgment, and shall condemn it because they repented at the preaching of Jonah; and behold, something greater than Jonah is here' " (Matt. 12:39-41). Jonah's experience was a type of Christ's death, burial, and resurrection. (The Hebrew idiom "three days and three nights" only required a *portion* of the first and third days.)

Micah

"He has told you, O man, what is good; and what does the Lord require of you but to do justice, to love kindness, and to walk humbly with your God?"

Micah 6:8

"Who is a God like Thee, who pardons iniquity and passes over the rebellious act of the remnant of His possession? He does not retain His anger forever, because he delights in unchanging love."

Micah 7:18

Focus	Retribution		Restoration		Repentance	
	1	2	3	5	6	7
D I V I S I O N S	Calamity upon Israel and Judah	Causes of Coming Judgment	Condemnation of Rulers and Prophets	Coming Kingdom and King	Controversy with Israel	Covenant Promises Fulfilled
	1	2	3	4	5	6	7
T O P I C S	Day of Condemnation		Day of Consolation		Day in Court	
	"Hear, O peoples, all of you" (1:2)		"Hear now, heads of Jacob" (3:1)		"Hear now what the Lord is saying" (6:1)	
	Judgment (1:2-2:11) & Hope (2:12-13)		Judgment (3:1-12) & Hope (4:1-5:15)		Judgment (6:1-16) & Hope (7:1-20)	
	Message of Punishment		Message of Promise		Message of Pardon	
Location	Judah and Israel					
Time	About 735-710 B.C.					

Talk Thru — Micah was the prophet of the downtrodden and exploited portion of Judean society. He prophesied during a time of great social injustice and boldly opposed those who imposed their power upon the poor and weak for selfish ends. Corrupt rulers, false prophets, and ungodly priests all become targets for Micah's prophetic barbs. Micah exposed judges who were bought by bribes and merchants who used deceptive weights. The pollution of sin had permeated every level of society in Judah and Israel. The whole earth was called to witness God's indictment against His people (1:2; 6:1-2), and the guilty verdict led to a sentence of destruction and captivity. But while the three major sections begin with condemnation (1:2-2:11; 3:6), they all end on a clear note of consolation (2:12-13; 4-5; 7). After sin is punished and justice is accomplished, "He will again have compassion on us; He will tread our iniquities under foot. Yea, Thou wilt cast all their sins into the depths of the sea" (7:19). The three sections of Micah are Retribution (1-2), Restoration (3-5), and Repentance (6-7).

Retribution (1-2): Micah begins by launching into a general declaration of the condemnation of Israel (Samaria) and Judah (Jerusalem). Both kingdoms will be overthrown because of their rampant treachery. Micah uses a series of word plays on the names of several cities of Judah in his lamentation over Judah's coming destruction (1:10-16). This is followed by some of the specific causes for judgment: premeditated schemes, covetousness, and cruelty. Nevertheless, God will regather a remnant of His people (2:12-13).

Restoration (3-5): In this section, Micah strongly contrasts Judah's present state of corruption (3) with Judah's future position of kingdom blessings (4-5). The prophet systematically condemns the rulers (3:1-4), the prophets (3:5-8), and the leading classes (3:9-12). Micah then moves into a two-chapter message of hope which describes the reinstitution of the kingdom (4:1-5), and restoration of the remnant (4:6-8), the rescue of the remnant (4:9-5:1), and the Ruler of the kingdom (5:2-15). The prophetic focus gradually narrows from the nations, to the remnant, to the King.

Repentance (6-7): In His controversy with His people, God calls them into court and presents an unanswerable case against them. The people have spurned God's graciousness, choosing instead to revel in wickedness (6). Micah summarizes their sins

(7:1-6), but closes with a sublime series of promises. The Lord will pardon their iniquities and renew their nation in accordance with His covenant.

Title — The name *michayahu* ("who is like Yahweh?") was shortened to *michaia*. In 7:18, Micah hints at his own name with the phrase "Who is a God like Thee?" The Greek and Latin titles of this book are *Michaias* and *Micha*.

Author — Micah's home town of Moresheth-gath (1:1,14) was located about 25 miles southwest of Jerusalem on the border of Judah and Philistia near Gath. Like Amos, Micah was from the country. His family and occupation are unknown, but Moresheth was in a productive agricultural belt. Micah was not as aware of the political situation as Isaiah or Daniel, but he showed a profound concern for the sufferings of the people. His clear sense of prophetic calling is seen in 3:8: "On the other hand I am filled with power — with the Spirit of the LORD — and with justice and courage to make known to Jacob his rebellious act, even to Israel his sin."

Date and Setting — The first verse indicates that he prophesied in the days of Jotham (739-731), Ahaz (731-715), and Hezekiah (715-686), kings of Judah. Although Micah deals primarily with Judah, he also addresses the northern kingdom of Israel and predicts the fall of Samaria (1:6). Much of his ministry therefore took place before the Assyrian captivity of Israel in 722 B.C. His strong denunciations of idolatry and immorality also suggest that his ministry largely preceded the sweeping religious reforms of Hezekiah. Thus, Micah's prophesies ranged from c. 735 to c. 710 B.C. He was a contemporary of Hosea in the northern kingdom and Isaiah in the court of Jerusalem.

After the prosperous reign of Uzziah in Judah (767-739), his son Jotham came to power and followed the same policies (739-731). He was a good king although he failed to remove the idolatrous high places. Under the wicked King Ahaz (731-715), Judah was threatened by the forces of Assyria and Syria. Hezekiah (715-686) opposed the Assyrians and successfully withstood an Assyrian siege with the help fo God. He was an unusually good king who steered the people of Judah back to a proper course in their walk with God.

During the ministry of Micah, the kingdom of Israel continued to crumble inwardly and outwardly until its collapse in 722 B.C. The Assyrian Empire under Tiglath-pileser III (745-727), Shalmeneser V (727-722), Sargon II (722-705), and Sennacherib (705-681) reached the zenith of its power and became a constant threat to Judah. Babylonia was still under Assyrian domination, and Micah's prediction of future Babylonian captivity for Judah (4:10) must have seemed farfetched.

Theme and Purpose — Micah exposes the injustice of Judah and the righteousness and justice of Yahweh. About one-third of the book indicts Israel and Judah for specific sins, including oppression, bribery among judges, prophets, and priests, exploitation of the powerless, coveteousness, cheating, violence, and pride. Another third of Micah predicts the judgment that will come as a result of those sins. The remaining third of the book is a message of hope and consolation. God's justice will triumph and the divine Deliverer will come. True peace and justice will prevail only when Messiah reigns. The "kindness and severity of God" (Rom. 11:22) are illustrated in Micah's presentation of divine judgment and pardon. This book emphasizes the integral relationship between true spirituality and social ethics. Micah 6:8 summarizes what God wanted to see in His people: justice and equity tempered with mercy and compassion as the result of a humble and obedient relationship with Him.

Contribution to the Bible — In some ways, Micah is an Isaiah in miniature. Both prophets addressed the same people and problems: compare 1:2 (Isa. 1:2); 1:9-16 (Isa. 10:28-32); 2:8-9 (Isa. 10:2); 2:12 (Isa. 10:10-23); 2:13 (Isa. 52:12); 3:5-7 (Isa. 29:9-12); 4:1 (Isa. 2:2); 5:2 (Isa. 7:14); 5:4 (Isa. 40:11); 6:6-8 (Isa. 58:6-7); 7:7 (Isa. 8:17); 7:12 (Isa. 11:11). But Micah focused on moral and social problems while Isaiah placed greater stress on world affairs and political concerns.

A quote from Micah 3:12 a century later in Jeremiah 26:18 concerning the coming destruction of Jerusalem was instrumental in delivering Jeremiah from death. Micah was also quoted in the New Testament: 5:2 (Matt. 2:5-6; John 7:42); 7:6 (Matt. 10:34-36; Mark 13:12; Luke 12:53). Compared with other prophets,

Micah's proportion of foretelling relative to forthtelling is high. He has much to say about the future of Israel and the advent and reign of Messiah.

Christ in Micah — Micah 5:2 is one of the clearest and most important of all Old Testament prophecies: "But as for you, Bethlehem Ephrathah, too little to be among the clans of Judah, from you One will go forth for Me to be ruler in Israel. His goings forth are from long ago, from the days of eternity." This prophecy about the birthplace and eternity of Messiah was made 700 years before His birth. The chief priests and scribes paraphrased this verse in Matthew 2:5-6 when questioned about the birthplace of Messiah. Micah 2:12-13; 4:1-8; and 5:4-5 offer some of the best Old Testament descriptions of the righteous reign of Christ over the whole world.

Nahum

"The LORD is good, a stronghold in the day of trouble, and He knows those who take refuge in Him."
"But with an overflowing flood He will make a complete end of its site, and will pursue His enemies into darkness."

Nahum 1:7-8
(Also see 1:2-3; 2:13.)

Focus	Destruction Decreed			Destruction Described			Destruction Deserved		
	1:1 — 1:15			2:1 — 2:13			3:1 — 3:19		
DIVISIONS	Disposition of the Judge	Decree against Nineveh	Deliverance of Judah	Declaration of Warning	Description of the Invasion	Defeat and Destruction of the City	Iniquity of Nineveh	Illustration of No-amon	Inevitability of Nineveh's Fall
	1:1 1:8	1:9 1:14	1:15	2:1-2	2:3 2:7	2:8 2:13	3:1 3:7	3:8 3:11	3:12 3:19
TOPICS	Proclamation of God's Displeasure			Prediction of Nineveh's Doom			Portrait of Nineveh's Downfall		
	What God Will Do			How God Will Do It			Why God Will Do It		
	Declaration			Details					
	God's Justice			God's Judgment					
Location	Against Nineveh, Capital of Assyria								
Time	About 660 B.C.								

217

Talk Thru — When God finally convinced his prophet Jonah to preach to the people of Nineveh, the whole city responded with repentance and Nineveh escaped destruction. The people humbled themselves before the one true God, but their humility soon changed to arrogance as Assyria reached its zenith as the most powerful empire in the world. About a century after the preaching of Jonah, God called Nahum to proclaim the coming destruction of Nineveh. This time there would be no escape, because their measure of wickedness was full. Unlike Jonah, Nahum did not go to the city but declared his oracle from afar. There is no hope of repentance. Nineveh's destruction is decreed (1), described (2), and deserved (3).

Destruction Decreed (1): Nahum begins with a very clear description of the character of Yahweh. Because of His righteousness, He is a God of vengeance (1:2). God is also characterized by patience (1:3a) and power (1:3b-6). He is gracious to all who respond to Him, but those who rebel against Him will be overthrown (1:7-8). God is holy, and Nineveh stands condemned because of its sins (1:9-14). Nothing can stand in the way of its judgment, and this is a message of comfort to the people of Judah (1:15). The threat of Assyrian invasion will soon be over.

Destruction Described (2): Assyria will be conquered but Judah will be restored (2:1-2). Nahum's description of the siege of Nineveh (2:3-7) and the sack of Nineveh (2:8-13) is one of the most vivid portraits of battle in Scripture. The storming warriors and chariots can almost be seen as they enter the city through a breach in the wall. As the Ninevites flee in terror, the invading army plunders the treasures of the city. Nineveh will be burned and cut off forever.

Destruction Deserved (3): Nahum closes his brief book of judgment with God's reasons for Nineveh's coming overthrow. The city was characterized by cruelty and corruption (3:1-7). Just as Assyria crushed the Egyptian capital city of Thebes (No-amon), Assyria's capital city will also be destroyed (3:8-10). Nineveh was so well fortified that defeat seemed impossible, but God proclaims that its destruction is inevitable (3:11-19). None of its resources can deter divine judgment.

Title — The Hebrew name *nahum* ("comfort, consolation") was a shortened form of Nehemiah ("comfort of Yahweh"). The destruction of the capital city of Assyria was a message of comfort and consolation to Judah and all who lived in fear of the cruelty of the Assyrians. The title of this book in the Greek and Latin Bibles was *Naoum* and *Nahum*.

Author — The only mention of Nahum in the Old Testament is found in 1:1 where he is called an Elkoshite. At least four locations have been proposed for Elkosh: (1) A 16th-century tradition identifies Elkosh with Al-Qush in Iraq, north of the site of Nineveh on the Tigris River. (2) Jerome believed that Elkesi, a city near Ramah in Galilee, was Elkosh because of the similarity of the consonants. (3) Capernaum means "city of Nahum" *(kephar-nahum),* and many believe that the name Elkosh was changed to Capernaum in Nahum's honor. (4) Most conservative scholars believe that Elkosh was a city of southern Judah (later called Elcesei) between Jerusalem and Gaza. This would make Nahum a prophet of the southern kingdom and appears to be more in line with his interest in the triumph of Judah (1:15;2:2).

Date and Setting — The fall of Nineveh to the Babylonians in 612 B.C. is seen by Nahum as a future event. Critics who deny predictive prophecy naturally date Nahum after 612 B.C., but this is not based upon exegetical or historical considerations. Nahum 3:8-10 refers to the fall of Thebes as a recent event, so this book must be dated after 664 B.C., the year this took place. Thus, Nahum can be safely placed between 663 and 612 B.C. Thebes was restored a decade after its defeat, and Nahum's failure to mention this restoration has led several scholars to the conclusion that Nahum was written before 654 B.C. The fact that Nahum mentions no king in the superscription to his book (1:1) may point to the reign of the wicked king Manasseh (686-642).

The conversion of the Ninevites in response to Jonah's message of judgment took place c. 760 B.C. The revival was evidently short-lived, because the Assyrians soon returned to their ruthless practices. Sargon II of Assyria destroyed Samaria, the capital of the northern kingdom of Israel, in 722 B.C. and scattered the 10 tribes. Led by Sennacherib, the Assyrians also came close to capturing Jerusalem in the reign of King Hezekiah in 701 B.C. By the time of Nahum (c. 660), Assyria reached the peak of its prosperity and power under Ashurbanipal (669-633). This king extended Assyria's influence farther than any of his predecessors. Nineveh became the mightiest city on earth with walls 100 feet high and wide enough to accommodate three chariots riding abreast. Dotted around the walls were huge towers that stretched an additional 100 feet above the top of the walls. In addition, the walls were surrounded by a moat 150 feet wide and 60 feet deep. Nineveh appeared impregnable and could withstand a 20-year siege. Thus, Nahum's prophecy of Nineveh's overthrow seemed unlikely indeed.

Assyrian power faded under Ashurbanipal's sons, Ashuretililani (633-629) and Sinsharishkun (629-612). Nahum predicted that Nineveh would end "with an overflowing flood" (1:8), and this is precisely what occurred. The Tigris River overflowed its banks and the flood destroyed part of Nineveh's wall. The Babylonians invaded through this breach in the wall, plundered the city, and set it on fire. Nahum also predicted that Nineveh would "be hidden" (3:11). After its destruction in 612 B.C. the site was not discovered until A.D. 1842.

Theme and Purpose — Beginning with 1:9, the single thrust of Nahum's prophecy is the retribution of God against the wickedness of Nineveh. Nineveh's judgment is irreversibly decreed by the righteous God who will no longer delay His wrath. Assyria's arrogance and cruelty to other nations will come to a sudden end — her power will be useless against the mighty hand of Yahweh.

Nahum 1:2-8 portrays the patience, power, holiness, and justice of the living God. He is slow to wrath, but He settles in full. This book concerns the downfall of Assyria but it was written for the benefit of the surviving kingdom of Judah (Israel had already been swallowed up by Assyria). The people in Judah who trusted in the Lord would be comforted to hear of God's judgment upon the proud and brutal Assyrians (1:15; 2:2).

Contribution to the Bible — Nahum is one of the three prophets who primarily focused on the judgment of Judah's enemies. The other two are Obadiah (Edom) and Habakkuk (Babylonia). In spite of Judah's wickedness in the time of Nahum, this book does not contain one word of

condemnation against Judah and it has no call to repentance or reformation. That was the calling of Nahum's younger contemporaries, Zephaniah, Jeremiah, and Habakkuk.

In this book, Jonah's hoped-for judgment upon Nineveh is dramatically decribed with brilliant imagery.

JONAH	NAHUM
The Mercy of God	The Judgment of God
c. 760 B.C.	c. 660 B.C.
Repentance of Nineveh	Rebellion of Nineveh
Emphasis on the Prophet	Emphasis on the Prophecy
Disobedient Prophet	Obedient Prophet
Obedient Nation	Disobedient Nation
Deliverance from Water	Destruction by Water
The Great Fish	The Great Fulfillment

Nahum's very specific prophetic details include: Nineveh destroyed by a flood (1:8; 2:6) and by fire (1:10; 2:13; 3:13,15), the profaning of Nineveh's temples and images (1:14), the city never to be rebuilt (1:14; 2:11,13), the leaders will flee (2:9; 3:17), the easy capture of the fortresses around the city (3:12), the destruction of the gates (3:13), and the lengthy siege and frantic efforts to strengthen its defenses (3:14). All these events have been authenticated in archaeological finds and historical accounts.

There are only 47 verses in this book, but it contains nearly 50 references to nature (see 1:3,10; 2:11; 3:15). Nahum is not quoted in the New Testament.

Christ in Nahum — While there are no direct Messianic prophecies in Nahum, the divine attributes in 1:2-8 are consistent with Christ's work as the Judge of the nations in His second advent.

Habakkuk

"I will stand on my guard post and station myself on the rampart; and I will keep watch to see what He will speak to me, and how I may reply when I am reproved."

Habakkuk 2:1

"Behold, as for the proud one, his soul is not right within him; but the righteous will live by his faith."

Habakkuk 2:4
(Also see 1:13; 2:20.)

Focus	Habakkuk's Perplexity				Habakkuk's Praise
	1			**2**	**3**
DIVISIONS	Habakkuk's First Problem	God's First Reply	Habakkuk's Second Problem	God's Second Reply	Habakkuk's Response of Praise
	1:1-4	1:5　　1:11	1:12　　2:1	2:2　　2:20	3:1　　3:19
TOPICS	Problems of Faith				Prayer of Faith
	First Dialogue		Second Dialogue		Concluding Monologue
	Faith Troubled: Questioning			Faith Taught: Listening	Faith Triumphant: Responding
	Oracle (1:1)			Vision (2:2)	Prayer (3:1)
Location	Kingdom of Judah				
Time	About 607 B.C.				

Talk Thru — Habakkuk was a freethinking prophet who was not afraid to wrestle with issues that tested his faith. He openly and honestly directed his problems to God and waited to see how He would respond to his probing questions. After two rounds of dialogue with the Lord, Habakkuk's increased understanding of the person, power, and plan of God caused him to conclude with a psalm of unqualified praise. The more he knew about the Planner, the more he could trust His plans. No matter what God brings to pass, "the righteous will live by his faith" (2:4). The two divisions of this book are Habakkuk's Perplexity (1-2) and Habakkuk's Praise (3).

Habakkuk's Perplexity (1-2): Habakkuk's first dialogue with God takes place in 1:1-11. In 1:1-4 the prophet asks God, "How long will you allow the wickedness of Judah to go unpunished?" The people of Judah sin with impunity and justice is perverted. God's startling answer is given in 1:5-11: "I am raising up the fierce Babylonians as My rod of judgment upon sinful Judah." The Chaldeans will come against Judah swiftly, violently, and completely. The coming storm from the east will be God's answer to Judah's crimes.

This answer leads to Habakkuk's second dialogue with God (1:12-2:20). The prophet is more perplexed than ever and asks, "How can you, the righteous God, punish Judah with a nation this is even more wicked?" (1:12-2:1). Will the God whose "eyes are too pure to approve evil" reward the Babylonians for their cruelty and idolatry? Habakkuk stood upon a watchtower to wait for God's reply. The Lord answered with a series of five woes upon the Chaldeans because of their greed and aggression (2:5-8), exploitation and extortion (2:9-11), violence (2:12-14), immorality (2:15-17), and idolatry (2:18-20). God is aware of the sins of the Babylonians and they will not escape His terrible judgment. But Judah is guilty of the same offenses and stands under the same condemnation. Yahweh concludes His answer with a statement of His sovereign majesty: "But the LORD is in His holy temple. Let all the earth be silent before Him" (2:20).

Habakkuk's Praise (3): Habakkuk began by questioning God but He concludes his book with a psalm of praise for the person (3:1-3), power (3:4-12), and plan (3:13-19) of God. He now acknowledges God's wisdom in the coming invasion of Judah and though it terrifies him, he will trust the Lord. God's creative and redemptive work in the past gives the prophet confidence in the divine purposes and hope at a time when he would otherwise despair. "Yet I will exult the LORD, I will rejoice in the God of my salvation" (3:18).

Title — *Habaqquq* was an unusual Hebrew name derived from *habaq*, "embrace." Thus his name probably meant "one who embraces or clings." At the end of his book this name became appropriate because Habakkuk chose to cling firmly to God regardless of what would happen to his nation (3:16-19). The Greek title in the Septuagint was *'Ambakouk*, and the Latin title in Jerome's Vulgate was *Habacuc*.

Author — In the superscription to the book (1:1) and the closing psalm (3:1), the author identifies himself as "Habakkuk the prophet." This special designation seems to indicate that Habakkuk was a professional prophet. The closing statement at the end of the psalm ("For the choir director, on my stringed instruments.") suggests that Habakkuk may have been a priest connected with the temple worship in Jerusalem. He mentions nothing of his genealogy or location, but speculative attempts have been made to identify him with certain unnamed Old Testament characters. In the apocryphal book of Bel and the Dragon, Daniel is rescued a second time by the prophet Habakkuk.

Some critics challenge Habakkuk's authorship of chapter 3 because it is a psalm, not a prophecy. But this praise psalm is a most appropriate response to God's declaration in 2:2-20.

Date and Setting — There are no explicit time references in Habakkuk except that the Babylonian invasion is an imminent event (1:6; 2:1; 3:16). Some suggest Habakkuk was written during the reign of Manasseh (686-642) or Amon (642-640) because of the list of Judah's sins in 1:2-4. But the descriptions of the Chaldeans indicate that Babylonia has become a world power, and this was not true in the time of Manasseh when Babylonia was under the thumb of Assyria. It is also unlikely that this prophecy took place in the time of King Josiah (640-609), because the moral and spiritual reforms of Josiah do not fit the situation in 1:2-4. The most likely date for the book is in the early part of Jehoiakim's reign (609-597). Jehoiakim was a godless king who led the nation down the path of destruction

(cf. 2 Kings 23:34-24:5; Jer. 22:17).

The Babylonians began to rise in power during the reign of Nabopolassar (626-605), and in 612 B.C. they destroyed the Assyrian capital of Nineveh. By the time of Jehoiakim, Babylonia was the uncontested world power. Nabopolassar's successor, Nebuchadnezzar, came to power in 605 B.C. and carried out successful military expeditions in the west, advancing into Palestine and Egypt. Nebuchadnezzar's first invasion of Judah occurred in his first year when he deported 10,000 of Jerusalem's leaders to Babylon. The nobles who oppressed and extorted from the poor were the first to be carried away. Since Habakkuk prophesied prior to the Babylonian invasion, the probable date for this book is c. 607 B.C.

Theme and Purpose — The circumstances of life sometimes appear to contradict God's revelation concerning His power and purposes. Habakkuk struggled in his faith when he saw men flagrantly violate God's law and distort justice on every level without fear of divine intervention. He wanted to know why God was allowing growing iniquity to go unpunished. When God revealed His intention to use Babylonia as His rod of judgment, Habakkuk was even more troubled, because that nation was more corrupt than Judah. God's answer in 2:2-20 satisfied Habakkuk that he could trust Him even in the worst of circumstances because of His matchless wisdom, goodness, and power. God's plan is perfect, and nothing is big enough to stand in the way of its ultimate fulfillment. In spite of appearances to the contrary, God is still on the throne as the Lord of history and the Ruler of the nations. Yahweh may be slow to wrath, but all iniquity will eventually be punished. He is the worthiest object of faith, and the righteous man will trust in Him at all times.

Contribution to the Bible — Habakkuk was a daring thinker who openly expressed his doubt to God. He was a man of integrity who was concerned with the character and program of Yahweh. Habakkuk's unusually extended dialogue with God (about two-thirds of the book) was initiated by the prophet. Normally, the prophetic process was begun by God. After receiving the divine oracle, Habakkuk transmitted it to the people of Judah.

Both Jonah and Habakkuk faced severe tests of their faith. But they approached their problems differently:

Jonah	Habakkuk
God called on Jonah	Habakkuk called on God
Jonah ran *from* God	Habakkuk ran *to* God
Prayer and trouble (ch. 2)	Prayer after trouble (ch. 3)
Ends in foolishness	Ends in faith
Salvation of God to the Gentiles	Sovereignty of God over the Gentiles
In the fish	On the watchtower 2:4

Habakkuk moves from burden to blessing, from wondering to worship, from restlessness to rest, from a problem to God's person, and from a complaint to consolation. The best known passage is "the righteous will live by his faith" (2:4). This concept was central to the argument of Habakkuk and influential in the thought of three New Testament books (Rom. 1:17; Gal. 3:11; Heb. 10:38). It also powerfully affected the lives of Luther and Wesley.

The concluding psalm of praise (chapter 3) is one of the greatest psalms in the Old Testament. This magnificent declaration of faith in the character and ways of God has much in common with Psalms 18 and 68.

Christ in Habakkuk — The word "salvation" appears three times in 3:13,18 and is the root word from which the name Jesus was derived (cf. Matt. 1:21). When He comes again, "the earth will be filled with the knowledge of the glory of the LORD, as the waters cover the sea" (2:14).

Zephaniah

"Near is the great day of the LORD, near and coming very quickly; listen, the day of the LORD! In it the warrior cries out bitterly. A day of wrath is that day, a day of trouble and distress, a day of destruction and desolation, a day of darkness and gloom, a day of clouds and thick darkness."

Zephaniah 1:14-15

Focus	Day of the Lord: Judgment						Deliverance of the Lord: Joy	
	1:1					3:8	3:9	3:20
D I V I S I O N S	Universal Judgment	Judgment upon Judah	Appeal to Judah	Judgment upon Surrounding Nations (West, East, South, North)	Judgment upon Jerusalem	Judgment upon all Nations	Cleansing of the Nations	Restoration of Israel
	1:1-3	1:4 1:18	2:1-3	2:4 2:15	3:1 3:7	3:8	3:9-10	3:11 3:20
T O P I C S	Judgment of Sin						Joy of Salvation	
	Judgment upon Judah			Judgment upon the Nations			Blessings after Judgment	
	Retribution in the Day of the Lord						Salvation in the Day of the Lord	
	"I will remove all things" (1:2)						"I will restore your fortunes" (3:20)	
Loca-tions	World	Judah		Sur-rounding Nations	Jeru-salem	All Nations	Israel/ Judah	
Time	About 630-625 B.C.							

Talk Thru— Zephaniah is a fierce and grim book of warning about the coming day of the Lord. Desolation, darkness, and ruin will strike Judah and the nations because of the wrath of God upon sin. But Zephaniah looks beyond judgment to a time of joy when God will cleanse the nations and restore the fortunes of His people Israel. The book begins with God's declaration, "I will completely remove all things from the face of the earth" (1:2), but it ends with this promise: "At that time I will bring you in" and "restore your fortunes before your eyes" (3:20). Zephaniah moves three times from the general to the specific: (1) from universal judgment (1:1-3) to judgment upon Judah (1:4-2:3), (2) from judgment upon surrounding nations (2:4-15) to judgment upon Jerusalem (3:1-7), (3) from judgment and cleansing of all nations (3:8-10) to restoration of Israel (3:11-20). The two broad divisions of the book are Day of the Lord: Judgment (1:1-3:8), and Deliverance of the Lord: Joy (3:9-20).

Day of the Lord: Judgment (1:1-3:8): The prophetic oracle commences with an awesome statement of God's coming judgment upon the entire earth because of the sins of men (1:2-3). Zephaniah then zeroes in on the judgment of Judah (1:4-18), listing some of the offenses that will cause it to come. Judah is polluted with idolatrous priests who promote the worship of Baal, nature, and Milcom, and her officials and princes are completely corrupt. Therefore, the day of the Lord is imminent, and it will be characterized by terror, desolation, and distress. But in His grace, Yahweh appeals to His people to repent and humble themselves to avert the coming disaster before it is too late (2:1-3).

Zephaniah pronounces coming judgment upon the nations that surround Judah (2:4-15). He looks in all four directions: Philistia (west), Moab and Ammon (east), Ethiopia (south), and Assyria (north). Then he focuses in on Jerusalem, the center of His dealings (3:1-7). Jerusalem is characterized by spiritual rebellion and moral treachery. "She heeded no voice; she accepted no instruction. She did not trust in the LORD; she did not draw near to her God" (3:2).

Deliverance of the Lord: Joy (3:9-20): After a broad statement of the judgment of all nations (3:8), Zephaniah changes the tone of the remainder of his book to blessing, for this, too, is an aspect of the day of the Lord. The nations will be cleansed and the Gentiles will call on the name of the Lord (3:9-10). The remnant of Israel will be regathered, redeemed, and restored (3:11-20). They will rejoice in their Redeemer, and He will be in their midst. Zephaniah opens with idolatry, wrath, and judgment, but closes with true worship, rejoicing, and blessing.

Title — *Tsephan-yah* means "Yahweh hides" or "Yahweh has hidden." Zephaniah was evidently born during the latter part of the reign of King Manasseh. His name may mean that he was "hidden" from Manasseh's atrocities. The Greek and Latin title is *Sophonias*.

Author — The first verse is very unusual in that Zephaniah traces his lineage back four generations to Hezekiah. This is probably Hezekiah the king of Judah, because this would best explain the long genealogy. If Zephaniah was the great-great-grandson of the godly king Hezekiah, he was the only prophet of royal descent. This may have given the prophet freer access to the court of King Josiah in whose reign he ministered. Zephaniah's use of the phrase "this place" to refer to Jerusalem coupled with his familiarity with its features (cf. 1:9-10; 3:1-7) makes him a likely inhabitant of Judah's royal city.

Date and Setting — Zephaniah solves the broad dating problem by fixing his prophecy "in the days of Josiah son of Amon, king of Judah" (1:1). Josiah reigned in 640-609 B.C., and 2:13 indicates that the destruction of Nineveh (612) was still a future event. Thus, Zephaniah's prophecy can be dated between 640 and 612 B.C. But the sins catalogued in 1:3-13 and 3:1-7 indicate a date prior to Josiah's reforms when the sins from the reign of Manasseh and Amon still predominated. It is therefore likely that Zephaniah's ministry played a significant role in preparing Judah for the revivals that took place in the reign of the nation's last righteous king. Josiah became king of Judah at the age of eight, and his heart had already begun to turn toward God by the age of 16. His first reform took place in the 12th year of his reign (628; 2 Chron. 34:3-7) when he tore down all the altars of Baal, destroyed the foreign incense altars, burned the bones of the false prophets on their altars, and broke the Asherim (carved images) and molten images in pieces. Six years later (622), Josiah's second reform was kindled when Hilkiah the priest found the book of the law in the temple (2 Chron. 34:8-35:19). Thus, the probable date of Zephaniah's prophecy is around 630 to 625 B.C.

The evil reigns of Manasseh and Amon (a total of 55 years) had such a profound effect upon Judah that it never recovered. Josiah's reforms were too little and too late, and the people reverted to their crass idolatry and teaching soon after Josiah was gone. As a contemporary of Jeremiah and Habakkuk, Zephaniah was one of the 11th-hour prophets to Judah.

Theme and Purpose — The bulk of Zephaniah (1:1-3:8) describes the coming day of judgment upon Judah and the nations. Yahweh is holy and must vindicate His righteousness by calling all the nations of the world into account before Him. The sovereign God will judge not only His own people but also the whole world — no one escapes from His authority and dominion. The day of the Lord will have universal impact. That day came for Judah and all the nations mentioned in 2:4-15, but there is a future aspect when all the earth will be judged. Zephaniah 3:9-20 speaks of another side of the day of the Lord: it will be a day of blessing after the judgment is complete. A righteous remnant will survive and all who call upon Him, Jew or Gentile, will be blessed. God will regather and restore His people, and there will be worldwide rejoicing.

Zephaniah was also written as a warning to Judah and a call to repentance (2:1-3). God wanted to spare the people but they ultimately rejected Him. His judgment would be great, but in His covenant loyalty God promised His people a future day of hope and joy. Wrath and mercy, severity and kindness cannot be separated in the character of God.

Contribution to the Bible — Both Joel and Zephaniah deal almost exclusively with the concept of the coming day of the Lord. Using different expressions, Zephaniah refers to it 23 times in only three chapters. This book expands this important theme and includes these elements: the day of the Lord will fall upon all creation (1:2-3), it is imminent (1:14), it is a day of terror and judgment upon sin (1:15,17), it will involve the nations of the world (2:4-15; 3:8), a remnant will return on that day (3:9-13), and it will bring great blessing (3:14-20).

Zephaniah, Habakkuk, and Lamentations chronologically

follow each other and deal with the fall of Jerusalem:

Zephaniah	Habakkuk	Lamentations
Decades before the fall of Jerusalem (c.630)	Just before the fall of Jerusalem (c.607)	Just after the fall of Jerusalem (586)
"God will judge"	"God, when will you judge?"	"God has judged"
Preview of trouble	Promise of trouble	Presence of trouble
Declaration	Dialogue	Dirge
Day of the Lord	Dominion of the Lord	Destruction of the Lord
"God is in your midst" (3:15,17)	"God is your strength" (3:19)	"God is your portion" (3:24)

Christ in Zephaniah — Jesus alluded to Zephaniah on two occasions (1:3 in Matt. 13:41 and 1:15 in Matt. 24:29). Both of these passages about the day of the Lord are associated with Christ's second advent. Although the Messiah is not specifically mentioned in Zephaniah, it is clear that He is the One who will fulfill the great promises of 3:9-20. He will gather His people and reign in victory: "The LORD has taken away His judgments against you, He has cleared away your enemies. The King of Israel, the LORD, is in your midst; you will fear disaster no more" (3:15).

Haggai

"Thus says the LORD of hosts, 'Consider your ways!' "
" 'Go up to the mountains, bring wood and rebuild the temple,
that I may be pleased with it and be glorified,' says the LORD."
Haggai 1:7-8

Focus	A Call to Completion	A Call to Courage	A Call to Cleansing	A Call to the Chosen
	1:1 1:15	2:1 2:9	2:10 2:19	2:20 2:23
D I V I S I O N S	Priorities Perverted: People	Past Preferred: Zerubbabel	Purity Preserved: Priests	Power Predicted: Zerubbabel
	1:1 1:15	2:1 2:9	2:10 2:19	2:20 2:23
T O P I C S	Sermon 1: Priorities	Sermon 2: Perspective	Sermon 3: Purity	Sermon 4: Promises
	Arousing	Assuring	Affirming	Anticipating
	"Take part" (1:15)	"Take heart" (2:4)	"I will bless you" (2:19)	"I will honor you" (2:23)
	Finishing God's Building		Finding God's Blessing	
Location	Jerusalem			
Time	August 29, 520 B.C.	October 17, 520 B.C.	December 18, 520 B.C.	

232

Talk Thru — Haggai is second only to Obadiah in brevity among Old Testament books, but this strong and frank series of four terse sermons accomplished its intended effect. The work on the temple had ceased, and the people became more concerned with the beautification of their own houses than with the building of the central sanctuary of God. Because of their misplaced priorities, their labor was no longer blessed by God. Only when the people put the Lord first by completing the task He had set before them would His hand of blessing once again be upon them. Haggai acted as God's man in God's hour, and his four messages are: A Call to Completion (1:1-15), A Call to Courage (2:1-9), A Call to Cleansing (2:10-19), and A Call to the Chosen (2:20-23).

A Call to Completion (1:1-15): When the remnant returned from Babylonia under Zerubbabel, they began to rebuild the temple of the Lord. But the work soon stopped and the people found excuses to ignore it as the years moved by. They had no problem in building rich dwellings for themselves ("paneled houses," 1:4) while they claimed that the time for building the temple had not yet come (1:2). God withdrew His blessing and they sank into an economic depression. But they did not recognize what was happening because of their indifference to God and indulgence of self, so God communicated directly to the remnant through His prophet Haggai. Zerubbabel the governor, Joshua the high priest, and all the people responded, and 23 days later they again began to work on the temple.

A Call to Courage (2:1-9): In a few short weeks, the enthusiasm of the people soured into discouragement; the elders remembered the glory of Solomon's temple and bemoaned the puniness of the present temple (also see Ezra 3:8-13). Haggai's prophetic word of encouragement at this vivid point reminded the people of God's covenant promises in the past (2:4-5), and His confident plans for the future (2:6-9): "The latter glory of this house will be greater than the former" (2:9).

A Call to Cleansing (2:10-19): Haggai's message to the priests illustrated the concept of contamination (2:11-13) and applied it to the nation (2:14-19). The Lord requires holiness and obedience, and the contamination of sin blocks the blessing of God. Because the people have obeyed God in founding the temple, they will be blessed from that day on.

A Call to the Chosen (2:20-23): On the same day that Haggai

233

addressed the priests he gave a second message to Zerubbabel. Yahweh will move in judgment, and in His power He will overthrow the nations of the earth (2:21-22). At that time, Zerubbabel, a symbol of the Messiah to come, will be honored.

Title — The etymology and meaning of *haggay* is uncertain, but it is probably derived from the Hebrew word *hag*, "festival." It may also be an abbreviated form of *haggiah*, "festival of Yahweh". Thus his name means "festal" or "festive," possibly because he was born on the day of a major feast like Tabernacles (Haggai's second message took place at that time; 2:1). The title in the Septuagint is *'Aggaios*, and in the Vulgate it is *Aggaeus*.

Author — Haggai's name is mentioned nine times (1:1,3,12,13; 2:1,10,13,14,20), and the authorship and date of this book are virtually uncontested. The unity of theme, style, and dating is obvious. Haggai is known only from this book and from two references to him in Ezra 5:1 and 6:14. There he is seen working alongside of the younger prophet Zechariah in the ministry of encouraging the rebuilding of the temple. Haggai returned from Babylon with the remnant under Zerubbabel and evidently lived in Jerusalem. Some think 2:3 may mean that he was born in Judah before the 586 B.C. captivity and was one of the small company that could remember the former temple before its destruction. This would make Haggai about 75 when he prophesied in 520 B.C. But this is just a guess, and it is equally likely that he was born in Babylon during the captivity.

Date and Setting — In 538 B.C., Cyrus of Persia issued a decree allowing the Jews to return to their land and rebuild their temple. The first return was led by Zerubbabel and in 536 B.C. work on the temple began. Ezra 4-6 gives the background to the book of Haggai and describes how the Samaritans hindered the building of the temple and wrote a letter to the Persian king. This opposition only added to the growing discouragement of the Jewish remnant. Their initial optimism upon returning to their homeland was dampened by the desolation of the land, crop failure, hard work, hostility, and other hardships. They gave up the relative comfort of Babylonian culture to pioneer in a land that seemed unproductive and full of enemies. Finding it easier to stop building than to fight their neighbors, the work on the temple ceased in 534 B.C. The pessimism of the people led to spiritual lethargy and they became preoccupied with their own building projects. They used political opposition and a theory that the temple was not to be rebuilt until some later time (perhaps after Jerusalem was rebuilt) as excuses for neglecting the house of the Lord.

It was in this context that God called His prophets Haggai and Zechariah to the same task of convincing the people to complete the temple. Both books are precisely dated: Haggai 1:1, August 29, 520; Haggai 1:15, September 21,520; Haggai 2:1, October 17, 520; Zechariah 1:1, November, 520; Haggai 2:10,20, December 18, 520; Zechariah 1:7, February 15, 519; Zechariah 7:1, December 7, 518. Zechariah's prophecy commenced between Haggai's second and third messages. Thus, after 14 years of neglect, work on the temple resumed in 520 B.C. and it was completed in 516 B.C. (Ezra 6:15). The Talmud indicates that the ark of the covenant, the Shekinah glory, and the Urim and Thummim were not in the rebuilt temple.

Darius I (521-486) was king of Persia during the ministries of Haggai and Zechariah. He was a strong ruler who consolidated his kingdom by defeating a number of revolting nations.

Theme and Purpose— Haggai's basic theme is clear: the remnant must reorder its priorities and complete the temple before they can expect the blessing of God upon their efforts. Because of spiritual indifference they failed to respond to God's attempts to get their attention. In their despondency, they did not realize that their hardships were divinely given symptoms of their spiritual disease. Haggai brought them to an understanding that circumstances become difficult when people place their own selfish interests before God's. When they put God first and seek to do His will, He will bring His people joy and prosperity.

Contribution to the Bible — Haggai was one of the few prophets whose message brought quick and tangible results. Only 23 days after his first oracle, the people began to work on the temple for the first time in 14 years. Founding the second temple marked a major turning point in God's dealing with His covenant people: "Yet from this day on I will bless you" (2:19). This was because of the centrality of the sanctuary to the whole religious life in the Mosaic law. It was not only the focus of the whole system of offerings and sacrifices, priests, and worship; it was also the symbol of Israel's spiritual identity and a visible reminder of the person, power, and presence of God. Now that the Davidic throne was gone, it was especially important that the temple be built to bind the remnant together as the continuing covenant people of God.

Haggai lacks the vivid imagery and poetry of other prophets like Isaiah and Nahum, but his concise and austere messages were successful. His words ring with divine authority ("thus says the LORD" and similar expressions appear 26 times in Haggai's 38 verses).

Christ in Haggai — The promise of Haggai 2:9 pointed ahead to the crucial role the second temple was to have in God's redemptive plan. Herod the Great spent a fortune on the project of enlarging and enriching this temple, and it was filled with the glory of God incarnate every time Christ came to Jerusalem.

Messiah was also portrayed in the person of Zerubbabel: "I will take you, Zerubbabel, . . . and I will make you like a signet ring, for I have chosen you" (2:23). Zerubbabel became the center of the Messianic line and was like a signet ring, sealing both branches together:

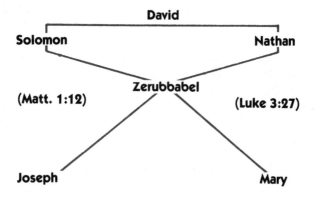

Zechariah

"Thus says the LORD, 'I will return to Zion and will dwell in the midst of Jerusalem. Then Jerusalem will be called the City of Truth, and the mountain of the LORD of hosts will be called the Holy Mountain.'"

Zechariah 8:3

Focus	Pictures			Problems	Predictions	
	1		6 7	8 9		14
D I V I S I O N S	Invitation to Repentance	Eight Night Visions	Coronation of Joshua	Question of the Fasts	First Burden: Introduction and Rejection of Messiah	Second Burden: Intervention and Reception of Messiah
	1:1-6	1:7 6:8	6:9-15 7	8 9	11	12 14
T O P I C S	Eight Visions			Four Messages	Two Burdens	
	Israel's Fortune			Israel's Fasting	Israel's Future	
	Judgment, Cleansing, Restoration			Fasting to Feasting	Messiah: First Advent and Rejection	Messiah: Second Advent and Acceptance
	Dated Prophecies: While Rebuilding the Temple				Undated Prophecies: After Rebuilding the Temple	
Location	Jerusalem					
Time	Nov. 520 B.C.	February 15, 519 B.C.		December 7, 518 B.C.	C. 480-470 B.C.	

Talk Thru — Zechariah uses a series of eight visions, four messages, and two burdens to portray God's future plans for His covenant people. The first eight chapters were written to encourage the remnant while they were rebuilding the temple, and the last six chapters were written after the completion of the temple to anticipate Israel's coming Messiah. Zechariah moves from Gentile domination to Messianic rule, from persecution to peace, and from uncleanness to holiness. The book divides into Pictures (1-6), Problems (7-8), and Predictions (9-14).

Pictures (1-6): The book opens with an introductory appeal to the people to repent and return to God, unlike their fathers who rejected the warnings of the prophets (1:1-6). A few months later, Zechariah had a series of eight night visions, evidently in one troubled night (February 15, 519; 1:17). The angel who was speaking with him interpreted the visions, but some of the symbols were not explained. The visions mixed the work of Messiah in both advents, and like the other prophets, Zechariah saw the peaks of God's program without the intervening valleys. The first five were visions of *comfort*, and the last three were visions of *judgment*: (1) The horsemen among the myrtle trees — God will rebuild Zion and His people (1:7-17). (2) The four horns and craftsmen — Israel's oppressors will be judged (1:18-21). (3) The man with a measuring line — God will protect and glorify Jerusalem (2:1-13). (4) The cleansing of Joshua the high priest — Israel will be cleansed and restored by the coming Branch (3:1-10). (5) The golden lampstand — God's Spirit is empowering Zerubbabel and Joshua (4:1-14). (6) The flying scroll — individual sin will be judged (5:1-4). (7) The woman in the ephah — national sin will be removed (5:5-11). (8) The four chariots — God's judgment will descend on the nations (6:1-8). The crowning of Joshua (6:9-15) anticipates the coming of the Branch who will be King and Priest (the composite crown).

Problems (7-8): In response to a question about the continuation of the fasts (7:1-3), God gave Zechariah a series of four messages: (1) a rebuke of empty ritualism (7:4-7); (2) a reminder of past disobedience (7:8-14); (3) the restoration and consolation of Israel (8:1-17); and (4) the recovery of joy in the kingdom (8:18-23).

Predictions (9-14): The first oracle (9-11) concerns the first advent and rejection of Israel's coming King. Alexander the Great will conquer Israel's neighbors but spare Jerusalem (9:1-8) which will be preserved for her King (Messiah; 9:9-10). Israel will succeed against Greece (the Maccabean revolt; 9:11-17), and though they will later be scattered, Messiah will bless them and bring them back (10:1-11:3). Israel will reject her Shepherd-King and be led astray by false shepherds (11:4-17). The second oracle (12-14) concerns the second advent and acceptance of Israel's King. The nations will attack Jerusalem, but Messiah will come and deliver His people (12). They will be cleansed of impurity and falsehood (13), and Messiah will come in power to judge the nations and reign in Jerusalem over the whole earth (14).

Title — *Zekar-yah* means "Yahweh remembers" or "Yahweh has remembered." This theme predominates the whole book: Israel will be blessed because Yahweh remembers the covenant He made with the fathers. The Greek and Latin version of his name is *Zacharias.*

Author — Zechariah was a popular name shared by no fewer than 29 Old Testament characters. It may have been given out of gratitude for God's gift of a baby boy. Like his predecessors, Jeremiah and Ezekiel, Zechariah was of priestly lineage as the son of Berechiah and grandson of Iddo (1:1,7; Ezra 5:1; 6:14; Neh. 12:4,16). He was born in Babylonia and was brought by his grandfather to Palestine when the Jewish exiles returned under Zerubbabel and Joshua the high priest. If he was the "young man" of 2:4, he was called to prophesy at an early age in 520 B.C. According to Jewish tradition, Zechariah was a member of the Great Synagogue that collected and preserved the canon of revealed Scripture. Matthew 23:35 indicates he was "murdered between the temple and the altar" in the same way that an earlier Zechariah was martyred (see 2 Chron. 24:20-21).

The universal testimony of Jewish and Christian tradition affirms Zechariah as the author of the whole book. But many critics believe that chapters 9-14 (the undated material) were written by an unknown author. The theory that this section was written before the exile is supported by weak arguments. These chapters fit the post-exilic period since they regard Israel and Judah as one (compare 1:19; 8:13; 9:10,13; 10:6-7). A more popular theory places 9-14 in the Grecian or Maccabean period in an attempt to make Zechariah a "prophecy after the event." The descriptions of Alexander's conquests (9:1-8) and what may be the later Maccabean revolt (9:11-17) are too specific for some commentators to believe that they were written in advance. It is true, however, that the Greeks were well-known in Zechariah's day (they defeated the Persian king Xerxes at Salamis in 480-479). The evolutionary view of the Jewish religion assumes that apocalyptic literature was the final stage, pointing to a very late date for chapters 9-14. This is mere assumption, but the best argument is the stylistic difference between 1-8 (unimpassioned prosaic visions) and 9-14 (fervent poetic prophecies). These stylistic differences can be attributed to the 40-year writing gap and the altered state of affairs. Also, the similarities outweigh the differences (the same unusual expressions and the purity of the Hebrew in both sections).

Date and Setting — Zechariah was a younger contemporary of Haggai the prophet, Zerubbabel the governor, and Joshua the high priest. The historical setting for chapters 1-8 (520-518) is identical to that of Haggai (see Haggai, Date and Setting). Work was recommenced on the temple in 520 B.C. and the project was completed in 516 B.C. Chapters 9-14 are undated, but stylistic differences and references to Greece indicate a date of about 480-470 B.C. This would mean that Darius I (521-486) had passed from the scene and was succeeded by Xerxes (486-464), the king who deposed Vashti and made Esther queen of Persia.

Theme and Purpose — The first eight chapters frequently allude to the temple and encouraged the people to complete their great work on the new sanctuary. As they built the temple, they were building their future, because that very structure will be used by the coming Messiah when He comes to bring salvation. Zechariah eloquently attests to Yahweh's covenant faithfulness toward Israel through the work of the Messiah, especially in chapters 9-14. This book outlines God's program for His people during the times of the Gentiles until Messiah comes to deliver them and reign upon the earth. This hope of glory was a source of reassurance to the Jewish remnant at a time when circumstances were trying. Zechariah was also written to promote spiritual revival so that the people would call upon the Lord with humble hearts and commit their ways to Him.

Contribution to the Bible — Zechariah is the "major minor prophet" — the longest of the minor prophets and second only to Isaiah among the prophets in Messianic passages. There is considerable variety in this book with its visions, messages, and apocalyptic oracles. As a counterpart to Daniel, Zechariah emphasizes the history of Israel during Gentile domination, while Daniel also develops God's prophetic plan for the Gentiles.

Haggai and Zechariah ministered together in motivating the remnant to build the second temple, but their approaches were different. Here are some *general* contrasts:

Haggai	Zechariah
Exhortation	Encouragement
More concrete	More abstract
Concise	Expanded
Present concern	Future concern
Take part!	Take heart!
Older activist	Younger visionary

Christ in Zechariah — Very clear Messianic passages abound in this book. Christ is portrayed in His two advents as both Servant and King, Man and Yahweh. The following are a few of Zechariah's explicit anticipations of Christ: the angel of the Lord (3:1-2); the righteous Branch (3:8; 6:12-13), the stone with seven eyes (3:9); the King-Priest (6:13); the humble King (9:9,10); the cornerstone, tent peg, and bow of battle (10:4); the good Shepherd who is rejected and sold for 30 shekels of silver, the price of a slave (11:4-13); the pierced One (12:10); the cleansing fountain (13:1); the smitten Shepherd who is abandoned (13:7); the coming Judge and righteous King (14).

Malachi

"Behold, I am going to send My messenger, and he will clear the way before Me. And the LORD, whom you seek, will suddenly come to His temple; and the messenger of the covenant, in whom you delight, behold, he is coming,' says the LORD of hosts."

Malachi 3:1
(Also see 1:2; 3:14; 4:5.)

Focus	Privilege of the Nation		Pollution by the Priests		Problems of the People		Promise of the Lord	
	1:1　　1:5		1:6　　　　2:9		2:10　　　3:15		3:16　　　4:6	
D I V I S I O N S	Care of God for Israel		Complaint of God against the Priests		Complaint of God against the People		Coming Blessing and Judgment	Concluding Warning
	1:1　　1:5		1:6　　　2:9		2:10　　3:15		3:16　4:3	4:4-6
T O P I C S	God Still Loves Israel	Obstacles to Divine Blessing					Future of the Righteous and Wicked	
	The Condemnation of the Lord				The Coming of the Lord			
	Repent: Prevailing Sins				Repent: Promise of Judgment			
Location	Jerusalem							
Time	About 432-425 B.C.							

Talk Thru — The great prophecies of Haggai and Zechariah were not yet fulfilled, and the people of Israel became disillusioned and doubtful. They began to question God's providence as their faith imperceptibly degenerated into cynicism. Internally, they wondered whether it was worth serving God after all, and externally, these attitudes surfaced in mechanical observances, empty ritual, cheating on tithes and offerings, and crass indifference to God's moral and ceremonial law. Their priests were corrupt and their practices wicked, but they were so spiritually insensitive that they wondered why they were not being blessed by God. Using a probing series of questions and answers, God sought to pierce their hearts of stone. In each case the divine accusations were denied: How has God loved us? (1:2-5); How have we (priests) despised God's name? (1:6-2:9); How have we (people) profaned the covenant? (2:10-16); How have we wearied God? (2:17-3:6); How have we robbed God? (3:7-12); How have we spoken against God? (3:13-15). In effect, the people sneered. "Oh come on now — it's not that bad!" But their rebellion was quiet, not open. As their perception of God grew dim, the resulting materialism and externalism became a settled characteristic that later gripped the religious parties of the Pharisees and Sadducees. In spite of all this, God still loved His people and once again extended His grace to any who would humbly turn to Him. Malachi explores the privilege of the nation (1:1-5), the pollution by the priests (1:6-2:9), the problems of the people (2:10-3:15), and the promise of the Lord (3:16-4:6).

Privilege of the Nation (1:1-5): The Israelites blinded themselves to God's love for them. Wallowing in the problems of the present, they lost perspective on God's works for them in the past. Yahweh gave them a reminder of His special love by contrasting the fates of Esau (Edom) and Jacob (Israel).

Pollution by the Priests (1:6-2:9): The priests had lost all respect for Yahweh's name and in their greed offered only diseased and imperfect animals on the altar. They had more respect for the Persian governor than they did for the living God. Moreover, God was withholding His blessings from them because of their disobedience to God's covenant and their insincere teaching.

Problems of the People (2:10-3:15): The people are indicted for their treachery in divorcing the wives of their youth to marry foreign women (2:10-16). In response to their questioning the justice of God, they receive a promise of Messiah's coming but also a warning of the judgment that He will bring (2:17-3:6). The people have robbed God of the tithes and offerings due Him but God is ready to bless them with abundance if they will put Him first (3:7-12). The final problem was the arrogant challenge to the character of God (3:13-15), and this challenge is answered in the remainder of the book.

Promise of the Lord (3:16-4:6): The Lord assures His people that a time is coming when the wicked will be judged and those who fear Him will be blessed. The day of the Lord will reveal that it is not "vain to serve God" (3:14). Malachi, the sunset of Old Testament prophecy, ends on the bitter word "curse." Although the people were finally cured of idolatry, there was little spiritual progress in Israel's history. Sin abounded, and the need for the coming Messiah was greater than ever.

Title — The meaning of the name *mal'aki* ("my messenger") has caused disagreement as to whether it is a proper name or a way of referring to an anonymous writer. In all probability it is the former, because this book would otherwise be the only unidentified writing prophet. The name is probably a shortened form of *mal'ak-yah*, "messenger of Yahweh," and it is appropriate to the book which speaks of the coming of the "messenger of the covenant" ("messenger" is mentioned three times in 2:7; 3:1). The Septuagint used the title *Malachias* even though it also translated it "by the hand of his messenger." The Latin title is *Maleachi*.

Author — The only Old Testament mention of Malachi is in 1:1. The Targum of Jonathan attributed this book to "Ezra the scribe," but there is no basis for this assertion. In fact, the authorship, date, and unity of Malachi have never been seriously challenged. The unity of the book can be seen in the dialectic style that binds it together. Nothing is known of Malachi (not even his father's name), but a Jewish tradition says that he was a member of the Great Synagogue (see Zechariah, Author).

Date and Setting — Although an exact date cannot be

established for Malachi, internal evidence can be used to deduce an approximate date. The Persian term for governor, *pechah* (1:8, cf. Neh. 5:14; Hag. 1:1,14; 2:21) indicates that this book was written during the Persian domination of Israel (539-333). Sacrifices were being offered in the temple (1:7-10; 3:8) which was rebuilt in 516 B.C. Evidently, many years had passed since the offerings were instituted, because the priests had grown tired of them and corruptions had crept into the system. In addition, Malachi's oracle was inspired by the same problems that Nehemiah faced: corrupt priests (1:6-2:9; Neh. 13:1-9), neglect of tithes and offerings (3:7-12; Neh. 13:10-13), and intermarriage with pagan wives (2:10-16; Neh. 13:23-28). Nehemiah came to Jerusalem in 444 B.C. to rebuild the city walls, 13 years after Ezra's return and reforms (457). Nehemiah returned to Persia in 432 B.C. but came back to Palestine around 425 B.C. and dealt with the sins described in Malachi. It is therefore likely that Malachi proclaimed his message while Nehemiah was absent between 432 B.C. and 425 B.C., almost a century after Haggai and Zechariah began to prophesy (520).

Theme and Purpose — The divine dialogue in Malachi's prophecy was designed as an appeal that would break through the barrier of Israel's disbelief, disappointment, and discouragement. The promised time of prosperity had not yet come, and the prevailing attitude that it was not worth serving Yahweh became evident in their moral and religious corruption. But God revealed His continuing love in spite of Israel's lethargy. His appeal in this oracle was that the people and priests would stop to realize that their lack of blessing was not caused by His lack of concern, but by their own compromise and disobedience to the covenant law. When they repent and return to God with sincere hearts, the obstacles to the flow of divine blessing will be removed. Malachi also reminds the people that a day of reckoning will surely come when God will judge the righteous and the wicked.

Contribution to the Bible — Malachi's structure is built upon a recurring pattern of accusation("You are robbing Me!"), interrogation ("How have we robbed Thee?"), and refutation ("In tithes and offerings"). Over and over, the false conclusions and rationalizations of the people ("but you say"

and similar expressions appear more than a dozen times) are overcome by irrefutable and convicting arguments. Of the 55 verses in Malachi, 47 are spoken by God, the highest proportion of all the prophets. Malachi is also the only prophet who ends his book with judgment. While Joel and Zephaniah present the theme of the day of the Lord with greater intensity than Malachi (3:2,17; 4:1,3,5), they end on a theme of hope and blessing. But Malachi is a fitting conclusion to the Old Testament because it underscores the sinful human condition and anticipates God's solution in the work of the coming Messiah.

Christ in Malachi — Malachi is the prelude to 400 years of prophetic silence, broken finally by the words of the next prophet, John the Baptist: "Behold, the Lamb of God who takes away the sin of the world!" (John 1:29). Malachi predicted the coming of the messenger who would clear the way before the Lord (3:1; cf. Isa. 40:3). John the Baptist fulfilled this prophecy, but the next few verses (3:2-5) jump ahead to Christ in His second advent. This is also true of the prophecy of the appearance of "Elijah the prophet" (3:5). John was this Elijah (Matt. 3:3; 11:10-14; 17:9-13; Mark 1:3; 9:10-11; Luke 1:17; 3:4; John 1:23), but Elijah will also appear before the second coming of Christ.

Prophecies Against the Nations

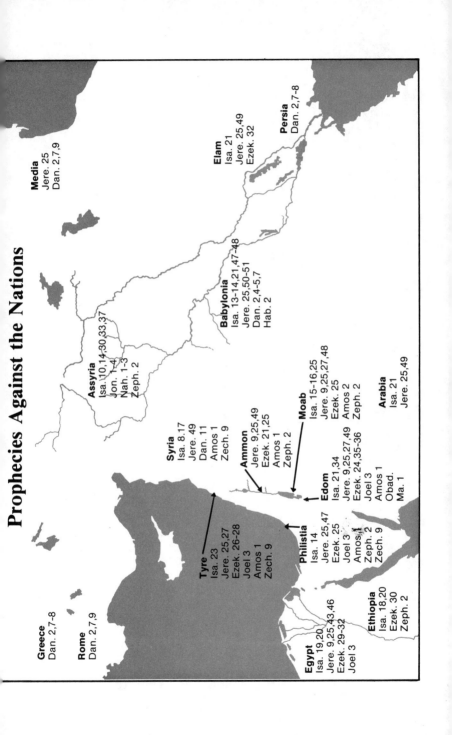

Media
Jere. 25
Dan. 2,7,9

Persia
Dan. 2,7-8

Elam
Isa. 21
Jere. 25,49
Ezek. 32

Babylonia
Isa. 13-14,21,47-48
Jere. 25,50-51
Dan. 2,4-5,7
Hab. 2

Assyria
Isa. 10,14,30,33,37
Jon. 1-4
Nah. 1-3
Zeph. 2

Arabia
Isa. 21
Jere. 25,49

Moab
Isa. 15-16,25
Jere. 9,25,27,48
Ezek. 25
Amos 2
Zeph. 2

Syria
Isa. 8,17
Jere. 49
Dan. 11
Amos 1
Zech. 9

Ammon
Jere. 9,25,49
Ezek. 21,25
Amos 1
Zeph. 2

Edom
Isa. 21,34
Jere. 9,25,27,49
Ezek. 24,35-36
Joel 3
Amos 1
Obad.
Ma. 1

Tyre
Isa. 23
Jere. 25,27
Ezek. 26-28
Joel 3
Amos 1
Zech. 9

Philistia
Isa. 14
Jere. 25,47
Ezek. 25
Joel 3
Amos 1
Zeph. 2
Zech. 9

Greece
Dan. 2,7-8

Rome
Dan. 2,7,9

Ethiopia
Isa. 18,20
Ezek. 30
Zeph. 2

Egypt
Isa. 19,20
Jere. 9,25,43,46
Ezek. 29-32
Joel 3